THE MORNING SIDE
OF
MOUNT DIABLO

An illustrated account of
Morgan Territory Road

Anne Marshall Homan

TABLE OF CONTENTS

INSTITUTIONS

FAMILIES II

Rainbow over section 29 in the Black Hills above Livermore. Photo by Don Homan.

Dedicated with my deepest love to the Spoog,
who so graciously allows me to travel
and travels with me.

Introduction: This Special Place

TOILET PAPER looped in the strong, gusty wind like a Chinese kite as I stood shivering in the crisp morning air, balanced on the boards that led to the portable outhouse. My bathrobe whipped wildly around my legs. I grabbed the flapping metal door, reeled in the toilet paper, tidily rolled up what had not escaped, and replaced it on its appointed shelf. On this hilltop even toilet paper seemed to have a life of its own.

The studio door at the side of the garage opened and shut with a bang, and I walked over to wish my husband, Don, good morning. The sun winked above the horizon and turned the few clouds a brilliant evanescent pink. A camera can never substitute for the human eye. Even a wide-angle lens could not have duplicated the hills spread out around us in the Black Hills section of Morgan Territory Road—an undulating ocean of myriad shades of green. Don and I held hands and strolled past our growing house to the brow of our hill. I said to him the wondering words we still occasionally repeat to one another: "Did you ever imagine that you would be here?"

Don grew up in Philadelphia, I in Baltimore. Though we were city dwellers, we both loved the outdoors and enjoyed hiking and camping. As a child, Don spent summers in the Adirondacks, and I had backpacked with Girl Scout friends. After we married, our favorite vacation camping spot was Cape Hatteras, North Carolina, where clean salty wind washed away the tensions of everyday life. For our summer vacation in 1963, we packed our Volkswagen bus with our two young children and our camping gear and headed west. In three weeks we made a gigantic loop—first down to the Southwest, then through central California, north all the way to the Canadian border of Minnesota, and back home to Maryland. We decided that we had to live in the West. By

1966 Don had managed to arrange a transfer to Boulder, Colorado, but after four years he lost his job, and we reluctantly moved from Boulder to Livermore, California, where Don began working as a physicist at Lawrence Livermore Laboratory.

We missed Colorado jeep roads and quick access to mountain hiking, so we began driving around and exploring back roads here. Our favorite turned out to be Morgan Territory Road. The rugged little one-lane road winding through an area of superb natural beauty reminded us of what we had left behind in the foothills of the Rockies. Ten years later we bought 13 acres on that road and began building our solar dream house. Don needed more space for working on his wood sculptures, so he planned a combination studio-garage as well.

I had heard the adage, "If you want to stay married, never build a house together." But I was pleasantly surprised at how easily we compromised and how well we complemented each other's efforts. When we moved to Morgan Territory in July of 1980, Don had finished the studio-garage by himself except that the roof was still only plywood, awaiting the finishing layers of tar paper and concrete tiles. Essentially, we camped out, but with the luxuries of electricity and a few pieces of furniture. A generous friend in Livermore let us use her shower; our only water on the hill was cold, from a hose. Our heat was a small wood stove, and our toilet was that portable one with the wind-driven paper. All of our clothes and most of our furniture were stuffed in the two-car garage. The larger side of the L-shaped sculpture studio functioned as our bedroom, living room, and kitchen, and the shorter side became the bedroom of our younger son, Andrew. Our older children, Becky and Ted, were away at college. My cooking helpers were a

Coleman stove, an electric frying pan, and a toaster oven.

On foggy nights moisture condensed on the roof and dripped over edges of the exposed plywood; we soon learned to wrap our furniture, clothes, and beds with plastic drop sheets even though the rainy season was many months away.

Don acted as his own contractor, but with the excellent advice of our lead carpenter. I was the decorator. The only hitch in this cooperative effort involved the bricks. I had chosen a tan-colored slumpstone, which Don accepted readily. When I showed our bricklayer a sample of what I wanted, he said that he would use his own supplier. One day when I arrived home from teaching, Don greeted me with the words, "The bricks were delivered today!" Sure enough, piled on pallets in the yard was a huge stack of bricks. Unfortunately, they were pink bricks. Not tan—pink. I told Don, but he did not believe me. Bringing out my sample brick, I laid it on a pallet, and even Don had to agree—the bricks were undeniably pink.

I said, "He'll have to take them back."

Thinking of the difficulties for the truck driver who had hauled all those bricks four miles up our steep, narrow road, Don replied, "I can't make him take them back."

I retorted adamantly, "I will NOT live in a pink house."

We argued for a while, and Don agreed to consult the bricklayer. The bricklayer accepted the situation matter-of-factly and ordered new bricks. I am happy to report that I do not live in a pink house, and that I am still married to the man I wed in 1957.

As we continued to live in this beautiful place, I became curious about the natural and local history around us. I began to ask questions that gradually led, after my retirement from teaching, to a more structured study, and this book.

The first section of the book describes the terrain and geology of Morgan Territory Road and tells what is known of the early Native Americans who passed through the area.

In the section "Families," the first four chapters are about the Hispanic settlers who started moving into the Black Hills in the late 1850s. They claimed somewhat hilly property initially and then moved northward onto steep and less desirable land. Other settlers along the road did not follow this trend; they generally stayed at one site.

The remainder of the chapters are not arranged chronologically but usually follow in spatial order the road and its adjacent landowners, from Livermore over the ridgetop to Clayton. Three chapters—"School Days, School Days," "Fire and Rescue Volunteers," and "A Pair of Rodeo Cowboys"—diverge from this organization. "School Days, School Days" tells of the five one-room schools supported by Morgan Territory Road residents. The development of the local fire departments is set out in "Fire and Rescue Volunteers," and "A Pair of Rodeo Cowboys" is the story of two local men who loved competing in rodeos; one lives on the Livermore side and one lived on the Clayton side of the road.

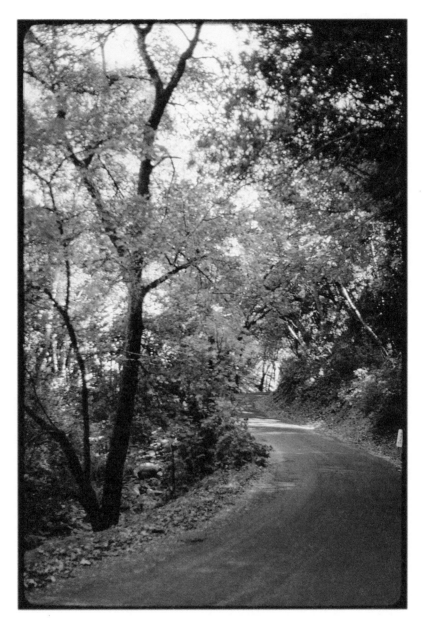

A shady section of Morgan Territory Road. Photo by Anne Homan.

The 1925 STAR

SPORT MODEL

That Good Looking Car

Behind its smart appearance it carries the sturdiest power motor ever built—the new Million Dollar Motor that develops 20% more power—real power.

Four-wheel brakes—the only car at its low cost so

equipped for your safety. **No** skidding in wet weather.

Full Force Feed Lubrication to all bearings and cam shaft. Never a burned-out bearing in a Star Car.

The 1925 Star Car is the greatest buy in the world (at the new low prices).

[See It Today—Drive In It—Compare It]

HIGHWAY GARAGE

F. H. DUARTE, Prop.

Million Dollar Motor

Smooth Disc Clutch

Four-Wheel Brakes

Tubular Backbone

From The Livermore Herald, *13 February 1925, page 7.*

A Muddy Wagon Track

Snowflakes were falling too fast for the windshield wipers to keep up. The truck kept slipping on the hill, its attached double horse trailer fishtailing around. Finally the driver gave up and steered her rig as carefully as she could onto the shoulder. ❧ *Climbing out, she shivered and slipped downhill to the back of the trailer, calling out to her horses. They nickered back, drumming restlessly on the trailer floor. Her ungloved hands were freezing. To avoid the cold metal latch, she grabbed a corner of her coat and opened the tailgate. The snow came down even harder, flakes sticking to her hair and eyelashes.* ❧ *Melinda Robles Koopman could have been in Montana, Wyoming, or North Dakota on that cold day in 1970, but she was not. She was in California, on a narrow byway about 30 miles east of San Francisco Bay called Morgan Territory Road. She had taken two horses into Livermore to the veterinarian, but after an unexpected late-afternoon snowstorm her truck could not negotiate the steep hill on her return.* ❧ *She finally rode one horse and led the other to the ranch three miles away. A neighbor brought down his tractor and pulled her truck and trailer the rest of the way up.*

MORGAN TERRITORY Road began as a muddy wagon track linking ranches in the Black Hills east of Mount Diablo. Although ranchers fenced most of the perimeter of their property, they did not at first fence along the road. Consequently, a traveler would frequently encounter gates at section lines that crossed the roadway.[1] Contra Costa County accepted the northern part of the dirt road in 1886, surveying and grading it as an official public road. In 1900 the county gave barbed wire to the landowners abutting the road "to erect a three wire fence on both sides" of the northern half from Marsh Creek Road to the summit.[2] The southern end of the road, after re-alignment at the summit, was accepted by the county as a public highway in 1895.

Early pioneer Jeremiah "Jerry" Morgan had settled at the northern end about 1857.[3] The area here is called "Morgan Territory," and the road was officially designated Morgan Road in 1892.

On a map the road travels through four townships in a wavering diagonal from southeast to northwest across surveyors' rigid section squares, from the Livermore Valley to Marsh Creek Road east of Clayton. The northern end of the road is only a little over one mile from the North Peak of Mount Diablo. As it exists now, the road is 14.5 miles long, and for most of its length it is barely wide enough for two cars to pass even if they go onto the shoulder. At several points, two cars cannot pass. Once, when a police officer tried to go through one of these areas too fast and met a car coming the other way, his cruiser ended up in the creek.

The road is so narrow that for 10 miles there is no center line. Fortunately, county workers do paint white side lines. Sometimes when the fog blows in from the west, finding a driveway—in fact, just staying on the road itself—is a tricky business. One of the more exhilarating moments

When winter comes to Morgan Territory Road, mud isn't far behind. Photo by Don Homan.

for today's driver comes when rounding a curve to confront a double-trailer gravel truck, especially when the steep drop-off is on the car's side. In the early history of Morgan Territory Road, a number of small intersecting dirt roads led to various nearby localities, such as Tassajara Valley to the west, the Vasco, and Round Valley to the east. Today these are only gated fire roads without public motor access. Along its entire length the road has no exit routes.

Beginning at its southern end down in the Livermore Valley at Manning Road, a short distance from North Livermore Avenue, the road weaves up into the Black Hills, rising in only five miles from the approximately 600-foot-elevation valley floor to an apex of 2,063 feet. En route, it ascends a 14 percent grade for about a quarter mile. This stretch is known as "the Levy," after early landowner Samuel Levy, who owned the property alongside the grade.

Since they did not have fuel pumps, many early cars could only climb the Levy backward. The Model T Ford with its elevated gas tank and the Star, Durant, and Flint with their vacuum tanks could make the grade forward. Early resident John Gleese's first car, chosen partly with that in mind, was a 1925 Star. His son Jack recalled that his dad bought the car at Frank

Duarte's Highway Garage in Livermore: "This was, I believe, the first lower-priced car with four-wheel brakes, and they were just what the doctor ordered for Morgan Territory Road."[4] Even by 1937, the road was gravel only from Manning Road to the Levy. Beyond that it was still dirt. Locals, according to Jack Gleese, called this graveled southern half, closer to Livermore, the "Black Hills Road."

Jack Gleese remembered working on the road for the county in the late 1920s and 1930s with his father and uncle, checking culverts and cleaning drainage ditches. In the spring they frequently had to hitch up the county grader with three teams of two horses each and scrape ruts out of the road. Ormond Smith, who lived on the ridgetop, worked four days on and four days off as a firefighter in Oakland in the 1930s. During the rainy season the county had to re-grade the road every four days when Smith returned home and left again. Often skid chains were necessary to negotiate the turns and gradients in the mud. The problem was not only with the wet dirt road itself, but with mud slides down the bank. Because of slides in 1982, residents had to park their cars at the Cardoza ranch at the top of the Levy grade and ride in four-wheel-drive trucks up the rest of the way to their homes. Mudslides are as slick as ice on the road, but sometimes there is real ice. Omery Smith, Ormond's son, remembered one snowy New Year's Eve in the '30s when the family car could not climb up the road. They had to borrow a sled and horses from the Cardozas.

The southern half of the road in its windings overlooks the broad landscape of the Livermore Valley and the gently rolling vistas of surrounding hills. On most days the blue dome of the sky blazes over the large valley oaks clinging to the hills. For a short distance the road is in Alameda County. In 1906 a number of ranchers petitioned the county to make this section of the road a permanent part of the Alameda County public road system; but as a result of the great San Francisco

Jeremiah Morgan's grandson Willard J. Morgan recalled the original Morgan Territory Road:

"Those were turbulent days. The road was so full of ruts, we were always turning out to pull stock and wagons out of the mud when it rained. It was just a 'summer' road. We had to drive our cattle and sheep over it on the way to market in Oakland. Rock was put down and that helped some. Cars brought more problems—they got stuck worse than the horses! It was during the '50s before we finally got the . . . macadam road it is now." [a]

earthquake, the business had to be brought to the Board of Supervisors again in 1907. They concluded: "The present road has been traveled for many years but as it has never been declared a county road it has never been cared for and during the long continued wet weather of the present winter it has . . . fallen into 'a most deplorable condition and is almost impassable.'"[5] The petition was granted, apparently, and that portion of the road was named for John Beck, whose nearby ranch home burned to the ground in 1917. An early ranch still surviving in Alameda County belongs to the Morris family. In the 1920s and 1930s, it was the only place on the road for miles where people who had an accident or who had run out of gas could find help or a phone.

A little north of the Morris ranch, after entering Contra Costa County, the road crosses over one branch of Cayetano Creek. At approximately two miles north of Manning Road, warned by some eucalyptus trees, the traveler finds that narrow one-car-wide section, the only place with a closed-in feeling on this half of the road, with a cliff to one side and Cayetano Creek, with its assortment of willows and wild almond trees, on the other. Scrub jays often flash by here, and occasionally a family of quail totters with quick baby-steps across the road. After the Levy, the panorama of the valley spreads out beyond the wild oats and leaning fence posts. Cattle have patiently trod the hills into ziggurats. In the summer this open hillside is the favorite haunt of red-winged blackbirds. Kestrels, red-tailed hawks, northern harriers, and golden eagles soar out over the hills in the daytime; owls taking off suddenly from fence posts startle drivers at night. Field mustard often yellows the pasturage in early spring.

Above the Levy the road follows a ridge for about two miles. Much of the ridgetop is treeless, and the winter north winds are especially strong, sometimes reaching hurricane force. The summer west winds, which bring cooling coastal fog, are more welcomed by the residents.

Morgan Territory Regional Preserve, a holding of the East Bay Regional Park District, begins just four-tenths of a mile after the highest point on the road. Immediately past the park staging area, the atmosphere changes completely as the road plunges into a dark wood pungent with aromatic bay laurel trees as well as big-leaf maples, buckeyes, and seven varieties of oak. The road follows down the narrow meandering canyon of northward-flowing Marsh Creek. Some turns are extremely and unexpectedly sharp, with steep drop-offs. A few small meadows allow the sun to dazzle the eyes, and then the tree canopy closes in again. About three miles of the road are inside Morgan Territory Preserve. Wildlife abounds in this isolated area. Travelers on their way up and down the road see bobcats, native gray foxes, coyotes, and red foxes as well as the ubiquitous black-tailed deer.

As the road finally comes down to fairly level ground, it zigzags over the creek on four one-lane bridges. The white bark of a sycamore occasionally interrupts the riparian greenery. As Willard Morgan pointed out all those years ago, Morgan Territory Road was originally only a "summer" road. Before the bridges were built, the only mode of travel left to isolated residents once the rainy season started was horseback. After the bridges the road acquires a white middle stripe, and the excitement of one-lane driving is over. This is the original "territory" claimed by Jeremiah Morgan. In the '30s the road was graveled from this point north. Although twisting, the road remains fairly level until it reaches Marsh Creek Road. This flat area now is much more developed than anywhere else on the road, with many houses and horse boarding facilities. The Curry Creek Park side road is to the west. Near the road's end, also to the west, are the tailings and catch pond of the old mercury mines. Mount Diablo's craggy profile looms in the western background.

When a ridgetop house was sold recently, everyone who toured the property loved the house and the view, but most complained, "How can you stand that road!" The primitive road, although admittedly more than a muddy wagon track today, still protects our isolation, reminds us daily of our history, and carves out a community. We hope that the time will never come when frustrated commuters can make a faster run from Clayton to Livermore or vice versa on this road than they can on wider county roads or the freeway system. Former residents who return to visit mutter about how many new houses have been built, but compared with housing developments around Livermore and Clayton, and considering its closeness to the urban communities around San Francisco Bay, the population density of Morgan Territory Road is still very low. Typical traffic consists of local residents, weekend visitors to the park, and lovers of back roads.

In this mobile modern society, neighbors often reach out only to the TV remote control or the Internet. George A. Pettitt commented in the foreword to his local history, *Clayton: Not*

Quite Shangri-La, that the modern community often "forgets that it has a past history, and that this story of the past, however humble and undistinguished it may be, is the community's most stable and distinctive possession. . . . If a community is to have spirit and morale it must start with this heritage. . . ." Only by knowing and understanding this, he says, can a community "make heirs of its citizens."[6]

1 Jack Gleese, letter, 14 Jan 1998.

2 *Contra Costa County Road Book,* Vol. 2, 5 Feb 1900: 237-238.

3 *Contra Costa County Old Road Records History Book,* Vol B: 35.

4 Jack Gleese, letter, 15 Apr 1997.

5 "Renew Petition for Road," *The Livermore Herald* 9 Feb 1907: 1.

6 George A. Pettitt, *Clayton: Not Quite Shangri-La.* Martinez, CA: Contra Costa Historical Society, 1969: vii.

a Sara Maloney, "A History of Morgan Territory Road," *Tri-Valley Herald, Brightside* 8 July 1979: 2,4.

Livermore Valley

Morgan Territory Regional Preserve

Highland Ridge

Cowell Ranch

Round Valley Regional Preserve

Bob Walker Ridge

Los Vaqueros watershed

Aerial view, looking southwest.
Photo by Bob Walker, ©IDG
Films/Oakland Museum.

Windy Point   San Ramon Valley   Mount Diablo
                                            North Peak

Black Diamond Mines Regional Preserve

Hillside Seabeds

RETREATING EARLY-MORNING fogs reveal the undulating skyline north of the Livermore Valley. In the dry season, golden wild oats contrast with deep green trees hugging the arroyos, and with the dark dormant chaparral that gives the area its name—the Black Hills. Summer weather in the Black Hills is hot as well as dry; winter brings cold wet storms from the Pacific. In the wet season a visitor can easily imagine that this green landscape is Ireland.

The hills begin on the west with double-peaked Mount Diablo at 3,849 feet and fade eastward into the San Joaquin Valley, with Brushy Peak standing guardian near the southeastern corner. From Diablo, rolling hills surge like waves east toward the edge of the distant San Joaquin Valley. The panorama includes not only 734 square miles of Contra Costa County, but the Golden Gate, the Sierra Nevada, and Mount Shasta, adding up to a total viewing area on a

21

clear day of more than 40,000 square miles—about the size of the state of New York.[1]

After California statehood in 1850, early officials chose Mount Diablo to play an important role in surveying because no other mountains are close by to obscure the vista. In July 1851 surveyor Leander Ransom and his party of six men found Diablo's highest rock and excavated a hole nine inches deep and six inches square as the point from which to run an east and west base line as well as a north and south meridian.[2] That carved rock is still the central survey point for northern and central California and Nevada.[3] Ensuing surveys divided the surrounding land into a grid of townships, each six miles square, which are in turn divided into 36 square 640-acre sections. These sections can be divided into halves (320 acres) or quarters (160 acres). A piece of property is located with these aids. For example, a person might own 320 acres: the east half of section 12, township 1 north, range 2 east. This is abbreviated as T1N/R2E. "North" indicates that the property lies north of the point at Mount Diablo's summit, and "east" that the property lies east of that point. The numbers correspond to the township grid.

In 1805, Spanish soldiers from the San Francisco Presidio, who were chasing some runaway Christianized Indians, became lost in a large scrub willow thicket near present-day Concord. At dusk the soldiers managed to withdraw from the swampy area and camped at the thicket's edge. By morning the Indians had completely gone, and the soldiers believed their disappearance was a supernatural phenomenon. Frightened by their experience, the soldiers called the area *Monte del Diablo* (Thicket of the Devil). This phrase, mistakenly translated because *monte* can also mean "mountain," became in English "Mount Diablo" and soon was applied to the mountain rather than the willows.[4]

Many local residents nourish the misconception that Mount Diablo is a dormant volcano;

after all, the name conjures up the image of hell's fires threatening beneath the surface. Diablo, however, is not of volcanic origin, but arose more benignly as a mass of old sedimentary rocks moving upward on a thrust fault. This active uplift started about 2 million years ago, and the mass is still moving today. As it pushed its way up, the new mountain caused rock layers above to tilt, creating the resultant rippling foothills. The tilted layers are composed of shale and a muddy sandstone (a turbidite). The shale eroded faster, leaving today's valleys. The more resistant turbidite formed the hills.

On a scorching September day, when probably not a drop of rain has fallen in the hills since May, local firefighters would be amused to know that much of this area was once underwater. Fifteen million years ago, San Francisco Bay was a large inland sea covering what is now Oakland as well as the Diablo, San Ramon, Livermore, and Pleasanton valleys. Mount Diablo had not yet appeared, and the weather was more temperate, with fewer fluctuations. Ten million years ago, the sea had retreated somewhat, and the Black Hills had begun to lift. Rhinoceroses, camels, horses, and hyenas lived here—wildlife similar to that of an African savanna. Various now-extinct mammals such as the mastodon and the saber-toothed cat roamed the land mass, while 65-foot sharks prowled the sea; their remains are still being uncovered in the quarry on the former Blackhawk Ranch.[5]

Occasional rocky outcrops prove that today's hills have a sandstone base, and fossil shells convince even the skeptic of that ancient sea. A landmark for hikers in Mount Diablo State Park is Oyster Point, so named for its fossil oyster bed. A similar bed exists farther south near the border between sections five and six T2S/R2E. Omery Smith, who lived at the summit of Morgan Territory Road, remembered that the highest hill on their property was called Oyster Peak. At first he thought that that was because of its shape—a

'The opposite coast'

When the county containing the mountain was being named, Mount Diablo County was first proposed, but some lawmakers objected to a county being named after the devil. Contra Costa, meaning "the opposite coast" (from San Francisco), was suggested and approved.

bald top surrounded by trees and brush—but he discovered that oyster shells littered its summit. As an eight-year-old paleontologist, he recalled, "I always figured it was caused by the great flood in Noah's time."[6] Another local family collecting nearby rocks to build their sandstone fireplace split one rock and discovered a perfect mussel shell inside. During his 1851 survey, Leander Ransom remarked in his field notes that "in some of these ridges very large oysters are embedded, the shell remaining perfect, while the oyster is replaced by stone. Large quantities of other sea shells are embedded in the same rock."[7]

Most of the Black Hills are gently rounded, with underlying rock layers concealed, but sandstone cliffs on section 29 T1S/R2E reveal those layers as a huge playground slide aimed at the Delta. Extending deep into the San Joaquin Valley, where the hinge of this great uplift of Mount Diablo is located, the sandstone contains both early- and mid-Cretaceous rocks, which make it about 100 million years old. Geologists say that the Pacific and North American plates have ground together, again and again, rearranging the landscape here as if a giant had grown angry over his inability to solve a three-dimensional puzzle and thrown all the pieces down.

Northern California dwellers can attest to the strength of that continual movement, even in the last hundred years. In January 1980 a Morgan Territory Road resident who was home at the time of Livermore's 5.6 earthquake ran outside with her baby and witnessed cattle falling down the hillside. The epicenter was close to her house. Another resident, Sandy Joyce, lived during her teenage years in the pioneer house that once stood near the Morgan Territory Preserve parking lot. She described the 1980 earthquake as "the highlight of my living there."[8] She had invited some friends for a trail ride, and they were high on a ridge when the horses started acting up. The riders dismounted to calm the horses; several minutes later the earthquake began. In a nearby grove small blue oak trees with diameters of six to 12 inches waved back and forth, shaking dust down. When the ground waves stopped, an eerie absolute silence prevailed for a while; not even a bird called. Dust plumed up from the valleys. And almost 72 years earlier the great 1906 quake had emptied the water trough at the Cardoza ranch on section 24 and moved a surveyor's stone marker, located in a pasture, enough to create disputes in future surveys of some Black Hills properties.

Morgan Territory Road follows two streams. The south-side hills are the origin of Cayetano Creek, named for Italian Saint Cayetano.[9] Coming down into Livermore, the road follows what used to be called the Cañada de San Cayetano. Cayetano Creek eventually drains into the Arroyo de las Positas, which runs along Interstate 580 near Livermore. North-side hills shelter the headwaters of Marsh Creek. Morgan Territory Road, after the preserve at the top of the hill, generally follows the natural curves of Marsh Creek northward to Marsh Creek Road east of Clayton. Eventually the creek empties into the San Joaquin River. Marsh Creek was named for Dr. John Marsh, who owned a rancho nearby.

1 *History of Alameda County, California* (Oakland: M.W. Wood, 1883) 28.

2 In Purcell's *History of Contra Costa County*, the name is spelled Ransome. In a copy of Dyer's survey in 1861-62, the name is spelled Ranson. In the source cited in note 3 following, the name is spelled Ramson. In Ruth Dyer's copy of the surveyor's field notes for the California Department of Park and Recreation in 1973, she spelled the name Ransom. Happily, in all these sources his first name is Leander.

3 "Surveyor Established Boundaries of Pleasanton Township," field notes of Leander Ramson in *The Livermore Herald-News*, Shopping Guide 16 June 1969: 8A.

4 George C. Collier, *A Narrative History of Contra Costa County* (El Cerrito, CA: Collier, 1983) 17. Bev Ortiz, "Mount Diablo As Myth and Reality," *American Indian Quarterly,* Fall 1989: 460-461. An apocryphal story about the naming of the mountain was told by Mariano Vallejo. He described a weird war-painted figure appearing on the slopes of the mountain during an Indian battle, which led to the idea of a devil inhabiting the area. The idea of monte meaning thicket is supported in alcalde and rancher John M. Price's story of Indians who fled from Captain John C. Fremont into "a dense monte of willows" near San Luis Obispo. Price's story also supports such a thicket as an impenetrable hiding place. He advised Fremont, "You might as well try to arrest a lot of quail as to find them [Indians] in that monte." *History of San Luis Obispo County, CA* (Oakland: Thompson and West, 1883) 67.

5 John Boudreau, "Call It Beast Bay: Ancient Animals Found Hospitable Home Here," *The Valley Times* 4 June 1995: 4A.

6 Omery Smith, letter, 15 Oct 1996.

7 "Surveyor Established" 9A.

8 Sandy Joyce, personal interview, 19 Jan 1998.

9 Canonized in 1671, Cayetano was born and lived much of his life in Vicenza, Lombardy. The scion of a highborn family, he renounced all claims to wealth or title and was ordained a priest in 1516. He founded the Theatrine Order, priests who lived as a community and engaged in work in local parishes.

Early Footsteps

As I WALK along Morgan Territory Road on my frequent excursions up to the Morgan Territory Preserve, I often imagine ghostly Native American footprints accompanying me. When my neighbors on the ridgetop bulldozed their driveways recently, they uncovered a time-worn pestle and a hand tool, both made of stone. Walking along the road one day, I found a charm-stone. Numerous bedrock mortars are at the pre-serve and on private lands along the road. Archeologists investigating near this area because of the encroachment of Los Vaqueros Reservoir found a number of aboriginal sites, including one within the dam footprint that had a carbon dat-ing of 8,000 to 10,000 years, the oldest ever dis-covered in the Bay Area.[1]

The Black Hills may or may not have been an area of permanent settlement, but evidence indi-cates that they were the site of large gatherings in the autumn when local tribes came to collect acorns, and probably also at other times for trade and barter along this highland border between their territories. Randall Milliken says in a report for the Los Vaqueros Project that the local Native Americans' "ability to prosper as a group de-pended as much upon their strategic trading lo-cation—on the pass between the Livermore Valley and the San Joaquin Valley—as upon their ability to extract resources from their own terri-tory."[2] Trade goods covered a wide range: salt, olivella shells, dried abalone and abalone shells, baskets and basket-making materials, soapstone, obsidian, tobacco, tanned skins, dog pups, bows and arrows, bird feathers, piñon nuts, ornamental pigments.

Of course, neither survey maps nor fences marked off territory belonging to a tribe. Milliken's approximation of tribal locations in the San Francisco Bay Area is based on the tim-ing of each tribe's capitulation to mission life. He

places the Volvon tribe, who spoke a Bay Miwok language, from the peak of Mount Diablo down its rugged east side through the arroyos of Marsh Creek, with two neighboring Bay Miwok-speak-ing tribes nearby: the Chupcans, who lived in the area that now comprises Concord and Clayton, and the Julpuns, who lived to the northeast of the Volvons, between present-day Antioch and Brentwood.

According to Milliken, two Ohlone groups, the Souyens and the Ssaoams, who spoke a differ-ent language from the Bay Miwok, were also close by. The Souyens probably occupied the north side of the marsh that once existed in the western Livermore Valley as well as the Tassajara Creek watershed and the southern foothills of Mount Diablo. The Ssaoams lived in the drier eastern Livermore Valley, in the Vasco and Altamont areas. Milliken's research places the Tamcans, a Yokuts-speaking tribe, where the town of Byron is today and along the west bank of the San Joaquin River.

Early records support the Volvon tribe's loca-tion in the Mount Diablo area. In his 1811 diary, Franciscan Father Abella refers to Mount Diablo as *Cerro Alto de los Bolbones* (High Peak of the Volvons). A Mexican land grant in the area was named *Rancho Arroyo de las Nueces y los Bolbones*, the Ranch of Walnut Creek and the Volvons. The letters "v" and "b" are virtually in-terchangeable in Spanish pronunciation, and this is often reflected in different spellings of California names. The tendency is apparent in the alternative spellings of the nearby land grant *Cañada de los Vaqueros*, sometimes given as Baqueros.

The Volvon and Ssaoam territories were im-portant to the spiritual beliefs of many central California natives. Mount Diablo, the Vasco Caves, Brushy Peak or *Loma de las Cuevas* (Hill

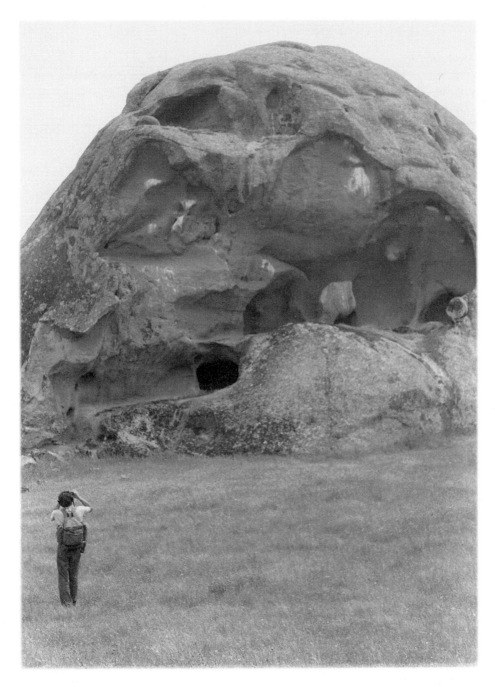

"Post Office Rock" near Brushy Peak, May 2000. Photo by Anne Homan.

with the Caves), as it was called long ago, all played central roles. Pomo and Wintun tribes to the north and Central Miwok groups to the northeast told stories of shamans and sacred dancers who would gather on Mount Diablo. J.P. Harrington's field notes in the 1920s included an informant who recalled a Volvon named Eusebio. Eusebio explained that his tribe had never settled high on the mountain's peak because his people considered it a place of special magic.[3]

The Ssaoam's tribal name meant "At the Rocks" or "Rocky Place,"[4] which fits with territory assigned to them by Milliken. On the northern side of Brushy Peak and farther to the north at the Vasco Caves, obtrusive sandstone has been shaped into caves by wind and rain. Brushy Peak was also the site of creation myths. In the beginning, says one Southern Miwok story, Coyote was human, only transforming himself into an animal after he had created human beings. The original Coyote left three giant footprints in the Bay Area before he changed. One was at Brushy Peak, one at Mount Diablo, and one at Pleasanton.[5]

Brushy Peak is now owned by the Livermore Area Recreation and Park District. Access is permitted only through ranger-led walks. On 13 May 2000, when I was on such a walk, we all were startled by a prairie falcon that emerged from a cavity in rocks high above us. It hovered briefly in front of the cavity and screamed "wek, wek" before wheeling away. Falcon was a major anthropomorphic being in the Bay Miwok cosmology. To the north of Suisun Bay his name was "*wek-wek*"; in the Black Hills area he was called "*cacnú*." The translation of the name is usually "duck hawk"; the most likely species meant is not the prairie falcon, but the peregrine falcon, which does prey on ducks. The name of an important Volvon chief baptized in 1805 at Mission Dolores was Cacnú.

Jeffrey Fentress says in another chapter in the Los Vaqueros Report that the Vasco Caves contain "the most extensive and best-preserved pic-

Bev Ortiz relates a creation myth that featured Mount Diablo:

"At that time the entire face of the country was covered with water, except two islands, one of which was Mount Diablo. . . . There was a coyote on the peak, the only living thing there. One day the coyote saw a feather floating on the water . . . as it reached the island, [it] suddenly turned into an eagle, and spreading its broad pinions, flew upon the mountain. Coyote was much pleased with his new companion, and they lived in great harmony together, making occasional excursions to the other island, coyote swimming while the eagle flew. After some length of time they counseled together and concluded to make Indians; they did so, and as the Indians increased the water decreased, until where the lake had been became dry land." [a]

tographs in the San Francisco Bay area."[6] Large numbers of raptors—marsh and redtailed hawks, prairie falcons, and golden eagles—nest in nearby rock formations, and many of the pictographs are of birds. The site's remoteness and protection by private land owners have succeeded in preserving this fragile rock art even though vandals have destroyed many similar areas in California. Now, because of the new Los Vaqueros Reservoir, the Vasco Caves will be administered jointly by the East Bay Regional Park District and the Contra Costa Water District, and these public agencies promise to maintain sufficient protection for this invaluable treasure.

Five caves contain representational bird forms drawn with charcoal. Other caves contain hand prints and bearlike and deerlike figures as well as nonrepresentational designs. Besides the charcoal pictographs, red, pink, white and yellow pigments appear. Recent researchers have collected

The birth of Falcon, grandson of Coyote and son of Condor, at the top of Brushy Peak:

"Condor always roosted on a certain large rock on a small hill between the west bank of the San Joaquin River and the eastern foot of Mount Diablo. He flew about hunting but always returned every night to roost on this rock. . . . When the rock became very hot, it suddenly burst with a loud report, and from it came Falcon. As he emerged, he gave his characteristic cry, 'wek.' The doctors then told Condor that his wife was well and had given birth to a boy." [b]

some evidence that the Vasco site might have been used for observing both the summer and winter solstice. Even if this theory is not correct, obviously the caves played an important spiritual role. Fentress says: "Pictographs, in particular, functioned to indicate places where supernatural power was present."[7] Many bedrock mortars and other indications of Indian occupation as well as a spring are nearby—possibly this was a major village site for the Ssaoam tribe.

Both men and women could be shamans, with special healing and spiritual powers, acting as doctor as well as priest. One of the Volvon women was named "Medicine Lady," and one of the men "Medicine Person."

The tribal name Volvon meant "natural springs." This foothill tribe relied on such springs for their water source. In Morgan Territory Preserve, one bedrock mortar area is near Marsh Creek, which rarely dries up completely in the summer, an indication that a spring may be nearby. A milling station with more than 20 mortars is thought to indicate a village site. This area has at least 28 mortars, and possibly more

that are obscured by dirt and mosses. Two large coastal live oaks and an immense valley oak provide shelter over the milling station. One rock also has numerous small indentations called cupules whose significance is unknown although they are believed to have been made by Native Americans. To the east is a large grassland valley, perfect for holding dances and other gatherings. Along the steep hillsides bordering the riparian corridor are many beds of brodiaea, globe lily, and soaproot. It is not difficult in this quiet place, with the stream gurgling gently behind, to imagine women digging springtime bulbs, carefully dividing and replanting some.

Another, larger village site is on the ridgetop outside the preserve where an excellent spring runs all year. Milling stations with more than 170 bedrock mortars occupy adjacent shady spots and open areas. The rock outcrops run for about 325 yards on the north side of the creek bed created by the spring. Sheltered in a bowl between hills, the site faces southeast and has easy access down to the Vasco, the valley containing the Vasco Caves site to the east. The open space could have contained many homes. Milliken surmises that the Volvons and Ssaoams had "two or three semipermanent villages of 40 to 100 people each for the winter and early spring, with dispersion throughout the summer and fall among temporary camps in . . . bands of 20 to 50 people."[8]

Members of East Bay tribes were for the most part a peaceful people. Their culture did not include specialized weapons for warfare, and as Malcolm Margolin points out in *The Ohlone Way*, "Their society was not built around booty, slavery, war rituals, or the worship of war heroes. Adolescents did not attain manhood by killing an enemy or 'counting coup.'"[9] Sometimes California tribes did wage a short bloody war, usually over territorial rights or wife-stealing, but individual ambushes or small group confrontations were more likely. Intertribal mar-

"Indian dance at Mission San Jose, 1806," in an engraving by Wilhelm von Tilenau, published in 1813 by Langsdorff. Courtesy of Contra Costa County Historical Society.

riages probably cut back on some of these clashes. Mission records reveal pre-mission marriages of Volvons with Souyens, Ssaoams and Julpuns, among others.

Ohlone tribelets closest to mission sites supplied the earliest baptisms at the missions. As mission populations grew, the priests' need for ever larger herds and flocks to feed and support their converts also grew. More grazing land was necessary. Starting in 1797, Mission San Jose claimed the Livermore Valley and lowlands south

of Suisun Bay as its grazing lands.[10] Gradually, this practice affected the Livermore Valley Ohlones. The missionaries baptized those closest to the mission—the Seunen tribe, who probably lived near the present city of Dublin—mainly between 1801 and 1804. The next tribe to the east were the Souyen, who abandoned the southern Diablo foothills and the Tassajara Valley between 1801 and 1805. As expansion of the mission herds and flocks with their attendants continued eastward in the period from 1803 through 1805, the Ssaoams left the Altamont Pass hills and the Vasco for Mission San Jose.

On 10 May 1805 a Christian Indian testified about a plot to burn down Mission Santa Clara and kill the priests. Seunens and Volvons were implicated. The majority of Seunens were already at Mission San Jose, but the Volvons had not yet come in. On May 13 the missions sent out a large mounted party of armed, leather-jacketed soldiers under Luis Argüello that swept for a month through the interior coast ranges. As Milliken says, "While the Spanish expedition was still in the field, the first large group of Volvon migrants arrived at Mission San Jose. Perhaps they were harassed into coming by the Spanish troops. Perhaps they had been planning to come anyway."[11] Between May 22 and May 30, 33 Volvons were baptized. About a year later, a measles epidemic struck particularly hard at Mission San Jose, where three-fourths of the children under five, half the adult women and a quarter of the adult men died. The epidemic killed 60 out of 126 Ssaoams and 28 out of 52 Volvons.[12]

The Volvons eventually totaled 55 members at the San Francisco mission and 55 at San Jose. Since such a wide split was fairly unusual, Milliken suggests that Spanish authorities, still wary after the Santa Clara plot, purposefully separated them.[13] As the influence of the San Jose priests ranged even more to the east, most of the Tamcan, the Yokuts tribe living next to the Vasco, were baptized at Mission San Jose by 1811. The majority of Julpuns, Bay Miwok neighbors of the Volvons to the north, entered Mission San Jose that year.

By 1806 the Ssaoams and Volvons had disappeared completely from the foothills of Mount Diablo, and they never returned. No anthropologists arrived to interview them before they left; the camera was not yet known in Alta California. A Volvon or Ssaoam Ishi did not miraculously appear years later. Although much physical evidence points to their being the earliest residents of the Black Hills and Morgan Territory, only skeletons and ghostly footsteps remain.

1 Jeff Rosenthal, "More Than 9,000 Years Ago," Beneath Our Feet, conference at Oakland Museum of CA, 18 Nov 2000.

2 Randall Milliken, "Contact-Period Lifeways," Native American History Studies for the Los Vaqueros Project: A Synthesis, eds. David A. Fredrickson, Suzanne B. Stewart, Grace H. Ziesing (Rohnert Park, CA: Anthropological Studies Center, 1997) 37.

3 Beverly Ortiz, "Sacred Geography of the Los Vaqueros Project Area," Native American History Studies for the Los Vaqueros Project: A Synthesis, eds. David A. Fredrickson, Suzanne B. Stewart, Grace H. Ziesing (Rohnert Park, CA: Anthropological Studies Center, 1997) 59.

4 Catherine Callaghan, "Analysis of Ssaoam, Souyen, Volvon, and Tamcan Indian Names," Native American History Studies for the Los Vaqueros Project: A Synthesis, eds. David A. Fredrickson, Suzanne B. Stewart, Grace H. Ziesing (Rohnert Park, CA: Anthropological Studies Center, 1997) 48. All subsequent references to Indian names and their translations are to Callaghan's essay.

5 Ortiz, "Sacred Geography" 62.

6 Jeffrey B. Fentress, "The Rock Art of Vasco Caves: A Summary," Native American History Studies for the Los Vaqueros Project: A Synthesis, eds. David A. Fredrickson, Suzanne B. Stewart, Grace H. Ziesing (Rohnert Park, CA: Anthropological Studies Center, 1997) 74.

7 Fentress 84.

8 Milliken, "Contact Period" 32.

9 Malcolm Margolin, The Ohlone Way (Berkeley, CA: Heyday, 1978) 113.

10 John Gerald Stokle, "Mission San Jose and the Livermore Valley, 1798-1842," MA thesis, U of CA, Berkeley, c1967- 1968, 45.

11 Randall Milliken, "Spanish Contact and Missionization, 1776-1806," Native American History Studies for the Los Vaqueros Project: A Synthesis, eds. David A. Fredrickson, Suzanne B. Stewart, Grace H. Ziesing (Rohnert Park, CA: Anthropological Studies Center, 1997) 104.

12 Randall Milliken, "The Mission and Rancho Eras, 1806-1845," Native American History Studies for the Los Vaqueros Project: A Synthesis, eds. David A. Fredrickson, Suzanne B. Stewart, Grace H. Ziesing (Rohnert Park, CA: Anthropological Studies Center, 1997) 108.

13 Milliken, "Spanish Contact" 105.

a Ortiz, "Sacred Geography" 55.

b Ortiz, "Sacred Geography" 62.

Unfenced Grazing Land

AFTER MEXICO WON independence from Spain and the new government secularized the missions, governors of Alta California became generous in assigning land grants to secular owners. The quiet interlude in California history from 1834 until the discovery of gold in 1849 is generally considered the rancho period. In his study *Land in California,* W.W. Robinson described it: "Great ranchos, thousands of acres in extent, used . . . for the grazing of long-horned cattle, provided the pattern of the pastoral age in California and determined the nature of its civilization."[1] About 500 new land grants were made, most between 1833 and 1846. These expanses of rangeland, previously claimed by missions, were used predominantly for cattle grazing

Beginning a rancho operation was simple. The ranchero borrowed some seed cows and a bull or two to start his own enterprise, then five years later paid livestock back to the loaner. The Bernal family's *Rancho el Valle de San José,* located southeast of what is now Pleasanton, had 1,000 head of cattle in 1839; by 1850 the rancho had 25,000 cattle, several thousand sheep, and 1,000 horses grazing the valley and surrounding hills.[2] Allowed to roam free without any fencing between ranchos, the long-horned cattle were wild, dangerous animals, particularly since no bulls were gelded. John Bidwell, who traveled through the Livermore Valley in 1841, complained, "That valley was full of wild cattle—thousands of them—and they were more dangerous to one on foot, as I was, than grizzly bears. By dodging into the gulches and behind trees, I made my way to a Mexican ranch [José María Amador's *Rancho San Ramon*] at the extreme west end of the valley."[3] At the time of Bidwell's visit, Robert Livermore was running 9,000 head of cattle and 6,000 sheep.[4] Particularly in late spring after the rainy season, the

cattle would have been concealed by the horn-high grass and mustard. The Black Hills and Morgan Territory were never claimed in any rancho *diseño* (rough map), but livestock nevertheless were free to roam through the rugged hilly terrain that was considered communal grazing land for cattle, horses, and sheep.

The missions had trained California Indians and some early Mexican settlers in working with livestock. The most skilled of these men were called vaqueros. When the missions were dissolved, the vaqueros, who were fabulous horsemen, easily found work on the ranchos. Rancheros and their sons were usually excellent riders. Artist and historian Jo Mora said of them, "A Californio used his hind legs as a biped only when he danced or was hopelessly stranded out of arm's reach of a horse."[5] The large spurs preferred by these Californio cowmen dragged on the ground when the men walked. Early Livermore resident Mary Ann Harlan Smith remembered, "When we kept a store at Mission San Jose, the Spaniards, who came to trade with us, rode their horses right into the store, although there were four or five doorsteps. There would sometimes be five or six horses in the store at one time. The Spaniards very seldom got off their horses, unless it was really necessary."[6]

Californios and vaqueros were also highly skilled in the use of *la reata*—the lariat. "The riata in the hand of a Californian was a more dangerous weapon than gun or pistol. . . ."[7] Not only cattle and mustangs but wild animals such as bears were roped with the riata, as it came to be spelled.

The main industry of the ranchos was a continuation of the hide and tallow trade begun by the missions, although sheep also were raised for meat and wool. The ranchos closest to the Black Hills and Morgan Territory were Robert

Livermore's *Las Positas,* John Marsh's *Los Meganos,* and *Cañada de los Vaqueros,* which was initially claimed by a partnership of three men, Francisco Alviso, Manuel Miranda, and Antonio Higuera. Livermore bought the property from the three to enlarge his grazing land. *Los Meganos* was in today's Brentwood area; *Las Positas* lay north and south of Livermore. *Cañada de los Vaqueros,* containing the Vasco Caves and today's Los Vaqueros Reservoir, was directly east of the Black Hills.

Each spring, generally in April, rancheros within about a 50-mile radius held a rodeo, attended by their families and friends. The rodeo was not the modern version but similar to today's roundup. Vaqueros spread out through the surrounding hills and flushed out the cattle, which were gathered to the same spot each year and separated according to their brands and earmarks. This was also the time for calves to be marked and branded. *Cañada de los Vaqueros* was a major rodeo site. Neighbors Bernal, Marsh, Pacheco, and Livermore met there for annual rodeos until 1863, when the grant was fenced.

Early settler James D. Smith remembered seeing his first rodeo in the early 1850s at the Livermore rancho. He estimated that there were probably 2,000 head of cattle and possibly 150 men from different ranches on horseback. "Only two men were permitted to enter the herd at a time. They located their stock and carefully drove the animal to the edge of the herd, and then with a rush they would drive it outside and separate it from the large band and drive it some distance away, where other riders took charge."[8] An appointed official, the *juez de campo* (field judge), settled any ownership disputes and gave clearance to the rancheros to drive their stock back to their home range. Three days of celebration followed the rodeo, with drinking, gambling, dancing, feasting, cockfighting, and feats of horsemanship. Another rodeo was usually held in July.

In late summer or early autumn, the *matanza* (killing season) began. Vaqueros rode into the hills and rounded up three-year-old cattle. Down at the killing grounds, these skillful riders slaughtered each animal from horseback with a knife thrust to the neck. Indian workers did the laborious skinning and butchering, then removed the hides and staked them down to dry. Indian women stripped the carcasses of interior fat, melting it into tallow which they stored in leather bags called *botas.* The remaining fat from under the hide was rendered and made into soap. Cut into strips and pulled into shreds, the tenderest meat was dried in the sun to make jerky. Possibly the Indian workers carried out this process somewhere near Tassajara Road, because *tasajero* means the person who made this type of jerky. The rest of the meat was left on the ground for grizzlies, buzzards, and the rancho's dogs. Smith recalled that on a trip in 1850 from the San Ramon Valley to Livermore's rancho he saw "acres of ground near the Amador ranch covered with the bleaching bones of cattle previously slaughtered for the hides and tallow."[9]

Once the hides were dried, they had to be transported to the coast, where they were loaded in small boats and rowed over to large Yankee sailing vessels moored in San Francisco Bay. Each hide, sometimes called a California bank note, was worth about two dollars in trade. At the site of the *matanza,* Indians unstaked and loaded the dried hides into *carretas,* wooden carts with two wheels made of oak tree cross-sections. Drawn by oxen, filled *carretas* were driven to the coast by the rancho Indian workers. As lubrication for the axles, a pail of thick soapsuds was carried on the journey, but the squeaky cart still could be heard from far away.

In 1843 Robert Livermore received $100 and four *reales* in payment for two bags of tallow and 18 hides.[10] Like many of his fellow rancheros, Livermore had bought large iron kettles from a whaling vessel for melting the tallow. California

The paths of grazing cattle remain etched in the hills near the Levy/Cardoza ranch. Photo by Anne Homan.

exported 80 thousand hides, 15 million pounds of tallow, and $10,000 worth of soap in the year 1846.[11]

During the rancho period cattle were valued mainly for their hides. If a passerby needed meat while on a journey, an accepted practice was to kill a beef but leave the hide staked out for the owner to retrieve. Later, after the tremendous influx of hopeful seekers to the gold fields, meat became worth more than the hides. Miners had to be fed. In 1845 cattle were worth four dollars a head; by 1850 they were selling in Sacramento at $500 a head. Although that exorbitant price soon fell, for many years the price remained steady at $50 a head.[12]

A frequent pastime at fiestas in addition to bullfighting was a bear and bull fight. Before this could take place, vaqueros went up in the hills on a bright moonlit night to capture a live grizzly. For bait they killed a cow and left its carcass exposed. Hiding in nearby chaparral, the vaqueros waited until the bear was busy feeding before riding out to capture it with their leather-braided riatas and bring it alive to the bull ring. According to one observer, "The crowning feat of dexterity with the riata, and of horsemanship, combined with daring courage, is the lassoing of the [grizzly] bear."[13] A bull was brought to the same ring, and the two animals were pitted against each other. The old bullfighting arena in

James D. Smith reminisced about seeing and hearing a *carreta* in the San Ramon Valley in 1852:

"We could hear something coming a mile away —it proved to be a two-wheeled cart, the wheels being of solid wood about six inches thick, evidently made from the trunk of a large tree, with a hole in the center for an axle. On top of this was a crate about eight feet long and five feet wide. A pole was fastened to the axle and two oxen with immense horns were on either side of the pole, which was lashed to the horns by long rawhide straps, thereby balancing the cart and at the same time drawing it. In front of the oxen, with a pole over his shoulder reaching back to the oxen to guide them, was a barefooted and bareheaded Indian. Beside the oxen was another Indian, to keep the oxen moving, and every time the wheels turned, not having been greased, the noise could be heard a mile or more. In the cart was an Indian woman, some children, some poultry, and some dogs followed. That picture is in my mind as plain as if I had it before me." [a]

Dublin lasted into the 1860s, and the one in Laddsville, a small settlement near Robert Livermore's rancho, was in use until 1875. The Laddsville arena was about 30 feet in diameter and seven feet high, with several tiers of seats around the ring.[14]

With the American takeover of California, the Treaty of Guadalupe-Hidalgo in 1848 guaranteed all existing legal claims to real property. Californians had the right to keep their lands or sell them, to remain here as Mexican citizens, or to become U.S. citizens. As increasing numbers of gold-seekers realized that agriculture offered a more stable future than mining, the demand for California lands open to settlement also increased. Determining what land was available was not simple. On the East Coast and in Europe, people fenced their property to define it and to confine animals. In California no one had fenced the land, and rancho headquarters were far apart. Newcomers could easily assume that such large stretches of unfenced and unimproved land were unclaimed. In many cases they began to fence land and build houses, with the intention of claiming some acreage. To the ranchero who owned the place, these newcomers were squatters.

In 1851 the federal government created a Land Commission to evaluate the validity of Mexican land claims, and the Californians who thought that the Treaty of Guadalupe-Hidalgo had protected their property rights learned to their grief that Article X of the treaty placed the burden of proof of ownership and legal title upon the grantees. The Land Commission heard 812 cases in San Francisco from January 1852 until March 1856, but appeals dragged on, and the average time to secure a final court decision was 17 years.[15] The commission's decisions could be appealed to the district court and all the way to the U.S. Supreme Court.

Commission hearings were conducted in English, and none of the commissioners could read Spanish. Rancheros and their witnesses from throughout Northern California had to travel to San Francisco for trial proceedings. Meanwhile, the rancho owners were obligated to pay legal fees and a peculiarly American institution— property taxes. During all this legal hassle, of course, the land was not salable because titles were not clear. Hopeful settlers perched on the edges of land grants like vultures. The often illiterate Californios were at their lawyers' mercy. Roughly two-fifths of the contested land went to those lawyers.[16] Mortgages were available only at sky-high interest rates. Although about 600 land claims were ultimately confirmed, most rancheros went bankrupt in the process of clearing their titles.[17] If a rancho title was cleared, any squatter allowed to remain had to pay the landowner a prescribed price per acre. Some had paid previously, trying to ensure their rights. A rancho owner who made a squatter leave had to pay for the squatter's improvements.

The typical early rancho usually contained fruit trees and a vineyard as well as a few acres cultivated for beans, peppers, and melons. Some small fields of corn, wheat, and barley were sufficient for a household. With the influx of gold miners came a demand for grain for the production of bread flour. John Marsh reportedly planted the first wheat crop in Contra Costa County in 1837. The first wheat in Alameda County was harvested on 160 fenced acres of *Rancho Las Positas* in 1856, presaging the dramatic shift that took place in the Bay Area from cattle ranching to grain farming.

Weather influenced this shift. The winter of 1861–62 brought heavy rains that ultimately killed many cattle. On the heels of this disaster, a two-year drought in 1863 and 1864 nearly wiped out the remaining rancho herds. In 1860 approximately three million cattle had roamed the California hills; 10 years later, 630,000, or scarcely more than a fifth, remained.[18] This placed added strain on the embattled ranchero's ability to pay his taxes. These two years of drought mark the definitive transition in the state from grazing, the traditional rancho land use, to grain production.

Thus did American courts and property taxes, weather and the demands of an unfamiliar agriculture break up the rancho system. The Californios, like the Native Americans before them, surrendered to the pressures of a new age. By the 1870s many rancheros were working as day laborers in the towns.[19] The Californios no longer held wealth or community power.

Under the Spanish and Mexican governments, claimants had chosen only the best flat properties

Jo Mora wrote in 1949 in *Californios*:

The ranchero "was relieved of his rancho, his horses, and his cattle, legally or otherwise. . . . He belonged to another age, another way of thinking, another philosophy of life." [b]

with plenty of water for their large land grants. Once the United States took over the process, surveyors indiscriminately placed the township grid over unclaimed land. This meant that some sections of surveyed land were rocky and mountainous, some covered with forest, others without any water source. Once the land had been surveyed, California settlers had three possible methods for claiming land. One was called "preemption." An American citizen 21 years of age or older could choose ("pre-empt") an unclaimed area of not more than 160 acres (one quarter section), settle there and make improvements. Later the citizen could purchase the land for $1.25 an acre after establishing proof of settlement. The law allowing this sort of claim went into effect in 1852; in the mid-1870s the pre-emption price rose to $2.50 per acre.

The Homestead Act of 1862 permitted another type of claim. An American citizen 21 years or older could choose a maximum of 160 acres, and the land was free except for minimal filing fees. The homesteader had to live on and cultivate the property for five years. Within the next two years, proof of actual settlement and cultivation had to be filed, with the testimony of the claimant and of two witnesses. A homesteader who did not want to wait this long to own the land officially could at any time after six months of settlement "prove up" and pay for the land with cash or scrip.

Government scrip—paper issued by the U.S. government that entitled the claimant to a selected amount of public land for a certain fixed price—provided the third means of becoming a landowner. Agricultural college land scrip was one type. To encourage and help pay for the establishment of agricultural colleges, the federal government gave a certain amount of public land for individual states to sell. The resulting federal scrip could be sold by one state to another or to individuals. Between 1862 and 1903, holders of this scrip acquired 1,397,760 acres of California public land.[20] Another type of scrip was the military bounty land warrant. Former soldiers were sometimes awarded public land by the federal government as compensation for military service. A man could settle on and purchase 160 acres at the price of $1.25 an acre with military scrip issued by the government. After March 1852 these military bounty lands were made assignable, and a citizen could sell the scrip or buy it from a broker.

The final step in all the claims was a patent affirming ownership issued to the settler by a federal land office. The claimants along Morgan Territory Road dealt with the San Francisco General Land Office. Many early settlers along Morgan Territory Road were Californios. For them as for Californios in other areas, the process of acquiring land was difficult because many of them did not speak English, the language of the land office, and they were unused to U.S. legalities. And finally, the land now available was not the most desirable. Claimants after about 1855 were forced to choose land in the hills.

The communal grazing lands of the Black Hills and Morgan Territory had remained relatively untraveled by humans during the rancho period except for occasional excursions of wild game hunters or vaqueros in search of grizzly bears or straying cattle. Basic changes were occurring, however. John Bidwell in 1841 described the landscape around John Marsh's adobe as filled with countless thousands of free-roaming wild horses and tule elk.[21] In 1844 Robert Livermore realized $600 from the fat of elk and bear that he killed in the Tassajara area of the Black Hills.[22] By 1860 the antelope and tule elk had disappeared from the Black Hills and Morgan Territory to seek forage in less crowded meadows. Bunch grasses covered the hills before the area was used as rangeland. Today, those native perennial grasses have been almost obliterated by oats and similar non-native annual grasses spread by the wind and by mission and rancho livestock.

1 W.W. Robinson, *Land in California* (Berkeley, CA: U of CA P, 1948) 45.

2 Herbert L. Hagemann Jr, *Abstract of Title—Rancho el Valle de San José,* reprint from *Pacific Historian* May/August 1965 (Amador-Livermore Valley Historical Society, n.d.).

3 John Bidwell, *Life in California Before the Gold Discovery* (Palo Alto: Lewis Osborne, 1966) 18.

4 Flora L. DeNier, *Robert Livermore and the Development of the Livermore Valley to 1860,* MA thesis, U of CA, Berkeley: 82.

5 Jo Mora, *Californios* (Garden City, NY: Doubleday, 1949) 68. The term "Californio"—used by historians in referring to the years 1830 to 1880—means native-born Spanish-speaking Californian of Spanish-speaking parents. Leonard Pitt, *The Decline of the Californios* (Berkeley: U of CA P, 1966) ix and glossary 309.

6 Anna T. Siig and G.B. Drummond, transcribers, *Recollections of a Pioneer Mother,* published originally in *The Grizzly Bear,* June 1915 (Livermore: Livermore Heritage Guild, 1995) 34.

7 *History of Alameda County, California* (Oakland: M.W. Wood, 1883) 83.

8 G.B. Drummond, ed., *Recollections: Early Life in the San Ramon Valley As Related by Prof. James Dale Smith, Headmaster, Livermore College* (Oakland, CA: GRT Book Printing, 1995) 23.

9 Drummond 23.

10 Janet Newton, *Las Positas* (Livermore, CA: Newton, 1969) 108.

11 Mae Fisher Purcell, *History of Contra Costa County* (Berkeley: Gillick, 1940) 206.

12 Walton Bean and James J. Rawls, *California: An Interpretive History,* 4th ed. (NY: McGraw-Hill, 1983) 162.

13 Edwin Bryant, *What I Saw in California* (1848; Lincoln, NE: U of NE P, 1985) 447.

14 Gary Drummond, "Laddsville," *The Livermore Roots Tracer* (Livermore: Livermore Area Genealogical Society, Oct 1997) 686.

15 Robinson 106.

16 Leonard Pitt, "John S. Hittell Gives the Brief of the Original Claimants," *California Controversies,* 2nd ed. (Arlington Heights, IL: Harlan Davidson, 1987) 70.

17 Robinson 106.

18 Lawrence I. Jelinek, *Harvest Empire: A History of California Agriculture* (SF: Boyd and Fraser, 1979) 27.

19 Jelinek 27.

20 Robinson 183.

21 John Bidwell, *A Journey to California, 1841: The Journal Account in the Bidwell-Bartleson Party,* ed. Doyce B. Nunis Jr (Santa Cruz, CA: Western Tanager P, 1991) 53.

22 DeNier 82.

a Drummond 14.

b Mora 175.

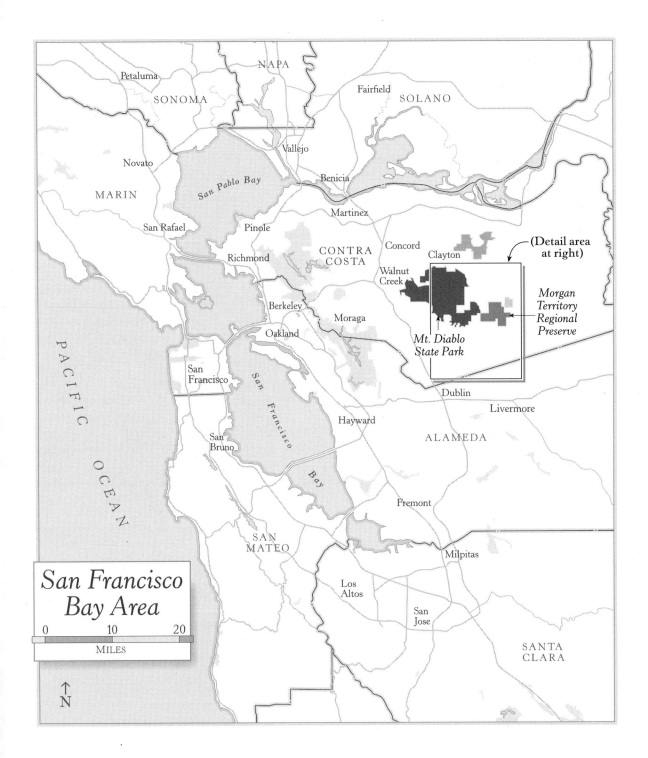

PACIFIC OCEAN

Petaluma

SONOMA

NAPA

Fairfield

SOLANO

Novato

MARIN

Vallejo

San Pablo Bay

Benicia

San Rafael

Pinole

Martinez

CONTRA COSTA

Concord

Clayton

(Detail area at right)

Richmond

Walnut Creek

Morgan Territory Regional Preserve

Berkeley

Moraga

Mt. Diablo State Park

Oakland

San Francisco

San Francisco Bay

Dublin

Livermore

San Bruno

Hayward

ALAMEDA

Fremont

SAN MATEO

Milpitas

Los Altos

San Jose

SANTA CLARA

San Francisco Bay Area

| 0 | 10 | 20 |
MILES

↑
N

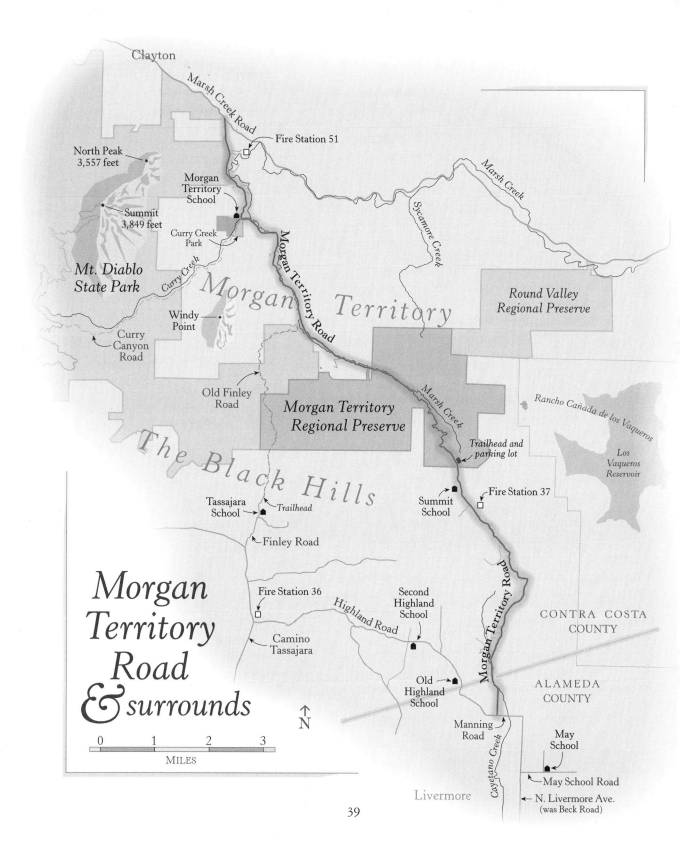

Clayton

Marsh Creek Road

Fire Station 51

North Peak
3,557 feet

Morgan
Territory
School

Summit
3,849 feet

Curry Creek
Park

Mt. Diablo
State Park

Morgan

Curry Creek

Windy
Point

Curry
Canyon
Road

Old Finley
Road

Territory

Morgan Territory Road

Sycamore Creek

Marsh Creek

Round Valley
Regional Preserve

Morgan Territory
Regional Preserve

The Black Hills

Marsh Creek

Trailhead and
parking lot

Rancho Cañada de los Vaqueros

Los
Vaqueros
Reservoir

Tassajara
School

Trailhead

Summit
School

Fire Station 37

Finley Road

Morgan
Territory
Road
&surrounds

Fire Station 36

Highland Road

Second
Highland
School

Morgan Territory Road

CONTRA COSTA
COUNTY

Camino
Tassajara

Old
Highland
School

ALAMEDA
COUNTY

0   1   2   3
MILES

↑
N

Manning
Road

Cayetano Creek

May
School

May School Road

Livermore

N. Livermore Ave.
(was Beck Road)

Tomás and Elicia Robles' youngest son, Steve Robles, was a member of the Livermore High School class of 1938.
Photo courtesy of Livermore High School.

40

Yaqui and Californio

THE JUST-RISEN sun cast long shadows from a group of travelers moving on foot over the red floor of the Sonoran Desert. Towering above the feathery *palos verdes,* giant saguaros dominated the stark landscape as far as the eye could see. Three of these travelers were a Yaqui Indian named Manuela Robles, her five-year-old son, Tomás,[1] and her brother, probably Manuel. Rumors of gold in California had reached the Sonoran villages in this year 1849, and many Indians had already headed north to seek a better fortune.

The Yaqui tribe still survives along the banks of the Yaqui River, which arises in the Sonoran Desert highlands of Mexico and flows down to the Gulf of California. In the fertile area close to the river, the Yaquis plant corn and cotton, living much like their relatives in the southwestern United States. Subsequent to the Spanish conquest, they accumulated large numbers of sheep, cattle, and horses.[2] "The Yaqui remained fiercely independent throughout Spanish and Mexican rule. . . . Although they pretended to convert to Catholicism, the Yaquis never abandoned their tribal customs."[3] Determined to control their own lands, they fought off both Spanish and Mexican armies.

The discovery of gold near Sutter's Fort in 1848 fueled enormous immigration not only from the eastern United States but also from Mexico, triggering impossible dreams for the majority. A U.S. dragoon stationed in Arizona described the northward immigration: "The whole state of Sonora is on the move, are passing us in gangs daily. . . ."[4] In the southern placer mine diggings of the San Joaquin River watershed, about 8,000 Sonorans and South Americans had gathered by June 1849.[5] In 1850 the new Foreign Miners' Tax Law prevented "foreigners," including Chinese and Sonorans, from filing claims. Those who already had claims were to be taxed $20 per month, an exorbitant sum at the time. California records do not reveal whether three Yaquis of the Robles family reached the gold diggings. Family legend has it that they did. About 12 years later, in 1862, Tomás Robles allegedly settled in Contra Costa County, as noted on the 1871 filing of his claim for the SW¼ of section 8 T2S/R2E.

By 1872 the tax collector for Contra Costa County recorded Tomás Robles living on section 8 and owning 700 sheep and 10 horses. When the *Contra Costa Gazette* published names of county taxpayers who paid more than $1,000 in 1872, Tomás Robles was listed at $2,585. On 10 March 1875 he scrip-purchased the SW¼ of section 8, and on 18 September 1886, after filing homestead entries in 1875 and 1879 for the SE¼ of section 4 T2S/R2E, he was, after some problems, granted a homestead claim there. He had not realized the necessity of submitting a final proof in order to receive his patent for the homestead. He missed the seven-year expiration date, and he had not applied for the necessary citizenship papers. "I am a poor Mexican, ignorant of the laws and customs of the United States regarding the Government lands, and speak English very indifferently, and did not know that I was required to make my proof within seven years. After I made my homestead in the Land office, I supposed the land was mine and nothing further was necessary, until I was informed by some friends that I must make final proof," was his explanation.[6]

The homestead ranch that belonged to Tomás Robles on the SE¼ of section 4 contains a semicircular stone corral, approximately 90 by 80 feet, at the edge of the *Cañada de los Vaqueros* land grant. According to his grandson Bernard Robles, Tomás built the corral for his sheep.[7]

This property was used mainly for grazing; by 1877 Tomás Robles' flock numbered 900 sheep, and he was cultivating 75 acres of wheat and barley.[8]

On the west side of Morgan Territory Road today, just 1.1 miles north from Manning Road, the Doubletree development sprawls out with large homes on five-acre lots. Once the site of the Robles ranch on section 8, the area is a bowl, a small canyon surrounded by gently rounded hills and bisected by a major artery of Cayetano Creek. The United States censuses for 1880, 1900, and 1910 include the household of Tomás Robles—each time with a different wife and different children. His first wife, Merced, died in June 1883, leaving him—at the time of his 1884 homestead proof—with one child, probably Rosa listed on the 1880 census.[9] His daughter Juanita, born of his third wife when Tomás was 71, described him as a "Don Juan," and although she was not aware of the two earlier families of 1880 and 1900, she agreed that this scenario was certainly possible. The third wife was Elicia García de Palomares, whom he married on 27 February 1891[10] when he was 46 and she was 13.[11] Elicia was an orphan, and Tomás promised her uncle who was her guardian that he would not consummate the marriage until she was 15. Apparently he did not quite keep his promise; their first child, Thomas, was born in late 1892.

Tomás and Elicia's last surviving child was Juanita, who was born in 1915 and died 21 February 2001. "My father . . . didn't look like an Indian. He had grayish eyes, white hair, and [was] little—he was a little bit of a man. He had a fairly good personality because he laughed a lot. He laughed a lot, and he drank a lot."[12] The Contra Costa voting register of 1892 showed his height as five feet five, his hair black, and his complexion and eyes dark.

Besides running sheep and cattle, Tomás owned a hay press, which he hired out to various farms in the area with a crew of workers. Elicia

Summer garden, winter stew:

Each year Elicia Robles planted a garden with bitter lettuce, bell peppers, onions, cilantro, parsley, tomatoes, and artichokes. She made and sold cheese, and she cut beef into thin strips for jerky, added spices, wrapped it with cheesecloth, and hung it up to dry. In the winter rainy season, when her family was unable to travel into town for groceries, she would pound on the jerky, pull it apart, and make a savory stew with potatoes and onions. With a metate she ground a fine table salt from rock salt.

had to prepare lunches for the crew. She was famous for her good cooking, which included menus from many different cultures—Basque, Italian, Portuguese, Spanish—reflecting the makeup of the local press crews. "She learned how to cook every one of those kinds of foods. She was a great cook," recalled her daughter.[13] Tomás transported the food for the workers with a horse-drawn wagon. An excellent horseman, he bought wild horses and trained them for the hay press.[14]

The family had a small orchard at the ranch, with a pear and an apple tree, and also planted fruit trees on their property in Livermore. Juanita remembered canning many different fruits: "So I learned how to can. Pears, peaches, my mother canned everything. Peaches, pears, we had in town, we had apricot, quince, figs. . . ."[15] One of Juanita's brothers, Leo, would pickle a large keg of olives each year from their tree in town. They also made butter and raised chickens, chiefly for eggs. Whenever visitors arrived, which Juanita noted was frequently, Elicia served them some canned fruit as well as coffee and a sweet bread. "And when you left, you always left with a jar of peaches or whatever. And I was always surprised my mother was so generous."[16]

Elicia Palomares Robles (l.) and her daughter Sarafina. Another daughter, Della Robles Buffo, is in the photo at right; the young girl's name is not known. Both photos courtesy of Cal and Beverly Buffo.

All cooking was done on a wood stove, which heated the small kitchen very quickly. On cold winter days the room was merely snug and warm, but most canning was done in the summer heat, as the fruit ripened. Before air conditioning and refrigeration, the women of a family could be at the stove throughout the day and night to finish canning a fruit or vegetable that would have spoiled if they had waited longer. Summer temperatures in the area can often reach the 100-degree mark. Of course, clothes manage to acquire dirt in all seasons—more work at the wood stove, heating wash water and then the irons. At least in summer weather, the washing itself could be accomplished outdoors, but hot water for the weekly Saturday baths also had to be heated on the stove. Besides surviving this woman's working world, Elicia bore at least 12 children, seven sons and five daughters, between 1892 and 1917—Thomas, Leo, Della, Angela, Sarafina (Sadie), Vincent, Virginia, Michael, Salvador, John, Juanita, and Steve.

With her daughter Juanita and her three young sons, Salvador, John, and Steve, Elicia moved away from her husband and other sons down into Livermore about 1922. Angela had died, and probably the other girls were married. Tomás had started making *grappa* in addition to his usual red wine. *Grappa* is an un-aged brandy made from must—the skins and other material left after the wine pressing. Tomás and the older sons took care of the ranch livestock and engaged in bootlegging. During the Prohibition years, many hardscrabble ranchers in the Black Hills—always strapped for ready cash—set up stills and secretly made liquor besides their traditional

Juanita Robles Hargraves told 'how they did years ago':

"We had pigs that we raised here in town, and he [brother Salvador]'d go out, and there was a cheese factory here. And he'd go after the swill and bring it home. And he had one of these wagons that you pull . . . but he'd fight with somebody along the way and the swill would be spilled and the pigs would have nothing to eat. And then my mother would call my father and then he'd come over and give him a spanking—you know how they did years ago. And that's how I remember my father."[a]

wine. Sometimes, Tomás also stayed in Livermore, at a house near that of his wife.

During this spell in town, Elicia worked at the Coast Manufacturing Company, a major Livermore employer at the time that manufactured safety fuses used to ignite explosives. In town she could also more regularly attend church and see to the baptisms and confirmations of her children. Tomás was not very religious. Juanita clarified her father's position regarding the church: "The men were against the religion. . . . My mother would still take us to church and everything but it wasn't something my father wanted. He didn't believe in baptizing. . . . it was too bad. But my mother raised us Catholic and she went to church when she could. She walked most of the time."[17] Juanita emphasized that this attitude was not only her dad's but that of men in general in her culture. Quite possibly, the stance of Tomás reflected the Yaqui rejection of Roman Catholic worship in Mexico. In his study of Californios, Leonard Pitt noted the trend: "The new generation deliberately rejected Spanish forms of piety. Domestic devotions fell off among the male part of the population until, by the end of the Mexican regime, Sunday mass had become

an affair for women, children, and neophyte Indians. . . ."[18] Juanita rarely saw her father except when he was invited to her mother's house in Livermore Heights to discipline her brother Salvador, "a feisty little thing."

The Robles family had acquired rental property in Livermore, and Elicia kept an eye on their tenants. They owned two town lots in Livermore Heights, near Junction Avenue and Enos Way; one lot in the Ladd Tract, and two in the Northern Addition. Laid out by Alexander Esdon in 1875, the Northern Addition north of downtown Livermore includes seven east-west streets from Pine to Chestnut and seven north-south streets from I to P Street. This early housing development attracted many Hispanic residents.

In town Elicia also served as a midwife for many Spanish-speaking women and helped many of her own grandchildren and great-grandchildren into the world. Bernard Robles was born on the old property off Morgan Territory Road with the help of his grandmother. His official birthplace, in 1930, was "Black Hill Canyon." Later, when each of Bernard's children was born, his grandmother took care of his wife, Rose, for two weeks. Neighbor Antoinette Morris praised the Robles' varied attempts to support their family. "They were really enterprising, exceptional, I think."[19]

Manuela Robles, Tomás' mother, died in April 1913 at age 90. Tomás died in 1926 at age 81, but of course Elicia was only in her forties. After the death of her husband, Elicia moved back and forth between the Black Hills ranch and her home in Livermore. Her son Michael managed the ranch with the help of her grandsons Bernard and Vince, sons of Vincent Robles. Bernard and Vince attended Highland School in the Tassajara area full time and did almost all the ranch work—milking the cows, training them to the milking stanchion, haying, feeding the cattle on section 4 and checking their water supply. Michael daily commuted north on Morgan Territory Road to Pittsburg, where he worked as a cement finisher for his brothers-in-law, the Buffos. Elicia's grandson Cal Buffo often rode to the ranch on weekends in Michael's battered old truck, which was doorless on the driver's side. Bernard recalled his grandmother's coming to the ranch, usually for two-week stretches. On Sundays, however, she always attended church in Livermore.

As Juanita described it, the exterior of the ranch house was constructed of wide vertical unpainted redwood boards that measured 1 by 12 or maybe 1 by 16 inches. On the interior the redwood boards were papered.[20] Upon entering the house via a screened porch, a visitor was in the heart of the home, the kitchen with its centerpiece—that wood stove—along with a large table and a number of wooden chairs. Elicia and the girls slept in the two bedrooms off the kitchen; the boys slept out in the bunkhouse. An outhouse was nearby.

Minnie Robles Pederson is the widow of Elicia's son Michael Robles, who managed the ranch. After Minnie married Michael in 1941, he brought her from Los Angeles, where she had grown up, to the rustic Robles ranch. Shocked at its condition, she insisted that he add a living room and a bathroom with tub and running water. He also installed a generator for electricity and built a milking barn. Minnie helped to milk 25 cows every morning. She separated off the cream and took it to the Southern Pacific Railroad depot at Livermore and Railroad avenues on her way to work for the telephone company. The house had a basement where Michael continued the family tradition of making red wine. Minnie said that she worked hard to make the place more livable, painting and wallpapering. Although Elicia cooked on her wood stove whenever she came out to the ranch, Michael installed a two-burner butane stove for Minnie. The family still raised pigs, sheep, cattle, and chickens.

Michael and his family moved down into Livermore in 1943, and without a regular caretaker the ranch began to fall apart. Elicia's grandsons Bernard and Vince had moved back to Danville to live with their mother and father. Elicia Robles leased out the property on section 8 to Al Morris and the section 4 land to Ed Smith. She often left her Livermore house to stay with her daughters and their families in Pittsburg. She and Tomás are buried at St. Michael's Cemetery in Livermore. At her death in 1958, she left 10 children, 38 grandchildren, 31 great-grandchildren, and an estate worth an estimated $77,000.[21]

Elicia and her six sisters were Californios, daughters of the Mexican-born Miguel García de Palomares. Elicia's mother, Virginia Miranda, was also of Californio heritage. Virginia's father was ranchero Manuel Miranda, one of the three original claimants of the *Cañada de los Vaqueros* land grant. Apparently Manuel Miranda no longer owned grazing lands by 1880. In August of that year, he opened a saddlery in the Whetmore building on First Street in Livermore.[22] James D. Smith described the expertise of Manuel Miranda in his memoirs: "A Mr. Miranda was a very skilled mechanic, made spurs and Spanish bridle bits inlaid with gold and silver, Spanish saddles complete, fine hair ropes, Macarta and rawhide ropes, 'Riatas,' or 8 strand ropes and hair cinches to secure the saddles to the horses. I have never seen any finer work in his line than he made."[23]

Elicia and her mother had been proud that they spoke Spanish with a Castilian accent rather than a Mexican accent. Juanita, too, was proud of this: "My mother, oh God, my mother could speak the best Spanish. Everybody used to comment: 'You speak so well.' Even the Mexican people would tell her this."[24] Elicia and at least one of her sisters attended Highland School for a while. "My mother was a very very smart lady, so [the teacher] wanted her to go, continue on to school. But you know, she just couldn't."[25]

Thornton Taylor, a local rancher who talked with Elicia a number of times about the possibility of buying her property, described her as an "effervescent" person who "loved life," a personality asset in any era and culture.

1 I have used the Spanish spelling *Tomás* throughout this book although he later used the anglicized spelling *Thomas*. I have also used the Spanish name *Elicia* throughout for his wife's name, although in many references she is called *Eliza* or *Elizabeth*. Some hearsay exists that supports the third party as Tomás' brother, rather than his uncle. In either case, the name of the third party is not certain. In the 1860 census for Contra Costa County township 2, page 100, a Manuel Robles, age 33, is listed as living with Cassildo Figaroa. Both men are from Sonora, Mexico. Manuel is thus quite a bit older than Tomás, who would have been 16 in 1860. Manuela, on the other hand, was about 37 years old in 1860 and could more likely have been Manuel's sister. The 1871-2 Alameda County Directory lists Manuel Robles, laborer, Livermore. The 1871-2 Contra Costa County Directory lists another possibility, Francisco Robles, farmhand, in township 2.

2 Hubert H. Bancroft, *The Wild Tribes, The Native Races of the Pacific States of North America*, Vol. 1 (NY: Appleton, 1875) 587.

3 Carl Waldman, *Encyclopedia of Native American Tribes* (NY: Facts on File, 1988) 255.

4 William Perkins, *Three Years in California* (Berkeley: U of CA P, 1964) 20.

5 Perkins 27.

6 San Francisco General Land Office, Homestead Entry 2647, National Archives, DC.

7 Bernard Robles, personal interview, 2 Dec 1998.

8 Karana Hattersley-Drayton, *Report on Oral History Completed Under the Historic Property Treatment Plan for Construction of the Los Vaqueros Dam and Reservoir and Related Requirements, Los Vaqueros Project* (Rohnert Park, CA: Sonoma State U Academic Foundation, 1996) 23.

9 Homestead Entry 2647.

10 Contra Costa County Marriages, Book 4: 102.

11 The 1900 census not only lists a different wife, Mary, but also three different children, John, Andrew and Frank. Perhaps at the time Tomás had two wives, or maybe these were his stepchildren. The census lists a marriage 11 years earlier, two years before the marriage to Elicia. Mary's given age in 1900 is 50.

12 Karana Hattersley-Drayton, "Interview with Juanita Robles Hargraves," Sonoma State Anthropological Studies Center, for the Contra Costa Water District, 9 Nov 1995: 12.

13 Hattersley-Drayton Interview 8.

14 Bernard Robles interview.

15 Hattersley-Drayton Interview 31.

16 Hattersley-Drayton Interview 33.

17 Hattersley-Drayton Interview 23.

18 Leonard Pitt, *The Decline of the Californios* (Berkeley: U of CA P, 1948) 4.

19 Antoinette Gattorna Morris, personal interview, 9 Sep 1996.

20 Hattersley-Drayton Interview 42-43.

21 "Estate Valued at Nearly $77,000," *The Livermore Herald* 4 Dec 1959: 13.

22 *The Livermore Herald* 5 Aug 1880: 3.

23 J.D. Smith, "Gringo," *The Livermore Herald* 10 July 1925: 7.

24 Hattersley-Drayton Interview 16.

25 Hattersley-Drayton Interview 24.

a Hattersley-Drayton Interview 4.

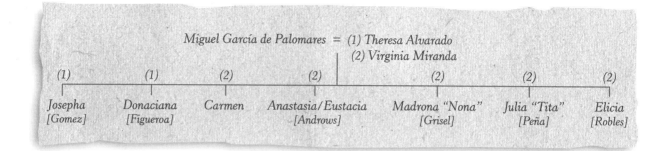

Miguel García de Palomares = (1) Theresa Alvarado
(2) Virginia Miranda

(1)	(1)	(2)	(2)	(2)	(2)	(2)
Josepha [Gomez]	Donaciana [Figueroa]	Carmen	Anastasia/Eustacia [Androws]	Madrona "Nona" [Grisel]	Julia "Tita" [Peña]	Elicia [Robles]

Seven Sisters

FATHER VINCENT VINYES often sailed on the ferryboat *Carquinez* from Benicia to administer sacraments to faithful Catholics in Martinez at the simple wooden church on Estudillo Street. On 19 March 1865 Father Vincent came over from St. Dominic's Priory to perform the marriage ceremony for Virginia Miranda and Miguel García de Palomares at the Martinez mission church that would later be named St. Catherine of Siena. Virginia, a Californio, was the daughter of Manuel Miranda and Carmen Alviso. Miguel was a native of Sonora, Mexico, and the son of Raymond García de Palomares and Michaela Valenzuela. After the ceremony, the families most likely celebrated with a fiesta at the Miranda rancho. The marriage was the first for 21-year-old Virginia, but Miguel, age 35, was a widower who had married Teresa Alvarado sometime before 1855.

Miguel's first marriage produced at least two daughters who lived to adulthood. According to records at St. Michael's church in Livermore, his daughter **Donaciana** married Cipriano Figueroa, the son of Casildo Figueroa and Rosa Miranda, on 22 December 1878. The couple settled in July 1879 on the NW¼ of section 20 T1S/R2E in the Black Hills. The patent for the Figueroa homestead was issued on 10 April 1885. On his land office proof, Cipriano Figueroa testified to having 10 fruit trees and 100 grapevines on the property

as well as a house and barn.[1] Cipriano died at age 46 in 1901, after suffering paralysis from a stroke, leaving Donaciana with a number of young children. Her obituary stated that she moved in 1906 from Livermore to Napa and then in 1925 to Yountville, where she lived until her death in 1934. Juanita Robles Hargraves remembered visiting her "Tía Chiana" in Napa as a child.

The other daughter from the first marriage of Miguel Palomares was **Josepha**, who married Pleasanton resident John Gomez in 1872 at San Jose. They settled in the Black Hills in summer of 1876. By 1885 Gomez had received a patent for an 80-acre homestead—the north half of the NW¼ of section 8 T2S/R2E. On his proof of residence for the land office, dated 18 December 1884, Gomez testified that Josepha had died just 10 days earlier, leaving him with their five children.[2] One Gomez son, Tino, stayed in the Livermore area; daughter Florence married John Merchant of Livermore.

From the marriage of Virginia Miranda and Miguel García de Palomares came five daughters. The first-born, **Carmen**, known as Carmelita, most likely died before 1886 as she is not mentioned in her father's deed of trust drawn up that year. The other four daughters—Anastacia, Madrona ("Nona"), Julia ("Tita"), and Elicia—settled along Morgan Territory Road very close

'Official' spellings:

Early recorders of public information such as tax payments or the census in Contra Costa County rarely were of Hispanic heritage and were not necessarily well-educated. Hispanic residents, many of them illiterate, often spoke heavily accented English. The resulting tortuous spellings of Hispanic names makes tracing family lines difficult. Records for Miguel García de Palomares, for example, spell his surname variously as Palomades, Palomedes, Palomario, Palomaro, Palomeres, Palamaries, Polomaries, Palamarsis, Palamaris, and Palomaseno. His first name is sometimes anglicized to Michael or rendered as Magell, Magil, or Maguel. In one index the tax recorder alphabetized his entry under "Magil" rather than by surname. Having two surnames also caused difficulties; occasionally his name was simply written "Michael García."

to one another, on land from their father's homestead. **Elicia**, the youngest, was discussed in the preceding chapter.

According to 1872 and 1874 tax records, Miguel García de Palomares was owner of the NW¼ of section 8 T2S/R2E. In 1880 Miguel received a homestead of 80 acres, the south half of the quarter.[3] Evidently he had allowed his son-in-law, John Gomez, to file for the northern 80 acres. Miguel Palomares listed a house, stable, and about 60 grapevines on his 1879 homestead proof. He had 60 acres planted in grain.[4] By the time of Miguel's death on 24 March 1886, his wife Virginia had already died. Miguel must have been aware of his approaching death because, in a deed of trust entered at Martinez on 22 March 1886, he had appointed his brother-in-law Francisco "Frank" Miranda trustee and guardian

of his orphaned minor daughters: Anastacia, 17, Madrona, 14, Tita, 11, and Elicia, 9. He entrusted Frank with the south half of the NW¼ of section 8 "in order to provide maintenance and support" for these four girls. When they had all reached their majority or had married, Frank was to sell the property and divide the proceeds with these four, but also give $100 from the sale to Miguel's son Evaristo and daughter Donaciana, now the wife of Cipriano Figueroa. Frank Miranda died in 1891, and Cipriano Figueroa became the new trustee.[5] In 1897 Cipriano settled the estate by dividing the remaining 80 acres of the property into 20-acre parcels and deeding one parcel each to Anastacia, Madrona, Julia, and Elicia, the four living Miranda/Palomares daughters.[6]

One 20-acre parcel was just north of the SW¼ of section 8 where Elicia Robles lived. Accessible by dirt road through the Robles' property, this plot had gone to her sister **Julia**, nicknamed "Tita," who married Mexican-born Basilio Peña in September 1893. "Local rancher [John] Gleese recalled the whole ranch was in grapes," noted an interviewer in 1996. "Peña sold wine during Prohibition and made 'the most wonderful claret.'"[7] John Gleese's son Jack remembered that customers would come from as far away as San Francisco to buy wine from Peña. A water tank is the only physical evidence of the family's ranch remaining on the property. Tita died at age 33 of tuberculosis, leaving her husband and six children shares in her property. The children were four young boys, William, Henry, Michael, and Antonio; a little girl, Mary, and a baby, Matilda, who died shortly after her mother. According to Juanita Robles Hargraves, Peña was a "very strange man, we didn't understand his ways because he was a foreigner. And when his wife died, when my aunt died, he sent for a woman from Spain and she was crazier than he!"[8] Actually, Peña's second wife, Evangelina Prieto, was a native of Colombia.

Basilio Peña died in 1927 of bronchial asthma. His sons Antonio and William had died nine years earlier in the influenza epidemic that struck Contra Costa County on its deadly march around the world. Eighteen-year-old Antonio died on 7 November 1918. His brother William, age 23, died the next day. Despite precautions such as California's "mask law," which required everyone on the public streets to wear a mask against contagion, one in four Americans caught the so-called Spanish influenza; 550,000 died of it.[9]

Madrona (nicknamed "Nona"), the second Miranda/Palomares sister, had married a tall, gray-eyed Frenchman, Adolphe Grisel, in 1852, when she was about 20. Grisel was a native of Lorraine and about 30 years older than she. Family lore suggests that Grisel had been pressed into service by the French navy. After having jumped ship in San Francisco in approximately 1867, he traveled to Livermore and by 1871 had settled down to an agricultural life, filing on the SE¼ of section 8 next to Tomás Robles. The San Francisco General Land Office issued him the patent on 3 May 1881, after he bought 160 acres with agricultural college scrip.[10] By 1885, however, John Beck owned this quarter section. After his 1892 marriage to Nona Palomares, Adolphe Grisel planted his wife's 20 acres in a vineyard and produced a red wine. This ranch was north of the Robles home ranch and the Peña place. His grandson August Grisel remembered that the living quarters consisted of a two-bedroom wood "shack."[11] From 1888 to 1899, Adolphe managed a Livermore saloon in E.S. Fergoda's store near the flagpole at Mill Square, the intersection of First and Livermore (then Lizzie Street). For the last 20 years of his life, he dedicated himself to his Black Hills vineyard. He died suddenly of pneumonia in 1920. After his death, and for some time earlier, Nona Grisel lived in the Northern Addition development at the corner of M and Pine Streets in Livermore until her own

HOW TO MAKE GAUZE SPANISH INFLUENZA MASKS

Masks for protection against influenza, according to the San Francisco Board of Health's circular issued this week, should be five by seven inches and made of four layers of fine gauze. Tape or strings should be sewed to the four corners. The upper pair of tapes are to be tied at the back of the head above the ears and lower pair around the neck.

The mask, says the circular, should not be medicated in any way. It can be cleaned by boiling for fifteen minutes.

During the epidemic, says the circular, all persons, and especially those who have come in contact with a case, should gargle the throat and spray the nose several times daily with Dobell's solution or Dickloramine T diluted in water. If these are not obtainable a solution of one tablespoonful each of borax, salt and bicarbonate of soda in one quart of warm water may be used. This, it is said, is about as good as Dobell's solution.

death in 1946. Grandson August remembered his grandmother as "a grand lady in all respects, and she respected everybody."[12]

Adolphe and Nona Grisel had five daughters and two sons. August, the younger son, kept up the vineyard and worked as a ranch hand. In June 1932 federal agents arrested the older son, Adolph, for sale and possession of an alcoholic beverage at 1289 Second Street, a building used as a saloon before Prohibition. Four other establishments were raided on the same day; six men were arrested in all. "While hundreds of people

The Androws' barn, still standing in the early 1980s, has since been removed for a home site. Photo by Anne Homan.

watched the performance, crowbars, sledge hammers and axes were wielded alike upon bars and fixtures that had cost thousands of dollars in the days before prohibition. . . . Cash registers, drink mixing machines, glassware, refrigerators, chairs and tables were loaded on trucks for removal to government warehouses in San Francisco," reported *The Livermore Herald*. Adolph was taken before the U.S. commissioner in Oakland and released on $1,500 bail.[13] Possibly he had been selling wine from the family's 20 acres on Morgan Territory Road.

The oldest sister, **Anastacia** (most often written "Eustacia"), married Charles Androws, who, despite his English-sounding surname, was a native San Franciscan of Mexican and Italian heritage. Eustacia's nickname, mentioned in her half-sister's obituary, was Tassie. She and Charles lived first in Brentwood, then moved to the Black Hills around 1900. Their 20 acres lay on the opposite side of Morgan Territory Road from the property of her sisters Elicia and Nona, toward the east. Here they maintained a vineyard and a family orchard of pomegranate, fig, apple, and orange trees as well as a number of almond trees. For the most part, the almond trees have migrated downhill, their nuts replanted by wind and ground squirrels along the roadside and nourished by the spring runoff. In 1971 the Androws' still-standing barn, fig tree, and apple tree identified their abandoned home site on what is now the property of Will and Marge Dias just before the eucalyptus grove some 1.8 miles north of Manning Road. Before building their home in 1984, the Diases had the original barn and fruit trees removed. The eucalyptus, which is not native to California, is a marker for the old ranches. Residents often planted these Australian trees in the late 1800s and early 1900s. Probably because of their strong herbal odor, they were "said to be a sure preventative against chills and fever, where grown in profusion."[14]

Eustacia Palomares Androws worked as housekeeper for Mrs. Patrick Gleese and tutored John Gleese in Spanish so that he could communicate better with his neighbors and ranch hands. John's son Jack supported Juanita's recollection that her aunt's pronunciation was Castilian.

A steep dirt track snakes up the hill above what is now the Dias home. Will Dias heard from longtime resident Al Morris that Charles Androws cut hay on the high meadows of the property, using horses to pull the mown hay down on skids to his barn. By 1920 the Androws family lived on a ranch near Greenville Road to the east of Livermore. Their house on Morgan Territory Road was gradually dismantled by neighbors and the curious and eventually disappeared.

Juanita recalled that her aunt and uncle were not officially married until Charles lay on his deathbed in 1935. They had four daughters and five sons. Eustacia died in 1941. Husband and wife are buried at St. Michael's Cemetery in Livermore.

1 San Francisco General Land Office, Homestead Entry 2555, National Archives, DC.

2 San Francisco General Land Office, Homestead Entry 2551, National Archives, DC.

3 *Contra Costa County Patents*, Book 5, application 3702, homestead certificate 1402.

4 San Francisco General Land Office, Homestead Entry 1402, National Archives, DC.

5 *Contra Costa County Deed Book* 49: 299-301.

6 *Contra Costa County Deed Book* 76: 474.

7 Karana Hattersley-Drayton, *Report on Oral History Completed Under the Historic Property Treatment Plan for Construction of the Los Vaqueros Dam and Reservoir and Related Requirements, for the Los Vaqueros Project* (Rohnert Park, CA: Sonoma State U Academic Foundation, 1996) 23.

8 Karana Hattersley-Drayton, "Interview with Juanita Robles Hargraves," Sonoma State U Anthropological Studies Center, for the Contra Costa Water District 9 Nov 1995: 22.

9 Nilda Rego, "More Die in Flu Epidemic than in WW I," *The Sunday Times* 12 Sep 1999: C7.

10 San Francisco General Land Office, Agricultural College Scrip, GA, Entry 557, National Archives, DC.

11 August Grisel, telephone interview, 9 July 1996.

12 Grisel interview.

13 "Federal Agents Raid Five Places," *The Livermore Herald* 17 June 1932: 8.

14 "Livermore," *Crofutt's New Overland Tourist and Pacific Coast Guide* (1880): n.p.

a From *The Livermore Herald*, 26 October 1918, page 2.

Raising the flag at the San Jose juzgado, site of Alcalde John Burton's courtroom, 1846. Courtesy of L. McKay.

Sons of a Yankee Alcalde

JOHN BURTON, a native of Provincetown, Massachusetts, arrived in Alta California in 1826 as captain of the *Young Tartar,* a 95-ton English coastal schooner used in the hide and tallow trade. The vessel was beached at San Diego in a November storm and condemned by an official survey of several captains.[1] By 24 July 1827 the remains of the *Young Tartar* were lying broken on the San Diego beach.[2]

John Burton chose to remain in Alta California. By 1830 he had made his way to San Jose, where he earned his living by farming and trade. On 6 November 1830 he was baptized into the Catholic faith at Mission Santa Clara, declaring himself to be 44 years old. The mission entry named him *"el Capitan Viejo"* (the old captain). He married Ramona Gonzales at Mission San Juan Bautista on 11 January 1832. Their son, Juan (John) Burton, had been baptized at Mission San Carlos in Monterey in 1831. Little more than a year after their marriage Ramona died, and on 29 November 1833 the elder John Burton married Juana Estafania Galindo at Mission Santa Clara. One of their seven children was Henrique (Henry).

When Americans occupied Alta California in 1846, they organized a military government that remained in authority over the former Mexican territory until establishment of California state government in 1850. Probably because he was a respected long-time community member with ties to both Americans and Hispanics, John Burton was elected alcalde (mayor/magistrate) of San Jose under the military occupation, serving from 19 October 1846 until September 1847. Although Burton had "but little book-learning," he was nevertheless "a man of considerable sound sense, and very honest,"[3] and he was fluent in Spanish. He died around 1848.

Two of Alcalde John Burton's sons, John and Henry, left San Jose and claimed property in the Highland area of Tassajara, near today's intersection of Manning and Highland roads. Signing with his mark on 10 December 1866, Henry Burton claimed a 160-acre parcel of land in Contra Costa County with military scrip, choosing the NW¼ of section 18 T2S/R2E.[4] He paid $215 for the property and stated that he had been living there since April 1866. In Henry's official declaratory statement filed with the San Francisco General Land Office in 1871, he described himself as 30 years old, with a wife and one child. He was six feet tall, with a dark complexion, brown eyes, black hair, and a crooked nose.[5] In 1871 he had 100 acres ploughed for wheat and barley; the rest was used for pasture. Improvements included a house, hen house, stable, and some fencing. A tax record in the same year showed Henrique Burton still living on section 18 and listed various livestock: eight horses, two cows, and 12 hogs. He satisfied two mortgages by selling his section 18 property in October 1875 for $2,209.

By 1877 Henry Burton was paying taxes on additional acreage in section 6 T2S/R2E. He had applied for a 102-acre homestead on section 6 in August 1874. On his proof of 5 December 1879, he testified that he had a house with an attached kitchen, a barn, 125 grapevines, and 41 fruit trees on that property. Cattle and horses grazed on most of the land, but he had planted about 55 acres in wheat and barley.

He received his new deed in 1880,[6] but the 1879 tax record showed Henry only at an 80-acre parcel, the north half of the NE¼ of section 6, with improvements worth $200. Section 6 is much farther up into the Black Hills, on steeper land than section 18. The record showed Azorean

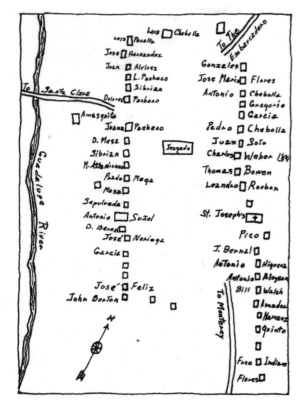

An early map of San Jose, c. 1840. Note "José Feliz" next to "John Burton," lower left. Another version of this map substitutes "El Capitán Viejo" for "John Burton." Map courtesy of the Amador-Livermore Valley Historical Society Museum.

rancher E.S. Fergoda now owning Burton's more desirable section 18 property.

In 1880 the census listed Henry Burton as divorced and living with his son, also Henry, and his widowed mother, Juana, who was 80 years old. Juana died in September 1881. Henry Burton's home was the polling place for a local 1884 school election in which Black Hills residents voted for a tax to finance their own schoolhouse. In 1889 and 1890, his son was attending Summit School at the top of Morgan Territory Road. Henry Burton paid taxes in 1888 on another 160 acres, the NW¼ of section 20

T1S/R2E, isolated property about eight miles up Morgan Territory Road from Manning Road. Although listed in the 1903 tax record as a resident of Summit School District, near the ridgetop of Morgan Territory Road, Burton apparently no longer owned real estate, and was assessed for personal property only. In 1901 he had sold his acreage in section 6 to Antone Bent Nunez for $1,000. The voting registers in 1896 and 1904 listed his son, Henry J. Burton, as a laborer, living in the Tassajara District. The son's death in Oakland at age 67 on 14 October 1941 was recorded in St. Michael's burial register in Livermore. According to the same church register, his father had died in October 1905.

The elder Henry Burton's half-brother, John, bought 160 acres on the NE¼ of section 18 with agricultural college scrip. In his declaratory statement, he claimed settlement on the property in June 1858; by 1873, he had built a house and barn and dug a well.[7] In about 1850 John Burton had married Symphorosa Félix. John Burton was listed in the 1871 tax records of Contra Costa with the 160 acres, two horses, and a cow; by 1874, he had $50 worth of improvements on the land. In September 1874 he took out a one-year mortgage on his property for $1,200 at one percent interest per month. Immediately after satisfying his mortgage on 20 July 1875, he sold the land for $2,200 to his mortgage holders, Philip and Simon Anspacher of Livermore.

John Burton's daughter Maria married Benjamin Guirado, who bought property in the Black Hills; Burton's son Frank married Isabel Mesa on 6 January 1898 at St. Michael's in Livermore; son John married Catherine Miranda on 8 June 1891. Another son, Michael, died at age 16. Daughter Maria Rosaria, "Rose," married Aurello Lemas. Her father gave permission for her marriage at age 14 to Lemas, who was 33 and from Pacheco.[8] The elder John Burton, his son John and probably another son Narciso appeared on the Contra Costa County Great Register, ages

62, 32, and 24 respectively, all farmers in the Tassajara District when they signed on 28 September 1888. The 1896 register added son Frank Burton as a laborer, age 21, living in Byron.

On 18 December 1897 *The Livermore Herald* Personal Mention column noted that Frank Burton had filed for a marriage license the day before and was upset to discover a three-day waiting period before it could be issued.[9] The 1900 census taker found him residing in Livermore with his wife, Isabel, and a six-month-old son, another Frank. After the 1906 earthquake and fire he found work in San Francisco as a teamster. He and his family lived there from 1907 until 1913, when Isabel died at age 36.

In 1910 John Burton's son John—grandson of Alcalde John Burton—was working as a laborer doing odd jobs and living in Livermore's Northern Addition with his wife, Katie (Catherine), four children, and his sister Rose. He died of throat cancer on September 17 of that year.[10] His father, the second John Burton, had died in 1904 and was buried at St. Michael's Cemetery in Livermore.

Many relatives of the second John Burton's wife, Symphorosa Félix, lived in the Black Hills. Their surname was often spelled Feliz or Felis. Symphorosa's father was Rafael Félix, a Mexican soldier stationed at San Francisco and San Mateo. By 1841 he had settled at San Jose with his wife, Juana Amézquita, and six children: Ramon, Urbano, Marcario, Julia, Symphorosa, and José. More children followed. The Contra Costa County voting register listed Urbano, Marcario, and José as farmers in the Tassajara area. Beginning in 1871, the records showed Urbano Félix paying taxes on the NW¼ of section 7 and Mrs. Juana Félix, presumably Urbano's mother, paying taxes on the SW¼ of section 7 T2S/R2E. They bought these properties with military scrip on 27 July 1875.[11] The Félix properties in section 7 were directly north of Burton's land on section 18

Urbano Félix at the Land Office:

"In November 1884, Feliz filed his Final Certificate. In his Homestead Proof, he testified that he was a native-born Californian, claiming citizenship under the treaty with Mexico, and could 'neither read nor write in any language.' This made Feliz's application more difficult than most. The person making out his homestead papers at the Land Office in San Francisco, 'being ignorant of the Spanish language,' mistakenly spelled his name Euvino; so Feliz had to establish that Euvino and Urbano were the 'identical person.' To complicate matters even further, Feliz had lost his receipt, having given it to his wife who reportedly misplaced it during the move to the homestead." [a]

and close to the Robles holdings. In 1879 Urbano cultivated 200 acres in wheat and 80 acres in hay. Manuel Altamirano acted as an interpreter in 1879 when Urbano applied for a homestead on the SW¼ of section 20 T1S/R2E and signed his mark on the documents. The 160 acres already held a house, but unlike his gently sloping property on section 7, section 20 was extremely steep and isolated high in the Black Hills. Besides the main house, described as measuring 20 by 40 feet, Urbano had built a smaller house where some of his eight children slept. He had put up a barn and set out 30 fruit trees and 100 grapevines.

Urbano Félix finally received the patent for his property on 10 April 1885.[12] This land abutted that of Henry Burton, which lay to the north. Urbano Félix Jr. attended Summit School in 1889 and 1890.

The Félix family did not appear on Contra Costa County tax records in 1885, and they were in financial difficulties in 1895. By 1900 the family no longer lived on section 20. The 1900 obituary of Urbano's brother Marcario mentioned the general loss of family property: "Felis had been a resident of the Livermore Valley since the pioneer days and was at one time the possessor of considerable property which frittered away until for a number of years past he eked out a living as a veterinary." He died while doctoring horses for a local rancher.[13]

The Burton and Félix family histories illustrate the typical Californio land ownership trend in the Black Hills. They acquired land, lost it, then bought less desirable acreage higher in the hills. Finally, they lost their property altogether before the turn of the century. Ironically, in the second half of the 1900s landowners began paying more for the privilege of owning hill property with a view. Aesthetics began to be worth more than agriculture.

1 Hubert H. Bancroft, *History of California*, Vol. 3 (San Francisco: A.L. Bancroft, 1885) Marine List 1825-30: 145-149. Other authorities list his ship as the *Juan Battey*. Still others call him a simple seaman who deserted from his vessel and merely assumed the title of captain. See Eugene Sawyer, *History of Santa Clara County, CA* (Los Angeles: Historic Record Co, 1922) 70.

2 *Vallejo Documents*, Bancroft Library, Berkeley, ms. C-B29: 143.

3 Frederic Hall, *The History of San José and Surroundings* (San Francisco: A.L. Bancroft, 1871) 171.

4 Act of 1855 Military Land Warrant 81230, National Archives, DC.

5 Contra Costa County Great Register 1892.

6 San Francisco General Land Office, Homestead Entry 1284, National Archives, DC.

7 San Francisco General Land Office, Agricultural College Scrip 1435, GA, National Archives, DC.

8 *Livermore Enterprise* 24 Apr 1875: 3. Contra Costa County Marriage Licenses, 8 Oct 1884: 356.

9 "Personal Mention," *The Livermore Herald* 18 Dec 1897: 7.

10 CA Death 22424.

11 San Francisco General Land Office, Cash Entry 5461; Act of 1855 Military Land Warrant 113943 and San Francisco Land Office, Cash Entry 5462; Act of 1855 Military Land Warrant 113945, National Archives, DC.

12 San Francisco General Land Office, Homestead Entry 2533, National Archives, DC.

13 "Obituary, Macardo Felis," *Livermore Echo* 3 Feb 1900: 6.

a Mary Praetzellis, Suzanne B. Stewart and Grace H. Ziesing, *The Los Vaqueros Watershed: A Working History* (Rohnert Park, CA: Sonoma State U Academic Foundation, 1997) 184.

Californio Sketches

FROM 1860 UNTIL about 1900, the rugged Black Hills area of Morgan Territory Road was home to descendants of more than a dozen Californio families, including the Robles and their Palomares/Miranda relatives as well as the Burtons. Many of them claimed U.S. citizenship under the Treaty of Guadalupe-Hidalgo. Tax assessments and land applications preserve many Hispanic surnames: Valenzuela, Félix, Robles, Palomares, Peña, Figueroa, Higuera, Guirado, García, Franco, Acosta, Gomez, Molina, Ramirez, Peralta, Castillo. Evans, Burton, and Goodfield were surnames of resident families descended from Hispanic mothers and American fathers. Most of the original Californio rancho families had large numbers of children, and legal problems involving their properties forced subsequent generations to leave the ranchos and claim their own land if they wanted to continue their agricultural heritage. Vaqueros and other rancho workers, as demand for their employment dried up with the decrease in stock raising, also had to find a place of their own.

Under federal laws allowing pre-emption, homesteading, and scrip purchase of military bounty or agricultural college lands, many Californios claimed property in the Black Hills. For most of them, however, life became a continuous struggle to come up with each year's mortgage payment and property taxes. Land use records show a variety of livestock—cattle, sheep, hogs, chickens—as well as plantings of orchards and vineyards and occasional fenced acreage for hay or grain. The families were frequently related by blood as well as culture. Only a few Hispanic landholders remained in the Black Hills by the twentieth century, and only Tomás Robles and his wife—with large holdings that included areas suitable for planting grain—had become prosperous and were able to hold onto their land until its real estate value outpaced its agricultural value.

Some displaced and disgruntled Californios ignored the agrarian life and became robbers and livestock thieves, especially after the tax on foreign miners became law in 1850. "Driven from the [gold] mines, mistreated by callous Anglos, and denied a means to earn their living, it is hardly surprising that many Californios and other Hispanics turned to robbery and theft."[1] Probably the most notorious bandit in the 1850s was Joaquin Murrieta. Numerous folk legends grew around his escapades. Some of these tales place him and his gang in the Vasco Caves area and up on Brushy Peak, where he could easily watch the San Joaquin Valley and the old Stockton Road for possible pursuing sheriffs or vigilantes.

In the next decade, Harry Morse, Alameda County sheriff first elected in 1864, searched through the Black Hills for a number of minor *banditos*. Morse's biographer noted, "These mountains and arroyos were ideal hiding places for fugitives and stolen stock. Here and there were *jacales* (huts), some made entirely of brush and others of adobe, where honest vaqueros and *borregueros* (shepherds) as well as horse thieves and cattle rustlers lived."[2]

In December 1867 Morse heard that Novato Ponce, a suspected horse thief and murderer, had been holed up recovering from wounds in Riggs Canyon, a northern extension of Finley Road into the Black Hills. After learning that Ponce planned to ride down into Alisal (now Pleasanton), Morse waited at a place called the Willows—the intersection today of Tassajara Road and Interstate 580. But Ponce escaped, and Morse later rode up into Riggs Canyon looking for his hideout. Ponce seemed gone for good, but Morse found an old Californio who had probably nursed Ponce back to health, and a cattle rustler whom Morse arrested.[3] At the foot of the Black Hills, near the southern Contra Costa County line, the deserted Casitas Ranch of Hiram Bailey was also a well-known hiding place. Bailey had married the stepdaughter of Robert Livermore.

Although the majority of Californios remained law-abiding, some East Bay banditos had familiar—and well-respected—local surnames: among them, Amador, Peralta, Sibrian. An occasional young Californio chose banditry over life on the dying ranchos. But familial ties remained strong enough that the lawbreakers were often given aid and shelter. San Quentin Prison held a disproportionate number of Hispanic inmates—whether from criminality or a biased court system is still a matter of debate.

By degrees, however, the Black Hills became ranching properties rather than outlaw hideouts. **Romualdo Valenzuela** purchased 160 acres in the SW¼ of section 4 T2S/R2E in the Black Hills in 1874 with a $400 mortgage.[4] According to his pre-emption claim, he had settled on this property in 1869; he lived there with his Mexican-born wife, Dorotea Castro, and "plenty of children."[5] Valenzuela was born in Los Angeles of Californio parents and had come to the Vasco area about 1850 at age 18, probably working as a vaquero.[6] In 1871 he was assessed for some Spanish horses and 150 sheep; in that year he listed himself in the Alameda County Directory as a vaquero. He had also been listed as a vaquero on the 1870 census, which named his wife and six children.[7] Soon after receiving title to the original 160 acres in October 1874, the family moved and filed for a homestead on a neighboring 80-acre parcel. Four neighbors testified in Valenzuela's behalf on the necessary new paperwork.[8] Romualdo and Dorotea Valenzuela sold the original 160 acres to Samuel Levy for $1,000 in 1876, signing the deed with their marks.[9] The Los Vaqueros Report for the Contra Costa Water District noted, "Romualdo Valenzuela was al-most constantly in debt. Each year when a mortgage would come due, usually worth $100, he would refinance by taking another mortgage. It appears that the family had to sell the 160-acre parcel in 1876 and move . . . because they could not pay off the mortgage on [the first property]. From the time that Valenzuela recorded his patent to the 80-acre homestead until his death in February 1892, the property was encumbered with a mortgage."[10]

Valenzuela rapidly made improvements to his new homestead, building a house measuring 20 by 12 feet and also a hen house. He dug a well. On the few tillable areas of this steeper property, about 30 acres in all, he planted wheat, barley, and corn.[11] The 1880 census listed the family with seven children; their closest neighbors were the Goodfields and the Francos.[12] The 1888 tax records showed the family still living on the 80-acre site, with $80 in improvements, and livestock including two horses, one colt, and two hogs.

Romualdo died on 5 February 1892 at age 60 of cerebral apoplexy. His will administrator sold his last piece of Black Hills property for $750 to Samuel Levy—the highest bidder—to pay the family's debts. A bill for $111.56 in the probate file was from Shuey and Galloway, a general store in Walnut Creek. The Valenzuelas had bought corn, beans, flour, sugar, salt, rice, bacon, soap, syrup, dried peas, bacon, and lard at the store from October 1891 to the end of April 1892. Their only luxury was a little bit of chocolate and tobacco. They received credit on their account for 23 dozen eggs and six hens. The probate record described the property: "There is a small dwelling house located on the said land in which the widow now resides; that said land is unfenced and open to the common, and is rough and hilly and fit only for pasture. . . ."[13] In 1900 Dorotea Valenzuela, age 66, was living in Livermore with two of her children. Although she had borne 16 children, only seven were still alive.[14] She died in

Fermin Valenzuela, foreman of the Bordes Ranch, c. 1925. The big barn in the background was the last original structure remaining in 1998. Photo courtesy of Frank M. Silva.

November 1902 and was buried at St. Michael's Cemetery in Livermore.

Two of the Valenzuela sons, Marcos and Fermin, probably lived up at the second Black Hills site until their father's estate was straightened out. They were unusually tall for their day, Fermin at six feet and his brother at six feet two. The 1900 census found Marcos and his family living in Livermore. After the death of his first wife, Marcos married Ramona Goodfield, the daughter of a Black Hills neighbor. In 1897 Fermin Valenzuela and another man were arrested for rustling eight steers from a nearby ranch. Fermin's neighbors were surprised. *The Livermore Herald* said, "Vallenzulla heretofore

has borne the reputation of a steady and reliable workman. He is well known among the valley farmers and was universally liked."[15] Turning state's evidence, Fermin Valenzuela acknowledged his guilt and regret.

When Sonoma State researchers were collecting oral histories for the Vasco area in the early 1990s, Fermin Valenzuela was easily remembered by old-timers. In spite of a drinking problem, which reportedly made him undependable at times, ranchers often called on him for his blacksmithing skills and his magical way with horses. By 1920 Fermin Valenzuela no longer had a place of his own, but moved from ranch to ranch as needed. He especially demonstrated his

Fred Mourterot worked with Fermin Valenzuela at the Bordes' ranch on the Vasco about 1917:

"[Valenzuela] worked at the Bordes when I was working up there one year and he'd go in the morning to feed the horses and [he'd say] 'Back, boys.' And they'd all back up out of their stall. And I'd go to feed mine and [laughing] I couldn't get them out of there!" [a]

"He was one of the best teamsters around. Whenever they had to hook up a bunch of horses they always went and got Fermin and never say nothin' to him. Just turn him loose. . . . He could handle . . . as many horses as you put in front of him. He even drove the first two wheelers, what they call the 'wheel horses' with his feet." [b]

skill at the Bordes' ranch when he served as foreman for harvesting crews.

Fermin was a thin, robust man who apparently never looked his age. People recalled him as being about 40 when in reality he was in his 60s. According to his ascribed age of 24 on his father's 1892 will, he was 71 years old when he died in 1939. Only one sibling of their large family outlived him, his sister Agnes.

Agustin del Carmen Vidful was the likely founder of another Black Hills family who were close neighbors of the Valenzuelas. According to his Mission Santa Clara marriage record, Agustin came to Alta California from his birthplace, Norfolk, Virginia. He was 35 years old when he married Ramona Gonzales, widow of a mission neophyte, on 19 June 1825. Twenty-five years later, after he and his wife had died, their son Agustin married Gertrude Juares at the same mission on 21 October 1850. In the later record, the surname for both Agustins was spelled

Guitfil. In a note signed 22 December 1849, an Augustine de Carmel Witfield promised to deliver a load of lumber worth $350, at the price of $165 per thousand board feet, to Robert Livermore's rancho by May 1850.[16] Although not specified in the agreement, the lumber was probably redwood, which was being harvested at the time in the Oakland hills.

The 1852 census of Contra Costa County listed Agustin, age 27, and Gertrude Whitfield. Josi Guttifield, age 24, was also listed, but separately. On 7 July 1880 Gertrude Juares de Whitfield sold part of section 2 T1S/R1E, at the north end of Morgan Territory, along Marsh Creek, to Y.F. Pacheco, without the participation of her husband in the transaction.[17] The 1870 U.S. census had listed Agustin Whitfield at the Stockton State Mental Hospital and described him as insane and not capable of voting.[18]

There is no proof that the José Whitfield who filed a Black Hills homestead entry on 24 September 1879 is related to these earlier Vidful/Guitfil/Whitfield families, but the prevailing problem with the spelling of their surname offers at least a tenuous connection. José could be the younger brother of Agustin Jr.

The homestead property of José Whitfield was the SE¼ of section 32 T1S/R2E in the Black Hills. His patent was issued on 9 May 1885. He testified in his homestead proof that he had settled on the land in June 1875, about five years after the Valenzuelas. José built two houses, a barn, granary, wash house, chicken house, and a second house for his sons. With a board and picket fence he enclosed 2.5 acres where he planted about 85 fruit trees and 500 grapevines. He also reported having cultivated 60 acres of grain each season. Neighbors Pascual Franco, Cipriano Figaroa, Jabiel García, and Victor Molina agreed to testify on Whitfield's behalf at the land office in San Francisco. Both Franco and García had known Whitfield for 25 years—15 years longer than they had been neighbors in the

Black Hills.[19] Franco filed his homestead proof on the same day as Whitfield. In 1880 the census listed José Goodfield, with his wife "Messa" and five children.[20] Often Anglo census takers could not understand the Hispanic practice of a woman's keeping her maiden name after marriage. José's wife was Narcisa Mesa. On 27 September 1880 the name Jose Gutifil appeared on the Contra Costa County Great Register of Voters. Fifty-two years old, he was born in California, lived in the Tassajara District, and earned his living as a carpenter.

The tax records of Contra Costa County illustrate the continuing saga of the various spellings of the Vidful/Guitfil/Whitfield/Goodfield name. In 1850 José Gutifull was on the county poll tax list. José Gootefield appeared on the 1855 tax list with one horse, one cow, a calf, and a wagon. The tax record of 1857 included José Guilfiela. In 1858 José Gutfield was living in a small house with his family on the property of José Jesus Mesa, his father-in-law, east of today's Alamo in the San Ramon Valley.[21] On the 1878 poll tax list he was named Joe Goodfield and now lived in the Tassajara District. Jo Goodfield and his son David were both listed on the 1879 tax record at the section 32 site although their improvements amounted to only $25. In 1880 Gatrudes J. Guitifild was taxed for her parcel on section 2 near Marsh Creek, apparently just before she sold it. J. Goodfield of Summit District in the same year paid taxes on the $250 evaluation of his property and $30 worth of improvements. Soon after receiving the final certificate for his homestead in 1885, Joe Whitfield mortgaged his property to George Beck.[22] In 1885 José's son Jesus Guilifil applied for an 80-acre homestead on section 18 T1S/R2E, but the application was denied.[23] Although the worth of José Whitfield's personal property rose to $600 by 1888, he still had a mortgage on his land in section 32.

In 1888 Valentin Alviso, a literate Californio friend, was a witness to—and most likely helped José Whitfield draw up—a deed of trust. Whitfield gave Tomás Acosta his section 32 property, along with nine horses, a set of harness and a spring wagon, two milk cows and calves, a two-year-old heifer, and the buildings, in trust for the following purpose: If José should die, Acosta should sell the property and purchase an acre in or near Livermore in the names of José Whitfield's son Theodore and daughter Juana. A house should be built there where Theodore and Juana could care for their mother. The monies remaining from the sale of the property and livestock should pay José's debts. José Whitfield signed the deed on July 30 with his mark.[24] According to Theodore Whitfield's affidavit, his father, José Whitfield, died on 1 August 1888 at Livermore, only two days after signing the deed of trust.[25] Two pupils at Summit School in 1889 and 1890 were Phillip and Edward Goodfield, probably sons of Jesus. In 1902 George Beck sold Whitfield's 160 acres along with Pascual Franco's quarter section to the north to Mary Gleese, whose sons were planning to use the properties as a stock range.[26] The Livermore city tax lists of 1917–18 show Theodore and Juana Goodfield owning lots 2, 3, 4, 5 in block 48 of the Northern Addition and Mary Goodfield, widow of Jesus/Jesse, owning lot 5 in block 39. Jesus had died of kidney disease in 1913 at his Northern Addition home, leaving his wife and seven children.[27] Whether or not the intentions of José Whitfield were carried out through his deed of trust, Theodore and Juana Goodfield/ Whitfield did succeed in owning property in Livermore. After José's death, the family surname remained "Goodfield," no doubt because family members were now literate.

Juan Mesa, grandfather of José Goodfield's wife, Narcisa, was the progenitor of another Black Hills family. Born at Altar, Sonora, Mexico, in 1775, he emigrated to California and enlisted in the military, probably at the usual age of 16. As a *soldado de cuera* (leather-jacketed soldier), he was stationed at Mission San Antonio and the presidios at Monterey and San Francisco. He married Maria Rafaela Soto at Mission Santa Clara in 1795, and, after his retirement from the military, settled in San Jose. He was buried at Mission Santa Clara in 1817. Juan Mesa's ninth child, José de Jesus Mesa, married Juana Serapia Miranda, sister of Manuel Miranda, one of the three claimants to *Rancho Cañada de los Vaqueros*. José de Jesus was a soldier like his father before him. He served at San Francisco from 1823 until 1833 and again from 1838 through 1839.[28] In 1841 José de Jesus's family was in San Jose, but by the time of the 1852 census, he was a ranchero living with a group of other Californios, including members of the Miranda and García families, near today's Alamo. In 1854 the tax assessor listed him with 12 cattle, five horses, 10 sheep, and 25 acres of land. By 1855 José de Jesus's cattle herd had increased to 70 head. In 1857 his holdings were two yoke of Spanish oxen, 10 Spanish cows and calves, three Spanish horses, two mares and colts, six pigs, and 55 sheep. Narcisa Mesa, José Goodfield's wife, was a daughter of José de Jesus. Before settling in the Black Hills, José and Narcisa Goodfield had lived in the Alamo area near her parents.

One of Narcisa's younger brothers, Dolores Mesa, was baptized at Mission Santa Clara three days after his birth on 3 April 1846.[29] In the Oakland directories of 1870 and 1876, Dolores Mesa listed himself as a vaquero. On the Contra Costa Great Register for 1872, he was a horse tamer, age 26, living at Alamo. At age 50 he was described as five feet four, still with dark hair.[30] The *amansador* (horse breaker) was a specialized vaquero who broke wild mustangs for general rancho use. Dolores Mesa's short stature would have been an advantage in this occupation. He married Incarnation Pacheco, and four of their children were baptized between 1878 and 1893 at St. Michael's church in Livermore, an indication that the family had moved from the

Alamo area to Livermore. His sister and brother-in-law Narcisa and José Goodfield moved up into the Black Hills in 1878; Dolores Mesa and family may have moved to Livermore then. The 1880 census taker found the family in Livermore and listed Dolores Mesa as a teamster and farm laborer.[31]

In 1880 he applied for a homestead of 80 acres on the east half of the NW ¼ of section 18 T1S/R2E. Although he began making improvements on the property, the family did not move up into the Black Hills until March 1882. On his proof in 1887, witnesses described his redwood house with a matched pine floor and four windows. José Goodfield had helped him to build it and said he had known the younger man since Dolores Mesa's birth. Other improvements mentioned were an adobe house, about 8 by 18 feet, and a barn, chicken house, and well. Dolores Mesa had planted about 15 acres in wheat, corn, beans, peas, and other vegetables as well as some fruit trees and vines. The rest of the land was too steep and mountainous for cultivation. His final certificate was issued on 20 October 1887.[32] His daughters, Ida and Isabel, attended Summit School in 1889 and 1890, but by 1892 they were at school in Livermore.[33] Dolores Mesa died in February 1902 of pneumonia.[34] At the time of the death of their daughter Isabel Mesa Burton in 1913, Dolores Mesa's widow, Incarnation Pacheco, was living in Pleasanton.

Another daughter of José de Jesus Mesa and Juana Miranda was Dolores Mesa's older sister, Delfina de Jesus Mesa, born 12 February 1844 and baptized a week later at Mission Santa Clara. On 23 April 1860 she married Pascual B. Franco at St. Catherine's in Martinez. Their daughter, Mary Pascual Franco, was baptized there in 1863.

According to family legend, **Pascual Franco** had arrived in California with the American army, who urged him into service in New Mexico because they needed a blacksmith.[35] José Goodfield testified that he first met Franco in

1858.[36] By 29 September 1869 Pascual Franco was a widower with three infant children; he claimed 160 acres, including a dwelling house, stable, and other improvements, by signing his mark. He had registered his brand PF with Contra Costa County in 1867. The SE¼ of section 6 T2S/R2E became his officially in 1873 when he claimed it with military scrip and paid $200.[37] One witness on his pre-emption claim was John Burton, who had known him since 1864. Three times during 1873 and 1874, Pascual Franco borrowed money from Alexander Esdon with mortgages on his land. In January 1875 his property appeared on the delinquent tax list.[38] Finally, in August of that year, he sold the land to Esdon.

The 1880 Contra Costa County Great Register listed Pascual Franco as a blacksmith, age 35, and a native of New Mexico.[39] He applied for a homestead grant of 160 acres in 1879 and was assigned his patent on 9 May 1885 for the NE¼ of section 32 near the top of Morgan Territory Road, in more rugged landscape than his property in section 6. He had settled on the new property soon after selling out to Esdon in 1876. On his final proof on 15 January 1885, Franco and his witnesses testified that he had a barn, blacksmith shop, granary, 20 fruit trees, "a few vines," and a large house approximately 16 by 38 feet.[40] In 1884 Franco was elected school trustee for the newly created Summit School District at the top of Morgan Territory Road. The trustees called for an election to vote on a proposed residential tax in order to raise the $200 needed to build the schoolhouse.[41] Franco sold his remaining Black Hills property to George Beck on 16 May 1894.

Pascual Franco's son Salvador married Sarah García around 1890. Salvador worked as a teamster at the Tesla coal mines east of Livermore. His wife was a laundress. Salvador invested some of his earnings in calves before the Black Hills property was sold, and asked his father to keep an eye on them. When Salvador checked on his cattle later, he discovered some of them missing.

Salvador Franco's granddaughter told of visiting Californio relatives in San Jose in the 1920s:

"I do know that when I was very small, our family went to San Jose to see family. The Mirandas, who were very musical, were there, and my brother and I would go to sleep with the old Spanish songs played on violin, mandolin and guitar. There were also tamales—much finer than are sold now anywhere I know. They were too spicy for me when I was 4 years old and made me sick even though I had begged to be allowed to eat them. My WASP mother never learned to speak Spanish, but she fit right in in learning how to make tamales." c

Pascual Franco admitted selling one now and then because "he needed money to go over and see a woman in Black Diamond because it gets lonely up here."[42] Salvador soon sold the rest of his animals. He died in 1907 at age 43 of "pulmonary trouble." His obituary called him an "honest and industrious young man."[43] His father was living in the Northern Addition of Livermore by then. Sarah García Franco, Salvador's widow, married Angelo Miranda, and the family lived in the Northern Addition at North L and Elm streets. Salvador and Sarah had had two sons—Cornelius, known as Connie, and Alfred. Alfred's daughter remembered her family visiting her grandmother Sarah in Livermore in the 1920s and recalled her father at the time showing her some large fancy wrought-iron gates that had been made by her blacksmith great-grandfather, Pascual Franco, for local wineries and homes.[44] Her grandmother Sarah was talented at creating drawn work, a needlecraft.

James D. Smith recalled the Californio families' welcome when his family arrived in the San Ramon Valley in 1850:

"Quite a settlement of Spaniards were located near some springs east of Alamo, across the San Ramon Creek. They were very friendly and soon came to see us, and the first cow we had in California a Mr. [José] Miguel Garcia gave to my mother—a gentle Spanish milk cow with long slender horns and yellow and white in color. . . .

"My mother in return invited him to bring his family to have dinner at our house, naming the day. They came on horseback, several couples. I remember the ladies of the party seated in the saddle and the men seated behind and guiding the horses, and I have no recollection of having seen any Spanish lady riding alone and directing her horse.

"My recollection of the Spanish people is that they were very liberal and accommodating and I recall that more than once Mr. [José] Miguel Garcia with a vaquero to assist, drove a fat animal to our home, butchered it and hung the meat in the tree standing near our house, with no charge for it. I recently passed the location of our first home in the San Ramon valley and the tree is yet standing in a corner of a small field south of Danville owned by the Flournoy family, and if I had the price I would buy that location for the memories of long ago." [d]

Sarah García's father, **Javier García**, also settled in the Black Hills. Javier (variously spelled Xavier, Javiel, Jabiel, Havriel, Gabriel, or Gabiel) García was born on 6 November 1843 and baptized Francisco Javier Leonardo García at Mission San Jose. He grew up on the family ran-

cho east of Alamo near the Mesas and the Mirandas. His father was José Miguel García, and his mother was Rafaela Miranda, another daughter of Manuel Miranda.

In the 1852 census Javier is listed with his large family as "Havire," age 10. The Garcías had owned a quarter of the Romero Grant, but in 1857 the courts ruled the Romero Grant invalid, so most of their rancho property was lost. The Garcías had borrowed money with a loan in 1863 from financiers Simon Wolf and Michael Cohen, but had been unable to repay it. They owed $508. The sheriff ordered a tax sale in 1866 of their remaining 140-acre property to the highest cash bidder.[45]

Javier García married Lucy Miranda, a sister of his mother. The Alameda County marriage records show that he was issued a license on 27 September 1870. At first Javier and Lucy were married in a civil ceremony, perhaps because the priest was unhappy that an aunt and nephew would marry. Their church wedding at St. Mary's Catholic Church in Oakland took place on 20 October 1875. Three of their children were baptized in Oakland, one at Mission San Jose, and then four more at St. Michael's in Livermore. The Livermore baptisms run from 1881 to 1889.

In March 1881 "Jabiel" García applied for a 41-acre homestead on section 4 T2S/R2E in the Black Hills; he was issued the patent on 10 April 1885. The November 1884 proof claims his settlement, directly north of the 80-acre homestead of Romualdo Valenzuela, in November 1879. He owned a house and barn, an enclosed vegetable garden, a two-acre orchard, and 10 acres planted in grain for hay. He and Lucy had six children, including daughter Sarah.[46] Sons Robert and Isaac García were attending Summit School in 1889 and 1890. Lucy Miranda García died of pneumonia in Livermore at age 41 on 6 January 1892. Her husband had used his 40-acre plot on section 4 for mortgage security in 1891.[47] However, the 1893 tax assessment map showed

George Beck as the owner of Javier García's 80 acres. After losing or selling his Black Hills property, García moved into Livermore. He died suddenly at the Northern Addition home of his daughter, Sarah García Franco Miranda, on 9 December 1909.[48]

Although the steeper Black Hills acreage on which most of the Californio families eventually settled was unsuitable for large vineyards or orchards or for growing grain—and not extensive enough to support cattle or sheep—the Californios did make use of the area's dense oak groves.

Denny Mallory, until recently a resident of that area in the Black Hills, told of the stories of neighbor George Cardoza about the Californio families' lumbering activities:

"He told us a lot about the early days of lumbering up through these hills. He showed us where we can still see the remains of a wagon trail, the remnants of the old Spanish road. They would bring in a team of four horses pulling these big sleds. And then they would lumber and take the oak trees down for fuel. You know, everything ran on wood in those days. . . . They would use sleds on the tough part and then probably reload them [the logs] on wagons when they got to Morgan Territory Road. They missed a few monarchs, but basically cleaned out the large trees."[49]

George Cardoza's father had purchased property on the north side of Morgan Territory Road in 1887, and later property on the south side. Young George spent his childhood wandering the hills and became familiar with their history. As late as 1897, a timber claim was filed for 80 acres in section 18 T1S/R2E.[50] Settlers such as the Cardozas continued the practice of cutting oak wood, but on a smaller scale, trading it a wagonload at a time to town merchants for credit when needed.

One by one, the Californio families moved to town, and most sold their Black Hills proper-

Wood for Sale:

In 1903 a realtor was advertising 480 acres of excellent grazing land for sale in the Black Hills country 10 miles from Livermore, with these incentives: "Abundance of water; with 2000 cords white and live-oak wood. Accessible to wagon; county road runs across corner of land. Wood sells for $6.00 per cord on premises." [c]

ties to Irish and Azorean immigrants who were eager to own land. The transition was occasionally rocky. Juanita Robles Hargraves, whose Californio family managed to retain their land, remembered: "Yeah, well, the people around us, didn't like us. They would stand up on the hill and call us every name under the sun. . . . Because we were different. They were the Portuguese—all Portuguese."[51] George Cardoza's Azorean father at one time fought with the five Irish McCormick brothers when they challenged him over a fence and dragged him from his horse. On the other hand, Irish rancher John Gleese struggled to learn Spanish in order to communicate better with his neighbors and enjoyed a close relationship with his French neighbor, Sylvain Bordes.

1 John Boessenecker, *Lawman* (Norman, OK: U of OK P, 1998) 42.
2 Boessenecker 28.
3 Boessenecker 88-91.
4 *Contra Costa County Mortgage Book* 10: 442.
5 San Francisco General Land Office, Cash Entry 4544, National Archives, DC.
6 Mary Praetzellis, Suzanne B. Stewart and Grace H. Ziesing, *The Los Vaqueros Watershed: A Working History* (Rohnert Park, CA: Sonoma State U Academic Foundation, 1997) 166.
7 Township 2: 385.
8 San Francisco General Land Office, Homestead Entry 1399, National Archives, DC.
9 *Contra Costa County Deed Book* 31: 332.

10 Praetzellis 169.

11 Homestead Entry 1399.

12 Township 2: 34.

13 Contra Costa County Probate Record 2156.

14 US Census 1900, Contra Costa County, ED 334: 17B.

15 "Hans Christensen Robbery on Sunday Night," *The Livermore Herald* 13 Mar 1897: 1.

16 Janet Newton, *Las Positas* (Livermore, CA: Newton, 1969) 147.

17 *Contra Costa County Deed Book* 38: 353.

18 US Census 1870, San Joaquin County, Stockton Ward 2: 170.

19 San Francisco General Land Office, Homestead Entry 2566, National Archives, DC.

20 US Census 1880, Contra Costa County, Township 2: 343.

21 *Contra Costa County Tax Assessment Book 1858*: 18.

22 *Contra Costa County Mortgage Book* 23: 163.

23 San Francisco General Land Office, Homestead Entry 6715, National Archives, DC.

24 *Contra Costa County Deed Book* 54: 150.

25 *Contra Costa County Deed Book* 96: 546.

26 *Contra Costa County Deed Book* 96: 545.

27 "All Around Town," *The Livermore Herald* 22 Nov 1913: 8.

28 *Bancroft Pioneer Register and Index* (Baltimore: Regional Pub, 1964).

29 Besides the mission records themselves, the following sources were helpful for Californio family genealogies: Dorothy G. Mutnick, *Some Alta California Pioneers and Descendants* (Lafayette, CA: Past Time Publications, 1982), available at the Contra Costa County History Center, and Marie E. Northrup, *Spanish-American Families of Early California 1769-1850*, Vol. 1 (New Orleans: Polyanthos, 1976). José Dolores Mesa was usually called simply "Dolores."

30 Contra Costa County Great Register 1896.

31 US Census 1880, Contra Costa County, ED 27: 41.

32 San Francisco General Land Office, Homestead Entry 3091, National Archives, DC.

33 "School Report for Feb 1892," *Livermore Echo* 3 Mar 1892: 3.

34 "Local Echoes," *Livermore Echo* 13 Feb 1902: 3.

35 Hazel Franco Tawney, personal interview, 28 Oct 1997.

36 San Francisco General Land Office, Homestead Entry 2565, National Archives, DC.

37 San Francisco General Land Office, Cash Entry 4463; Act of 1855 Military Land Warrant 109600, National Archives, DC.

38 "Delinquent Tax List," *Contra Costa Gazette* 30 Jan 1875: 1.

39 In other records Pascual Franco listed his place of birth as Mexico. Presumably he was born in New Mexico when it was a Mexican possession. In 1885 homestead proof he again listed New Mexico.

40 Homestead Entry 2565.

41 "Summit School District," *Contra Costa Gazette* 8 Mar 1884: 3.

42 Tawney, personal interview, 23 June 1998.

43 "Death of Salvador Franco," *The Livermore Herald* 19 Jan 1907: 1.

44 Tawney, personal interview, 28 Oct 1997 .

45 *Contra Costa Gazette* 6 Oct 1866: 2.

46 San Francisco General Land Office, Homestead Entry 2538, National Archives, DC. García family tree, property of Hazel Franco Tawney.

47 *Contra Costa County Mortgage Book* 27: 533.

48 "Local Brevities," *The Livermore Herald* 11 Dec 1909: 4.

49 Denny and June Mallory, personal interview, 4 May 1997.

50 San Francisco General Land Office, Timber Culture Entry 20087, National Archives, DC.

51 Karana Hattersley-Drayton, "Interview with Juanita Robles Hargraves," Sonoma State U Anthropological Studies Center, for the Contra Costa Water District, 9 Nov 1995: 17.

a Karana Hattersley-Drayton, *Report on Oral History Completed Under the Historic Property Treatment Plan for Construction of the Los Vaqueros Dam and Reservoir and Related Requirements, Los Vaqueros Project* (Rohnert Park, CA: Sonoma State U Academic Foundation, 1996) 28.

b Hattersley-Drayton 29-30.

c Tawney, letter, 19 Aug 1997.

d "'When the Gringo First Came'—Life History of Prof. J.D. Smith," *The Livermore Herald* 10 July 1925: 7.

e *Livermore Echo* 11 June 1903: 3.

The Beck Brothers

IN 1863 LEONARD and Caroline Beck with their two sons and three daughters crossed the Great Plains by ox team from Iowa to Virginia City, Nevada. The obituaries of both Caroline and her younger son, George, who was 10 years old when the family made the trek, testified to their strenuous wagon train journey.

Probably because this feat of crossing the country seems so heroic to the modern mind, the wagon itself has become exaggerated in size. Actually, travelers like the Becks typically used two or three small wagons that could each carry a ton of goods. The interiors would sleep only two adults, so tents were carried for any additional family members. Three to four yoke of oxen—cheaper than mules, the other beast of burden favored for the task—pulled each wagon. Hollywood to the contrary notwithstanding, horses were not as good a choice. A driver controlled the oxen by walking alongside the beasts, using a few commands and a whip. Indian presence was still threatening even as late as 1863. In that year, at Twin Sisters Rock on the Hudspeth Cut-off from the Oregon Trail to the California Trail, Bannack Indians attacked and killed all the members of a seven-wagon train.[1]

To finance their undertaking, the Becks sold their land in Iowa. Besides wagons and oxen, they had to purchase beef cattle, riding horses, firearms, and basic food supplies: bacon, crackers, salt, flour, corn meal, sugar, coffee, tea, rice, vinegar, dried fruit. The total cost would have been about $2,000.[2] They traveled approximately 2,000 miles across what are now the states of Nebraska, Wyoming, Idaho, and Nevada, averaging about 14 miles per day for five months, from early May through September.[3] From 1842 until the completion of the transcontinental railroad in

George Beck, c. 1913.
Courtesy of the Livermore Heritage Guild.

John Beck, from The Livermore Herald *special school edition, 2 June 1896, page 2. Courtesy of the Livermore Heritage Guild.*

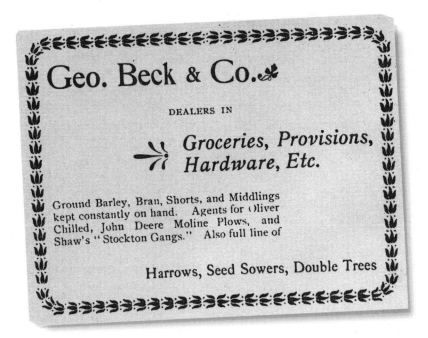

From The Livermore Herald, *5 August 1899, page 4.*

1869, an estimated 200,000 people used this route.[4]

The Becks' journey took place during the Civil War. On 2–3 May 1863, just as the Becks would have left Iowa, Lee won the battle of Chancellorsville, in which Stonewall Jackson died. In July, about halfway on their journey, as their wagon train would have reached Fort Hall, Idaho, the Battle of Gettysburg was raging back in Pennsylvania.

Leonard Beck's birthplace was in Westmoreland County, Pennsylvania. On 26 December 1836 he had married Caroline Sherwood in Perry County, Ohio. Like their mother, the children were natives of Ohio except for the youngest child, George, born in Indiana. U.S. census records show the Beck family still farming in 1840 in Perry County. In 1850 they were in Washington County, Indiana, and by 1860 they were farming in Van Buren County, Iowa. From here they began their cross-country trek to California.

After short stays in several other California cities, the Beck family came to Livermore about 1869. Leonard Beck erected the downtown Livermore building later occupied by the drugstore firm of McKown and Mess and started a merchandising business. He had a home and several rental cottages built on Second Street, and he bought 160 acres of flat farming land along May School Road to the north of Livermore. George Beck chose to follow in the steps of his father as a Livermore merchant with a general store, which carried not only groceries but hardware and even farm equipment such as harrows. An 1896 advertisement for George Beck's store in *The Livermore Herald* boasted, "The stock of groceries, provisions, cutlery, hardware and farming implements, is not only an extensive one, but thoroughly up to date."[5] Beginning in 1879, George Beck was in partnership with C.J. Stevens, but upon his partner's death he bought out Stevens's share of the estate to form "Geo. Beck & Co" and

John Beck's barns as they appeared in 1998. Photo by Anne Homan.

later "Geo. Beck & Sons."[6] Eventually he amassed a considerable amount of property in Livermore.

Leonard Beck's son John, 10 years older than George, chose to be a farmer and stock raiser. Just under six feet, John was a little taller than George, with gray eyes instead of his brother's blue. The 1878 *Murray Township Business Directory* advertised that John Beck owned 160 acres; this property was in section 16 T2S/R2E, which he had acquired with agricultural college scrip.[7] Alameda County is divided into townships, and Murray is the name of the township that includes Livermore. In 1878 John Beck built a hay barn with a capacity of 200 tons on his ranch; he added another barn, 52 by 80 feet, and a granary, 12 by 26 feet, in 1881. The 1880 agricultural census for Murray Township listed John Beck with 844 acres of improved land and 110 acres of unimproved. On this acreage in

1880 he raised 200 tons of hay, 300 bushels of barley, and 3,400 bushels of wheat. His ranch in the same year also produced 300 pounds of butter and 200 dozen eggs. *The Livermore Herald* announced that he raised 130 tons of summer fallow wheat and a good crop of apples in 1881.[8] By 1903 he was offering to sell 1,030 acres of land.

Until 1956 the portion of Morgan Territory Road that lies in Alameda County was named Beck Road. North Livermore Avenue was called Beck Road until even more recently; in fact, the latest available United States Geological Survey map in 1999 still labels both sections as "Beck Road." The county named these roads for John Beck, to whose property the roads led, honoring not only his status as a rancher but also his service as a road supervisor and contractor for the area from about 1880 to 1904. In one instance, *The Livermore Herald* reported on 30 March 1882 that Beck was working on Livermore Avenue from the railroad crossing to the town line, as well as on the Dublin grade, with a team of six men and 18 horses, a county grader, and a plow. His grandson Robert Beck told of his grandfather's having had a major part in the building of Mines Road, and in 1898 John Beck completed the grading for a new road to the coal mining town of Tesla.[9] Besides his usual work of grading and graveling as "road master" of Murray Township, he put in an $8,000 water system for the city of Suisun in 1897 with 10 Livermore workmen.

John Beck and his brother were also active in community affairs. George Beck was Livermore's postmaster during the Grover Cleveland administration from 1885 to 1890; the post office was inside his store in the Odd Fellows' Building. *The Livermore Herald*'s special school edition of 1896 has photographs of John Beck, Livermore Union High School director for May District, and George Beck, high school trustee. From 1895 through 1896, George was a Livermore City trustee, and from 1913 to 1916 he served as a Democrat in the California Assembly.

The "corner ranch" site that belonged to John Beck is slightly northeast of the right-angle turn between North Livermore Avenue and Manning Road. The original house has been replaced by a trailer, but numerous outbuildings are still standing. In about 1915, John Beck built a fancier country home, "El Cayetano," half a mile up Morgan Territory Road from Manning Road on section 17 T2S/R1E. Soon after a driver turns onto Morgan Territory from the south, after the small orchard of the Fagundes family to the east and just beyond a large eucalyptus tree, a gravel road dips down and crosses Cayetano Creek, while the blacktopped Morgan Territory Road veers to the west. Down that gravel road are two large palm trees that ornamented either side of the fashionable John Beck home. A number of cypress trees march along a straggling fence line

to the north, and two olive trees are growing on the east side of the gravel road. A cistern and two dilapidated barns are the only structures remaining at the site. John Beck married twice and raised six children, three girls and three boys. After his children became adults, tragedy seemed to stalk the family.

In 1909 John Beck's second wife, Priscilla, choked on a bone while eating her lunch alone at the corner ranch. John found her unconscious and rushed her to the hospital, but she died of blood poisoning sustained from scratches she had made in her throat when she was trying to remove the obstruction.[10]

John's oldest son, George L. Beck, had moved to Washington state with his wife and three young children in 1908. Several years later, they decided to travel by train to visit relatives and friends in Livermore. A sudden heavy snowfall trapped their train, the Spokane Limited with 40 passengers, as well as a westbound transcontinental Fast Mail with no passengers, high in the Washington mountains on 24 February 1910. In the early morning of March 1, an avalanche swept both trains, along with 30 workmen attempting to free them, down the side of a mountain, killing 96 people—still the highest avalanche death toll in U.S. history. George had informed his father they were coming by steamer but changed his plans just before departure, so until authorities notified him, John Beck had not even been aware that his son's family was traveling on the train.[11] All of the young family are buried together at Livermore's Roselawn Cemetery.

In December 1909 widower John Beck was married a third time to Anna Wallace, and gave her more than $3,800 to help her sick mother and pay off a mortgage. She managed to deceive him by living part-time with him and part-time with her first husband and five children. Beck had his marriage to Anna annulled in October 1910.[12]

John Beck traveled to the eastern seaboard in

October and November 1911 and visited a number of cities, but spent the majority of his two-month excursion in Boston, where he had relatives. He returned to Livermore by train via the southern route through Louisiana and Texas. During his vacation he shaved his beard, and the *Herald* observed that his friends barely recognized him on his return.[13]

In 1915 John's string of misfortunes continued when he broke his leg while in San Francisco. The break was severe enough to limit his activities; he was still using a crutch two years later when his house caught fire on a late November evening. All the contents of the house were lost except for one trunk.

An emergency telephone call had been made to Livermore, and the fire bell was rung, but the volunteers probably would have been unable to save the wooden structure anyway. The firefighters' arrival at the blaze was delayed because they thought the caller had meant a fire at Beck's rental property on Second Street in Livermore, and the firefighters went there first. Estimators judged the loss of house and contents at $5,000. Insurance covered less than half the loss.[14] Several weeks later, a depressed John Beck journeyed to San Francisco, where he rented a hotel room and poisoned himself with potassium cyanide. News of his suicide first came to his brother, George, in a telephone message from the San Francisco coroner's office.[15]

'Burning Lamp Sets Fire to Farm House'

"Mr. Beck, who was alone in the house, was in the kitchen. He started to go into another room carrying a small glass lamp by its handle in his left hand, holding onto his crutch at the same time. This action tilted the lamp and the chimney fell off. It did not break as it struck the floor and Mr. Beck was attempting to recover it. He did not realize that he was holding the lamp at a dangerous angle until it exploded, scattering the burning oil about the room. Mr. Beck himself fortunately escaped contact with the blazing fluid but it soon spread to the walls. Being lame, he could do nothing to extinguish the fire but he made his way to the porch and shouted for help. John Johnson, his nearest neighbor, hurried to the scene with his men. They worked hard to extinguish the fire but it had gained too much headway under the stimulus of the oil stove and a wall lamp, which both burst and added fury to the fire." [a]

1 Albert and Jane Salesbring, *Here Rolled the Covered Wagons* (NY: Bonanza, 1948) 38.

2 Timothy Foote, "1846: The Way We Were—and the Way We Went," *Smithsonian* April 1996: 46.

3 George R. Stewart, *The California Trail* (NY: MacGraw-Hill, 1962) 141.

4 Salesbring 29.

5 "Geo. Beck & Co," *The Livermore Herald*, Midwinter Edition 25 Jan 1896: 22.

6 "Building Razed Two of Oldest," *The Livermore Herald* 22 Apr 1932.

7 *Alameda County Record of Patents*, Vol. B, 1876-1891: 131.

8 " Local Brieflets," *The Livermore Herald* 1 Sep 1881: 3.

9 Dan Mosier and Earle E. Williams, *History of Tesla* (Fremont: Mines Road Books, 1999) 91.

10 "Mrs. John Beck Dies From Blood Poisoning," *The Livermore Herald* 10 July 1909: 1.

11 "Entire Family Meets Death," *The Livermore Herald* 5 Mar 1910: 1.

12 "Court Annuls Beck Marriage," *The Livermore Herald* 22 Oct 1910: 1.

13 "People You Know," *The Livermore Herald* 2 Dec 1911: 3.

14 "Burning Lamp Sets Fire," *The Livermore Herald* 1 Dec 1917: 1.

15 "John Beck Commits Suicide in City Hotel," *The Livermore Herald* 22 Dec 1917: 1.

a "Burning Lamp Sets Fire."

Antoinette and Albert (Al) Morris on their wedding day in 1939. Courtesy of Antoinette Morris.

"Guv'nor" Al Morris and His Little Genovese

Six people crowded the utilitarian cabin of the SS Giuseppe Verdi. The mother and three of her daughters chattered in rapid Italian as they moved about, folding clothes into open trunks in preparation for the end of the voyage. In one corner Papa sat, hidden behind his newspaper, but once in a while he lowered it and with a deeper note of advice briefly joined the chorus. ❧ Off to one side on a small straight-backed chair sat the youngest daughter, her legs, too short to reach the carpet, swinging back and forth. Two braids pulled her chestnut-colored hair back from her face. Hunched over, with her arms stiff at her sides and hands clutching the seat of the chair, eight-year-old Antoinette was deep in thought, and very worried. ❧ Their ship was fast approaching New York harbor. Authorities on board had warned passengers that if anyone were found to be sick that person would not be allowed to enter the United States but would be sent back to Italy. If one of them were ineligible, would the whole family be turned away? Would only that one be sent back? What if she were that one? What would she do without her family?

ANTOINETTE AND HER three older sisters, Lena, Augusta, and Marie, had enjoyed playing with other children in the huge sitting room of the liner from Genoa to New York City, but now the 14-day journey was almost ended, and a new country about to engulf them. Antoinette Gattorna's memories of that scene in the ship's cabin are still strong, but she needn't have worried. For her family the move to the New World was a good one.

The girls' parents, Giovanni and Rosa Gattorna, had run a small coal business in Genoa, but World War I hostilities were spreading over Europe, and in 1916 the Gattornas decided to immigrate to California, where Rosa's father and brother were already living in Livermore. They disembarked at Ellis Island, waited through the tedious bureaucratic process, and were ultimately permitted to enter the country. The overland train journey to California took four days. Antoinette recalled her family's surprise at the late-September weather on their cross-country ride. "What most of us remember was heat, heat, heat."[1]

Their relatives met them at the train station in Oakland and brought them to Livermore, where the Gattornas settled down on the old Robert Livermore Jr. property on Las Positas Road. A fifth daughter, Josephine, was born in 1917. They raised vegetables and delivered them to regular customers along a country wagon route that included Vasco Road to the east and San Ramon to the west. Later they bought a truck. In those days salesmen frequently drove around to ranches and sold all sorts of goods and groceries—needles, fabrics, shirts, vegetables, fish. "They'd stop in the yard and you'd buy. It was a godsend, I guess," mused Antoinette 80 years later. Women rarely left the ranches. The Gattorna family also entered into partnership with their relatives in a grocery store; the building is now part of the Livermore Cyclery, next door to the Bank of Italy building near the flagpole in downtown Livermore.

The Gattorna sisters and their parents in 1948; Antoinette is at left in the back row, behind her mother. Courtesy of Antoinette Morris.

The older four girls struggled with their new language at St. Michael's parochial school in Livermore. Helpful nuns gave extra lessons to these eager students. Antoinette remembered well the girls' frustration: "Every night we'd come home. One of us had a little clue. 'I think when they say this, it means that!' Just a little clue, any little clue." Educators say that to be able to perform, write, and think comfortably in a new language takes an average of seven to eight years. Antoinette agrees that the task is difficult, but she has little patience for those who do not try. "I'm angry, very angry at some of these people that sit back and don't learn the language. If you have knowledge of the alphabet and know how to read, you can learn. It's embarrassing, but you can learn." The Gattorna family had come to Livermore in September. The following February, Antoinette realized with excitement that she had understood all that a neighbor had just said to her in English.

"Several years later," Antoinette remembered, "a student at St. Michael's told me that I could get books for free at the Carnegie Library. She gave me directions, and I went there. It was true! That was so wonderful, to get books for free. I introduced my whole family to the library. My aunt had to sign for us since she was a taxpayer."

Antoinette graduated from Livermore High in 1926 and worked after graduation at the family grocery store, which she described as "not fancy," with shelves for canned goods and boxes on the floor filled with various vegetables and fruit. Customers bought many items by the pound, in bulk—rice, brown sugar, white sugar, crackers, cookies—but the store did not carry meat. Soon after frozen foods became available, the little store closed, after 30 years in business. Although Antoinette stressed that their meeting was anything but romantic, she first met her husband, Albert George (Al) Morris, when he came into the store as a customer.

The Morris family had changed their surname from Morais, the original Portuguese name. Al's father, John J. Morris, emigrated from the Azorean island of São Jorge to Contra Costa County about 1898. Subsequently, two brothers, Julio and Joe, came also. Albert, a fourth brother, may have been here briefly and returned to the Azores.[2] Many Azorean immigrants like the Morrises bought property along Morgan Territory Road, and they were all from that one tiny island—São Jorge (Saint George).

On 28 November 1906 John Morris married Annie Bent Nunez, daughter of Manuel Bent Nunez, at St. Catherine's in Martinez. Annie's nephew Fred Bloching clearly remembered John's large handlebar mustache.[3] The three Morris brothers and Annie occasionally piled supplies, including bottles of wine, into a wagon and headed for a Monterey beach where they camped out for several days.

By 1910 Annie and John Morris had bought their own ranch in section 17 T2S/R1E on the west side of Morgan Territory Road, beginning at its intersection with Manning Road. They moved their first wooden frame home from Vasco Road to this site and altered it so that nowadays it serves as a granary, just next to the road. Their son, Al, was always proud to tell visitors that he was born in the tumbledown granary, on 19 October 1907. Al's sister, Madaline, was born in 1911. The children attended the one-room Highland School until Al graduated, and then Madaline finished at May School.

Around 1914 John Morris built a new home, where his daughter-in-law Antoinette still lives, about one-half mile north from Manning Road. The Morrises' original wooden hay barn erected north of the ranch house burned in 1993, and they have replaced it with a metal barn. As did many of his neighbors, John Morris ran cattle on his properties and cut firewood to barter in town. The three Morris brothers were skilled at carpentry and even made musical instruments. Joe

Jack Gleese remembered the 1920s bootlegging activities of John Morris:

"In those days he drove a big Buick sedan, four-door sedan. And he would drive to Livermore and turn . . . around at Livermore and come back and park at the side of the road, usually where Jensen's place is. He'd be sitting by the side of the road. Nobody knew what was going on. He might be having a stroke or something. But he had his deliveries and those who were getting their whiskey would stop and pick up their jug and pay him and he'd be on his way. So he delivered his whiskey at the roadside. And I don't think he ever got caught." [a]

spent some time working at a dairy farm in Hanford. After the suicide of John Beck, the Morris brothers bought his property, which included two large barns and the site across the road from the Morris ranch where Beck's home had burned. Joe Morris died of influenza at age 35 in 1919. Because of financial disagreements, John bought out his brother Julio's share of the property, and Julio returned to São Jorge. John J. Morris died at age 70 in April 1939.

John Silva, who lived on North Livermore Avenue for many years, remembered that John Morris made moonshine whiskey in his basement during Prohibition—reputedly a very good whiskey. Local legend had it, according to John Silva, that if you drank "jackass" whiskey you would not catch the flu, so his family was a regular customer of John Morris. He affirmed that the Silva family never caught the flu.[4]

Antoinette Morris and Will Dias both recounted a story told by Al Morris about authorities coming to the Morris home and searching for

Annie Morris and her son, Albert, c. 1908; her husband, John Morris, is in the portrait above and flanked by his brothers Joe and Julio in the photo below. Photos courtesy of Antoinette Morris.

Annie Morris (above, right) and haying crew on the Morris ranch, c. 1910. Photo courtesy of Antoinette Morris. A windmill still stood on the Morris property in 1971. Photo by Don Homan.

a basement still. *The Livermore Herald* reported that in July 1920 John Morris' car was damaged by another at Livermore Avenue and old Highway 50 (now Portola Avenue).[5] The news account did not mention smashed moonshine jugs, but this accident might have led local law enforcement officials to Morris's basement. Presumably he had had the foresight to remove the evidence.

Antoinette and Al were married in Reno on 16 November 1939. Antoinette remembers first coming to live on the isolated Morris ranch when it had the only phone for miles around. She tried working in town for a while but found that too difficult. She'd come home after a long day, and the first words from her family would be, "When do we eat?" She elected to stay at home, dealing with ranch life and working alongside her mother-in-law, who died in 1966. Antoinette and Al Morris had two children, Albert and Beatrice. Now Antoinette is isolated again, but this time by age. In her early nineties, she can no longer drive, which has greatly affected her independence. "It's terrible not being able to drive," she says. However, she still loves living on the ranch, being able to feel close to the natural world: "I really enjoy the hills and the weather and the trees. I like to see the cattle come up and drink." She keeps busy reading biographies, her favorite selections from the Livermore library. She often sits during the day at her kitchen window, which overlooks a water trough and commands a good view of Morgan Territory Road. After 60 years, she has difficulty imagining living anywhere else.

Antoinette describes herself as "a very private person." She is shy in contrast to her husband, Al, who was a great socializer, and the pair were also a contrast in appearance. Al was a barrel-chested man, about five feet eight, whereas Antoinette is a petite five feet one. Neighbor and friend Will Dias called Al "guv'nor." Al always seemed to be aware of the latest news and liked to visit over coffee, especially with Will and close friend Ernie Basso. "He was our local newspaper," Will noted—he would visit ranch to ranch and spread the word, not as gossip, but in friendship.[6] Al and Ernie Basso frequently drove to the stock sales in Stockton together. Al had a phenomenal memory, his friends say. For example, he could recall annual rain and drought statistics or the numbers of stock he had run in any year. Al died in 1993, and he is sorely missed. "Al would have known!" people lament when asked questions they cannot answer about local history and customs. Will Dias commented, "Gee, the guy you should have here is Al Morris. I mean, between him and his father, they was here over 100 years!"

For three generations the Morris family have raised cattle on their land; young Al now runs the ranch for his mother. Al Senior had a '52 Chevy truck that he called "Greenie," which Morgan Territory Road residents recognized easily because Al never drove faster than 10 miles per hour on his way to and from the section 14 Nunez property he had inherited from his mother, on the north end of the road. His little terrier would sit in the passenger side. Al loved the Livermore rodeo and, from its founding in 1918, he attended every one until his death.

1 Antoinette Morris supplied much information in this chapter through continuing personal interviews, 11 Feb 1995, 9 Sep 1996, 31 Jan 1997, 31 May 2000.

2 Alberto Morais, letter to Annie Nunez Morris, 2 Apr 1954. Return address at Velas, São Jorge. Translated by Manuel Rosa, 25 Jan 1998. In the letter, Alberto said he was brother-in-law to Annie, and mentioned that his sister Rita, married to João Fontes, had cancer. He also said that two of his children, Julio and Rita, had recently settled in Africa, necessitating the sale of his two cows since he was too old and tired to climb the rocky cliffs above their house on São Jorge.

3 Fred Bloching, personal interview, 21 Jan 1997.

4 John Silva, personal interview, 13 Oct 1995.

5 "John Morris' Auto Damaged," *The Livermore Herald* 3 July 1920: 8.

6 Will Dias, personal interview, 21 Sep 1995.

a Jack Gleese, personal interview, 26 Nov 1996.

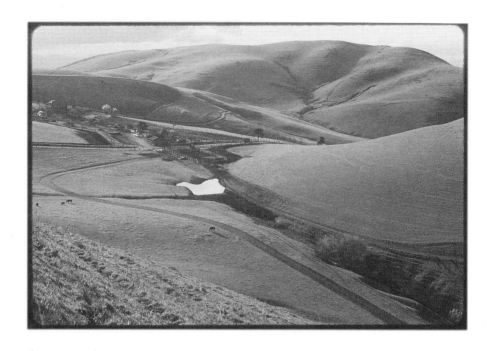

Murder at the Levy Grade

GERMANY WAS briefly united as a confederation in 1848, but its legislature soon dissolved because of aggressive actions by the northeastern kingdom, Prussia. Frederick William IV insisted on ruling Prussia by "divine right." He strictly monitored the press, took away many previously won civil liberties, and drafted thousands of young men into his army. The Prussian militaristic stance frightened peace-loving citizens, and many Germans fled from possible military conscription to the United States. Samuel Levy, a Prussian Jew, would be 18 in August 1851. Knowing that he would be eligible then for the draft, he emigrated from his native village of Miloslaw to the United States. He probably came at first to San Francisco. After marrying in about

1862, he moved to Washington Corners (now called Irvington) but settled in the Livermore area soon after, and purchased a Laddsville lot in November 1871.[1] Zylpha Bernal Beck [2] remembered the early sales career of Samuel Levy: "Before he had the store, he peddled his merchandise from a wagon that was fitted with shelves and drawers like a store. He was known all over the area. One of his stops was at El Niño Rancho near San Ramon, where Joel Harlan's family lived. He was always invited to have his midday meal with them."[3] Levy's wife, Dorchan, also had emigrated from Prussia.[4]

Once settled in Livermore, Samuel Levy erected a large two-story building at the southwest corner of First and J streets, where he ran a

The Levy/Cardoza ranch, 1971. Photo by Don Homan.

First Street in Livermore, c. 1893. The first two-story building on the left is the Levy's Building, which housed the Palace Restaurant. Courtesy of the Livermore Heritage Guild.

general merchandise business downstairs. The family probably lived upstairs at first. Later, they lived in a cottage behind the store, and at one time used the upper floor of the building as a rooming house.[5] The business portion of the building was 26 by 52 feet and "appropriately laid out to accommodate the various departments." His general store carried almost everything, "from a wash bowl for the kitchen to a mirror for the drawing room; from a shoestring to the latest modes de Paris; from a pound of molasses" to a complete stock of food items.[6] In 1881 he built another, larger two-story structure that cost $3,500 and included two stores on the first floor, besides six offices on the second level.[7]

C.H. Christianson leased the west store area for a saloon. By May of the same year, Levy had built a sidewalk on First Street and laid 66 feet of a "substantial plank walk" on J Street.

His business, unlike that of George Beck, which was strictly cash and carry, allowed his customers credit. This policy led to his sometimes acquiring property rights because of the indebtedness of a customer. However, the policy likely also helped carry him into bankruptcy on 12 July 1888, when he declared debts of $18,000 to merchants of San Francisco, Sacramento, and Livermore, and assets of only $11,000. He listed $2,211 in doubtful customer accounts, and an additional $508 in collectible outstanding accounts.[8] Samuel and his son Albert were co-partners in S. Levy and Company, which included the store in Livermore and one in Jackson, Amador County.[9] Two weeks after declaring bankruptcy, Samuel had managed to reopen his Livermore store for business.[10] In 1893 Samuel Levy, proprietor of the Palace Restaurant, advertised in the *Livermore Echo*, offering "oysters in every style" and promising that "only skilled cooks and polite attendants" were employed.[11] Finally going out of business for good, he sold the complete stock of his store in 1897.[12]

The Levy family included four daughters and three sons: Anna, Albert, Hattie, Bertha, Benjamin, Nora, and Herman. Two of the sons became involved in general merchandising, but the third son, Benjamin, after training in San Francisco, operated jewelry stores in Newman, Fruitvale, and Los Banos. Dorchan Levy died 24 November 1887 and was buried in a Jewish cemetery on 19th Street in San Francisco, the site today of Mission Dolores Park. The bodies at that site were moved soon after the 1906 earthquake to the Hills of Eternity Cemetery in Colma. After selling his stock, Samuel left Livermore for Newman, a small town near Modesto. Shortly before his death, his only unwed daughter, Nora, married Abraham Jacobsen of San Francisco in August 1908. "Mr. Levy knew he had not long to live and was anxious to have the ceremony take place. . . ." Samuel Levy died in San Francisco on September 2 "after a lingering illness" and was buried next to his wife.[13] While they lived in Livermore, the Levys traveled often to cosmopolitan San Francisco where they probably had the comfort of worshiping and visiting with friends and relatives who shared their religion and culture. No figures exist for Livermore, but by 1883 San Francisco had a Jewish population of 17,000.[14]

At the peak of his real estate ventures, Samuel Levy owned seven lots in downtown Livermore, which he probably sold before leaving for

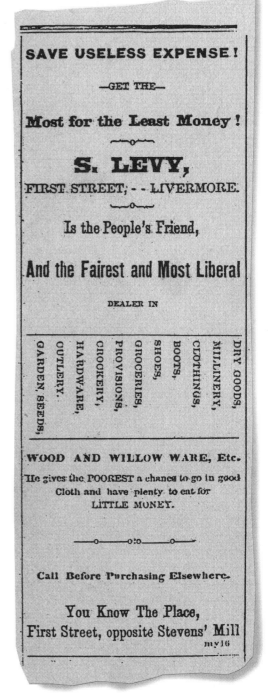

From The Livermore Herald, *16 May 1874, page 2.*

Newman. He also owned property on Morgan Territory Road, although the family most likely never lived here but used it as a rental property and investment. By 1876, not long after he first moved to Livermore, he had bought 160 acres in section 4 T2S/R2E from Romualdo Valenzuela. In his declaration of assets during his bankruptcy of 1888, he listed this acreage as worth $4,000. Later, he also purchased the adjoining western half of section 5, where he built a house, corral, barn, granary, and bunkhouse. These buildings were near the road at the top of the long steep grade that locals still call "the Levy." In 1882 he bought 5,000 grape cuttings to plant in a nursery at his "mountain ranch," planning to set them in his vineyard there the following season.[15] He had a number of tenants, including James Anderson in 1885 and later Manuel Garcia. The Levy family, however, must have worked and visited fairly often at their Black Hills ranch. They tended their vineyard, and Benjamin Levy knew the local ranchers' children since he chose to attend local dances at Highland School.

Samuel Levy's estate sold the ranch in 1913 to Antone Bent Nunez. Eventually, Joseph Souza Cardoza bought it in 1925, and the site has stayed in the Cardoza family ever since.[16] The original house was almost square, with a truncated pyramidal hip roof, typical of ranch houses of the late 1800s in this area. On 5 June 1996 this venerable piece of history burned to the ground, along with an old garage-shop and all the belongings of Russ Cardoza's family. Wood seasoned for more than 120 years burned very well; firefighters could do little but keep the barn and surrounding fields of dry grass from burning. The cause of the fire remains a mystery although it was not judged arson. The ready access of the home to the road and the helpfulness of the Cardoza family through the years created a haven for road travelers in any trouble. Russ and his family had a new home built in 1999 slightly to the east of the original site.

The Livermore Herald published details of the 1909 murder at the Levy:

"Garcia was killed in his corral, possibly while milking. The murderer approached him from behind and shot him in the back with his own rifle. He then clubbed the rifle and endeavored to dispatch him by repeated blows on the head. The rifle stock broke and he then dragged the body toward the house. Finding some signs of life he struck the unfortunate man in the back of the head several times with an ax, the sharp blade cleaving the skull. . . . The body was then dragged through the fence and into the cellar where it was found. . . . Robbery was apparently the motive of the crime." [a]

Ninety years ago, while the Levy estate still owned it, this bucolic ranch was the scene of a brutal murder. Manuel Garcia, a Portuguese rancher whose home was in Irvington, leased Levy's ranch. Antone Bent Nunez, a neighbor in the Black Hills, came to consult with Garcia about pasturage for his cattle but assumed when Garcia was not there that he had gone to Centerville or Irvington, where he owned ranches. Nunez returned the following day and realized something was wrong when he heard the whinnying of the horses in the barn. He investigated and determined that the animals had not been fed or watered for at least a day. "After watering them and giving them hay, he returned to the house and, after a thorough search of the premises, went into the cellar and there found Garcia's body in a huddled heap on the floor, as if it had been thrown down the steps by the slayer."[17] Nunez contacted the sheriff's department by sending word to Livermore. Alameda County Deputy Sheriff Jack Sherry and Contra

Costa County Sheriff Veale among others conducted the investigation.

Fortunately for the sake of justice, neighbors John Gleese and Willie Peña had noticed a stranger talking to Manuel Garcia on Sunday. They were able to describe him accurately to Sheriff Veale, and the sheriff recognized the description as that of John McFarland, a man he had already been seeking.

The murder occurred on 2 August 1909. Police picked up McFarland in San Jose on unrelated charges several days later and held him until Sheriff Veale took him into custody. McFarland admitted taking Garcia's money and trousers, but could not explain why his own trousers, which were found hidden at Levy's ranch, were bloody.[18] At first he denied committing the murder, but he later confessed.

Manuel Garcia Homem had emigrated from the island of Faial in the Azores. The coroner's report listed him as age 46. The cause of death was "compound fracture of the skull and laceration of the brain and gunshot wound through the right thorax."[19] He was buried in Centerville's Catholic Cemetery. His estate was estimated at $9,000; his only heir was his mother, who still lived on Faial.[20] Although residents have discovered other bodies left along this relatively deserted road, as far as is known this is the only murder that actually occurred on the Livermore side of Morgan Territory Road in the Black Hills.

1 Laddsville was a small settlement slightly east of Livermore.

2 Zylpha Bernal Beck was married to George W. Beck, cousin of John and George Beck.

3 Janet Newton, *The Livermore Valley 1878, 1889*, 2nd ed. (Livermore, CA: *The Livermore Herald*, 1988) 6.

4 Dorchan's name is spelled in various ways in public records: Dorothea, Douretta. Dorchan is the version on her tombstone and land records.

5 The proprietress was Lena Beck. Newton 6.

6 "Our Business Houses, Hotels and Places of Amusement," *Livermore Enterprise* 8 July 1876: 3.

7 "Murray Township Improvements," *The Livermore Herald* 29 Dec 1881: 1.

8 "Local Echoes," *Livermore Echo* 12 July 1888: 3.

9 *Alameda County Deed Book* 350: 451.

10 "Local Echoes," *Livermore Echo* 26 July 1888: 3.

11 *Livermore Echo* 14 Dec 1893: 2.

12 "Local Echoes," *Livermore Echo* 25 Mar 1897: 3.

13 "Passing of Two Pioneer Residents," *The Livermore Herald* 5 Sep 1908: 1.

14 Rudolf Ganz, *The Jews of California* (NY: Southern California Jewish Historical Society, 1960) 31.

15 "Local Brieflets," *The Livermore Herald* 6 Apr 1882: 3.

16 Karana Hattersley-Drayton, *Report on Oral History Completed Under the Historic Property Treatment Plan of Construction of the Los Vaqueros Dam and Reservoir and Related Requirements, Los Vaqueros Project* (Rohnert Park, CA: Sonoma State U Academic Foundation, 1996) 20.

17 "Brutal Murder of Manuel Garcia," *The Livermore Herald* 7 Aug 1909: 1, 8. "McFarland Held for Murder," *Contra Costa Gazette* 21 Aug 1909.

18 "MacFarland Makes Damaging Admissions," *The Livermore Herald* 14 Aug 1909: 4.

19 Contra Costa County Death Certificate #37.

20 "Estate of Manuel Garcia," *Byron Times* 8 July 1910: 8.

a "Brutal Murder of Manuel Garcia," *The Livermore Herald* 7 Aug 1909: 1, 8.

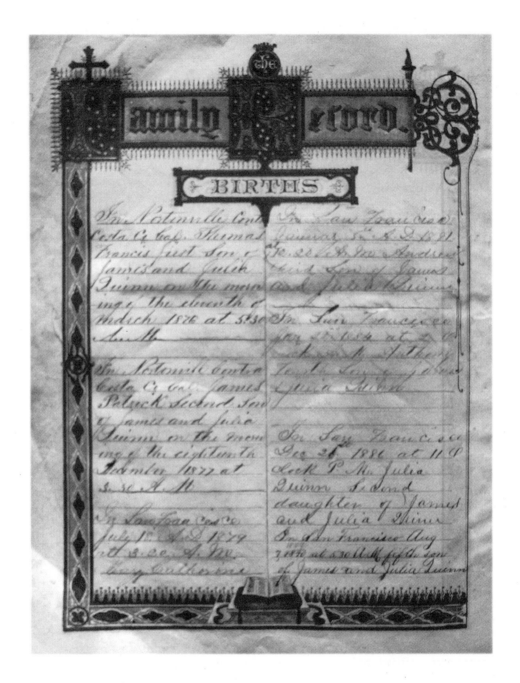

From the Quinn family Bible. Courtesy of Ruth Quinn.

"Burke & Quinn"

CALIFORNIA'S LARGEST coal mining development—the Mount Diablo coal field in the hills between Antioch and Marsh Creek Road—is now largely in Black Diamond Mines Regional Preserve, administered by the East Bay Regional Park District. Five towns grew up around the Contra Costa County coal mines; Nortonville and Somersville were the largest. They are all ghost towns now, with only slag heaps, covered mine openings, cellar holes, exotic trees, and one lonely cemetery to mark their town limits. The total coal production of the area between the years 1861 and 1902 was about four million tons, worth from $15-20 million.[1] This was a soft coal, lignite, not a very good quality. It had a bright black luster, but was brittle and crumbled easily.[2] The coal was in demand by river steamer owners who could buy it directly at local wharves more cheaply than at Sacramento, Vallejo, Stockton, or San Francisco.[3] By 1874 the mines had shipped 206,300 tons to San Francisco.[4] By 1907 they were closed permanently, although much coal remains in the area.

"There is in the mine and in the work almost a Zen-like quality. . . ."[5] John Waters, mining specialist with East Bay Regional Parks, described that feeling: "All there is in the world is what was in the beam of your light. That's all that exists. . . . There are no seasons. . . . It's always exactly the same. No time. No weather. . . . There is nothing else."[6] The grinding physical work was dangerous. Fear was always present with the knowledge of how far away escape was and how heavy that ceiling was over the worker's head. By 1880 Black Diamond Company's shaft reached almost 426 feet below the surface to the lower Mt. Hope tunnel.[7] Some fatal accidents were caused by methane gas, some by coal collapsing on working miners, some by carelessness.

Not so spectacular a danger, but working insidiously at their lungs, the unavoidable coal dust was the most serious threat to the miners' health. The rooms at Black Diamond varied in height. Miners could be working with picks on a ceiling anywhere from 18 inches to four feet above their faces. When coal fell from the vein, a giant cloud of dust flew up. The bucker boys who assisted the miners—some as young as eight—added more dust as they scraped the coal fragments over to a greased chute to be transported to a waiting ore car. After a time, despite the coolness underground, the workers removed their jackets and shirts. Their sweating torsos and heads soon became indelibly smeared with black dust. Black Diamond workers manned a 10- to 12-hour shift and received $1 per cubic yard of coal.[8] This amounted to about $3.00 for a normal day's work. In the winter months, a miner and his bucker boy would not see the sun at all, for the shift began in early morning before dawn and ended well after dark.

Miners Andrew F. Burke and James Quinn were Irishmen. Burke—probably also Quinn—was a native of Moylough, County Galway. "Moylough" means "Plain of the Lake," describing the town's situation on lowlands east of Lake Corrib.

In July 1870 the Contra Costa County census taker found the Irish miners living together at Nortonville, Quinn age 27 and Burke 30. Burke had become a naturalized citizen on 23 April 1868 at Martinez. While continuing to work as miners, they acquired property on Morgan Territory Road. The 1872 tax assessment showed Burke and Quinn paying taxes on the NW¼ of section 32 T1S/R2E, as well as on a watch, two saddles, three horses, six cows, 25 stock cattle, 500 sheep, and poultry. According to James

Quinn's 1873 pre-emption papers, he had used the section 32 property earlier for grazing, but settled there permanently when he built a house in March 1871 and added a corral, fencing, and well. He had planted about six acres in potatoes and owned 25 cattle and two horses grazing on the land. Andrew Burke, who had known Quinn for 20 years, testified as a witness. James Quinn bought agricultural college scrip worth $200 at the San Francisco General Land Office to pay for the 160 acres in May 1873.[9] In that year the tax assessor charged Burke and Quinn for four horses, 14 cows, 30 calves, 12 stock cattle, and two hogs. Apparently, they had switched to raising cattle rather than sheep.

Quinn still paid taxes on the original acreage in 1873, but now Andrew Burke paid taxes on the SW¼ of section 32. Burke had purchased these 160 acres in April 1872 for $400, claiming settlement there with his family in January 1872. He testified to having a house, barn, stable, corrals, and henhouse. About five acres were planted in grain for hay.[10] The west half of section 32 is on the ridgetop along Morgan Territory Road.

Both men married, Burke about 1871 and Quinn in December 1874.[11] Andrew Burke also maintained a Nortonville house and stable, both of which he bought on 17 July 1875 from butcher William G. Noakes. The house was on Black Diamond Railroad's north side opposite the lumberyard.[12] James Quinn and his family probably continued to live on Morgan Territory Road. Former residents recalled an old house at the site. A small dilapidated barn and what remains of a corral system are still adjacent to the road. When the current landowner recently put up a new windmill, he had to switch from the originally proposed site because he ran into the remains of an old well.

The two families raised animals in the Black Hills and sold meat in the coal mining towns, under the business name "Burke & Quinn." They

must have been doing well—in 1874 the firm paid $1,596 in taxes.[13] On the 1877 county voting register, James Quinn identified himself as a butcher. As early as 14 May 1870, the pair had registered the brand BB with Contra Costa County.

Both men seemed ambitious and eager to leave behind the grimy, dangerous work of coal mining. By 1878 Andrew Burke moved with his family to San Francisco, and the Quinns followed in 1879. The Burkes settled in at 529 Haight Street in the Northern Addition, the Quinns at 530 Noe Street in the Mission District. City directories listed both men as teamsters or draymen—a dray is a large horse-drawn wagon with removable sides—and occasionally as grading contractors. Andrew Burke and his Irish wife, Mary, had three children; James and Julia Quinn had seven. Both families held onto their Morgan Territory properties for some time. In 1903 Quinn was still running 26 head of cattle there.

Probably partly because of his own illiteracy, Andrew Burke was especially proud of his younger son's striving for an education. Signing his mark on the deed, Burke sold his land in 1903 to John Rafael, perhaps to finance his son's education at St. Mary's College—on the old Oakland "brickpile" campus—and later at Hastings Law School. Andrew F. Burke Jr. graduated from Hastings in 1907 and became a noted lawyer and advocate for the Roman Catholic Church. "He guided the archdiocese's complex legal affairs through three milestone constitutional cases, as well as handling all of its ordinary business over five decades."[14] The *San Francisco Chronicle* praised him in its obituary: "Soft-spoken, scholarly and deliberate in manner, he was noted for the painstaking research of his cases."[15] When the lawyer entered Golden Gate Hospital with the illness that led eventually to his death on 18 March 1964, he even took a portfolio of church business with him. The Quinns were also a devout Catholic family, and one of their daughters

Mary A. Geraghty Burke and Andrew Burke, 1896; "crayon" portraits by Marceau, San Francisco. Courtesy of Edward McGuirk.

became a nun. One of their sons and a colleague, however, embezzled $4,000 each from a San Francisco bank in 1916. The Quinns' son confessed to the crime and was not given any jail time, but made restitution for the sum.[16]

In San Francisco, of course, 17 April 1906 was a day of disaster, and these two families nearly lost their homes in the fires that followed the earthquake. The flames were stopped only a few blocks from both houses.

Many people who were not so fortunate needed transportation as they fled the fires with their possessions. Drays owned by teamsters like Andrew Burke and James Quinn were in constant demand. In fact, military authorities at times commandeered drays and other wagons. Once the fires were out, demand for the heavy wagons increased as supplies had to be distributed to the city's beleaguered citizens, and

mountains of rubble removed from city streets. Draymen who had charged $1 or $2 for a job before the quake now asked and received $50 and $75 for the same type of work.[17]

Andrew F. Burke Sr. died on 29 January 1912 at age 71. He was buried at Holy Cross Cemetery in Colma. Two residents from the Livermore Valley, John Sweeney and W.J. Fallon, attended his funeral because they knew him well. He had purchased workhorses for his drays from valley residents for many years.[18] According to family lore, the younger Andrew Burke had been born unexpectedly in Livermore while the Burkes were visiting their relatives, the Fallons.

James Quinn continued his ownership of property in the Black Hills. In 1906 and 1907 he signed a petition asking the Alameda County Board of Supervisors for a permanent road across section 17 at the Livermore end of Morgan

Territory Road. Not until 1916 did he sell his land to Joe F. Rose. James Quinn died 10 August 1925 at his Noe Street home at age 82. Like the Burkes, James Quinn and his family are buried at Holy Cross Cemetery.

After the two families moved to San Francisco, they probably used their Contra Costa County properties not only to run a few cattle and perhaps to lease but also to retreat from city life occasionally and enjoy the beauty of the Black Hills. A drive from San Francisco to purchase horses and visit relatives could have included a stopover for a pleasant picnic.

1 Raymond Sullivan and John Waters, "History of Mount Diablo Coalfield," *California Geology* March 1980: 51.

2 Sullivan and Waters 51.

3 W.A. Goodyear, *Coal Mines of the Western Coast of the United States* (San Francisco: A.L. Bancroft, 1877) 134.

4 Karana Hattersley-Drayton, "Community, Conflict and Change: The Oral History of the Mount Diablo Coal Fields," MA thesis, U of CA, Berkeley, 1996, 106.

5 Hattersley-Drayton 147.

6 Hattersley-Drayton 147.

7 Sullivan and Waters 56.

8 Sullivan and Waters 57.

9 San Francisco General Land Office, Agricultural College Scrip 523, Florida, National Archives, DC.

10 San Francisco General Land Office, Cash Entry 4891, National Archives, DC.

11 *Monitor* 2 Jan 1875: 5.

12 *Contra Costa County Miscellaneous Records,* 1:205.

13 *Contra Costa Gazette* 1 Aug 1874: 2.

14 "Andrew F. Burke Is Dead at 79," *San Francisco Chronicle* 20 Mar 1964: 26.

15 "Andrew F. Burke" 26.

16 "2 in Bank Accused of $8,000 Shortage," *San Francisco Examiner* 6 Oct 1916: 1.

17 William Bronson, *The Earth Shook, the Sky Burned* (Garden City, NY: Doubleday, 1959) 52.

18 *The Livermore Herald* obituary, 3 Feb 1912: 4.

Boyhood Adventures Cut Short

Dragging the splintery gray ladder to the rear of the house, the two boys worked in harmony, their high-top shoes crunching dried summer grass in the yard. Once the ladder was leaning against the wall, the older brother ran around to the front porch, grabbed up a black umbrella, and ran back. With a big grin, he glanced at the other boy before starting up the rungs to the roof. His brother just shook his head and rolled his brown eyes as he steadied the ladder. Built on an east-facing hill, the house was only one story at the back but two at the front, allowing for a large basement. As soon as his brother had climbed onto the shingles, the eight-year-old raced around to the front of the house. The figure of his brother appeared at the peak of the roof. "Dad'll kill you if you hurt his umbrella." "Oh, shut up! I'm not hurtin' nothin'!" The early sun lit up the older boy's eager face as he opened the umbrella. After maneuvering gingerly in order to avoid the half-porch, he straightened up. With the big wooden handle of the "parachute" clutched tightly in his hands, he leaped out, landing with a thud on his feet and then rolling, being careful to keep the umbrella from hitting the ground. Although 12-year-old Ormond Smith's experiment did not garner an exciting liftoff, it didn't injure him, either. "He was tough!" said his younger brother, Omery, 65 years later.

ORMOND AND OMERY Smith moved up to the ridgetop in the Black Hills from Oakland with their parents about 1932. Their father, Ormond C. Smith, was an Oakland firefighter. Their mother, Stella, had been in an automobile accident with their Model T Ford, and insurance money from a subsequent settlement paid enough for the Smiths to make a down payment on the SW¼ of section 30 T1S/R2E, which is west of the highest point on Morgan Territory Road, and to purchase a new Model B Ford as well. Before he became a firefighter, the elder Ormond Smith had been in the Navy. Omery remembered that his father had somewhat unusual difficulties in the service: Reared in a strait-laced family in the backwoods hill country of Georgia, his father took deep offense at any rude language.

"If they called him an S.O.B.," Omery said, "he'd just deck 'em."[1] Thus, his dad spent a good deal of time in the brig. Their little redwood house on the property, probably built by William F. Wattson when he acquired the land about 1910, had a living room, a kitchen, and two bedrooms.

Another, older home on the property, bought by Irish immigrant Hugh L. Beirne in November 1871, was still standing when the Smiths arrived. Beirne had paid $200 to Augustin E. Herrara for the house and for Herrara's future interest in the land up on "Black Mountain." The government approved Beirne's pre-emption and $400 payment for the SW¼ of section 30 T1S/R2E on 19 April 1875.[2] The pioneer home had a porch across its entire front, and the Smiths later used its basement as a garage for wagons and buggies. Outbuildings included a barn, chicken house, garage, and privy. The Summit School property next door, which Beirne had sold to the county, was still fenced off, but only fragments of the old building remained. In the rainy season, the headwaters of Marsh Creek flow through a gully near the school site. A bridge that is part of the ranch road spans the creek soon after the ranch entry gate. Just beyond the bridge to the north, the creek sprouts scrub willows, which graduate to oak, big-leaf maple and bay trees as the gully deepens. The trees shield the ranch buildings from passersby on the county road. After a period of winter rain, frogs croak insistently under the willows, and storm run-off rushes headlong down the creek bed.

Hugh Beirne lived here from November 1871 until he sold the 160 acres in 1910. His wife, Annie, came from Ireland in 1868, three years after Hugh. Their two sons, Joseph and James, attended Summit School. Joseph, the older by two years, died at age 14 of kidney disease, and James died at 24 of tuberculosis in Tucson, where he had traveled for relief from the symptoms of the disease. The sons and parents are buried at St. Michael's Cemetery in Livermore under the surname "O'Beirne." Reportedly Annie had raised flocks of chickens, but after she died in 1902, Hugh only ran cattle. He outlived all his family and died at age 84 at St. Joseph's Home in Stockton in 1911. The next year, according to *The Livermore Herald*—on 24 August 1912—a range fire broke out "on the old O'Bierne place in the Black Hills" and burned several hundred acres before local firefighters got it under control. A number of different owners occupied the property until the Smiths bought it.

From the Rowell Ranch, located along old Highway 50 in Dublin Canyon between Pleasanton and Castro Valley, Ormond C. Smith bought eight or 10 wild horses at a time for $20 a head and tried to break and tame them. He hoped to sell them for a profit. Neighbor Richard

A couple of close calls:

One day a cow belonging to John Gleese died in the creek mud. Young Ormond Smith got permission from Gleese to skin it. Some days earlier a skunk had come into their yard in the daytime, and Rule, their dad's favorite coon hound, had killed it. While the boys were skinning the cow, Rule walked toward them, frothing at the mouth. Ormond whispered sternly to his brother, "Don't move!" The dog passed within 10 feet of their rigid figures, continued down into the creek bed, where it did a flip, and came right back up the hill toward them. Once more Ormond said, "Don't move!" Once more the rabid hound passed close by, but continued on down the ranch road and out of sight. They never saw it again.

Omery Smith remembered another near miss: "Once while I was on top of Oyster Peak, the highest hill on our property, a commercial passenger plane almost crashed. I was watching it come toward the hill with my heart in my mouth and at the last minute it turned. It came so close to crashing that the wind from the propellers blew the snow into the air." [a]

Lawrence, a boy at the time, recalled that those mustangs "just about tore down all the fences in the county."[3]

Smith also bought coon hounds, at $100 apiece—a fortune then. Omery described "charging over those hills in the dark," using flashlights only when the dogs had treed a raccoon. The hunting party would follow Marsh Creek northward to flush out the water-loving animals.[4] Richard Lawrence remembered few raccoons being found; usually the hunters succeeded only in getting drenched in the creek.[5] After going with the Smiths just once, Richard never volunteered again. One year at Christmas, Smith insisted that his family would have their feast South Georgia-style, not with Yankee turkey. This meant raccoon or possum—Omery has forgotten which—and sweet potatoes. Omery did not have much appetite with the animal's four legs sticking up from the platter in front of him. "It wasn't a big hit with the family. I don't even think my dad liked it."[6]

In the first year the Smiths lived at the ranch, the boys received sleds for Christmas. On Christmas Eve—as if by special order from Santa —several inches of snow fell, not a frequent occurrence. During summer months when Summit Emergency School was not operating, they were rarely bored, thanks to the imaginative ideas of young Ormond. Omery fondly remembered days of skinny-dipping in the creek, hanging from grapevines, climbing the rock cliffs nearby (now in the preserve), and riding in the family pony cart. One of the boys' favorite pastimes was creating miniature roads for their toy trucks. Their dad often brought home firecrackers from Oakland's Chinatown, where he was stationed, and the boys used them like dynamite to blow up play roadbeds.

The daredevil nature of young Ormond was in evidence when he competed in a wild horse race at the Livermore Rodeo. Not old enough to enter, he lied about his age with the acquiescence of his father. A contestant's first challenge in such a race was to catch his horse. Then a partner (in this case his father) held the horse while the rider got on. Ormond was within 20 feet of winning the race when the excited crowd roared its approval. The noise scared the horse, and it promptly turned and raced the other way.

This idyllic life for young boys came to an untimely end when their parents separated, selling the property in 1936. The boys stayed with their mother, but the Depression and the war years were tough times for a waitress to earn a living. She had to change jobs so often that Omery attended six different elementary schools. Ormond

graduated from Amador High in Pleasanton in 1940 and attended Cal Poly for one year, majoring in aeronautical engineering. He left college to enlist in the Army Air Corps, and he worked in the Kaiser shipyards at Vallejo as a welder trainee until he was called to duty. With his shipyard pay, he bought himself a '34 Ford roadster that had been stripped and souped up so that it could go 115 miles per hour. It had no fenders and no windshield. The Ford replaced the motorcycle Ormond had had since he was 15. Generously, he also bought a Model A roadster for Omery, who was attending Livermore High. Both boys played football in high school, Ormond at guard and Omery at end.

Young Ormond entered the service in August 1942, was accepted in pilot training, and received his wings at Turner Field, Albany, Georgia. While stationed at Maxwell Air Base in Alabama for preflight training, he met and married Sallie Capps of Montgomery. Before shipping overseas, he was again stationed at Maxwell where he received specialized training in flying a B-24 Liberator bomber, the "flying boxcar." "It looked like a truck, it hauled big loads like a truck and it flew like a truck,"[7] as an historian noted later. It had 10 or more .50 caliber machine guns for defense, but because the plane had to fly lower than the B-17 Fortress, enemy flak hit the Liberator much harder. With a crew of 10 and a 4,000-pound bomb load, the plane had a 2,100 mile range.

Air Corps authorities cleared Ormond for overseas duty as a B-24 bomber pilot on 26 May 1944; he arrived to serve with the 466th Bomber Group, a part of the 785th Bomber Squadron at Attlebridge, near Norwich, England, on July 23.[8] While flying as co-pilot 16 days later, Ormond Smith was shot down over Europe and was officially declared missing on 9 August. Omery recalls a new regulation granting extra leave time to the crew of a plane that volunteered to lead a bombing run. On the first such volun-

Ormond (l.) and Omery Smith in 1934, with the family's horse, "Buck," and colt. Courtesy of Omery Smith.

teer mission by his crew, enemy antiaircraft fire had severely damaged Ormond's plane.

At first the family knew only that he was missing in action and presumed dead; finally, on November 21, the International Red Cross confirmed his death. Not until 18 months later, on 27 May 1946, did a letter from General Leon Johnson to Sallie Smith give details gleaned from a recent translation of captured German records. After the rest of the crew bailed out, Ormond and the pilot stayed with the plane and attempted a crash landing on an island near Rotterdam, Holland. German soldiers carried Ormond from the plane wreckage to an army hospital, but he died soon after being admitted on August 9. Buried first in a military cemetery in Holland, the body of Second Lieutenant Ormond B. Smith was returned to the United States in July 1949

and buried in the national cemetery at San Bruno. In downtown Livermore the plaque at the Carnegie Park flagpole lists his name with those of other Livermore World War II casualties. The Army awarded him the Purple Heart and Air Medal posthumously.

Other Morgan Territory Road families had anxiously watched the war news. August M. Grisel, grandson of Adolphe and Nona Grisel, flew in a B-24 from an Italian air base. Augie was a ball turret gunner and survived more than 35 bombing missions. In May 1945 he was awarded the Air Medal with three oak leaf clusters.[9] John Robles, son of Tomás and Elicia Robles, survived his three-year stint in the South Pacific. The Army awarded him the Silver Star for his service in New Guinea.[10] Down in Tassajara, the Bettencourts waited for news of their foster son, Richard

Lawrence, who had joined the Navy before the war began. He had been trained in helping Marines with beach landings. His most important landing and ground supply operation was on the South Pacific island of Tulagi, near Guadalcanal. After developing malaria, he was shipped to a hospital in Wellington, New Zealand. Once he had recovered, he was assigned to shore patrol there. He was discharged in 1945 at Boston as a bos'un's mate first class.[11]

At the time of the death of his brother, Omery Smith was a senior at Livermore High. He inherited his brother's souped-up '34 roadster and recalled driving fast down North Livermore Avenue, hitting each rancher's dirt driveway that intersected the road so hard that the Ford flew up into the air. After graduation from Livermore High, Omery attended Cal Poly, earning an electrical engineering degree. In the '50s he was the PG&E estimator of the cost to run an electric line from Vasco Road up to the property of John Gleese. The line was put in and later extended to all the new homes along the ridgetop. In 1998 PG&E tore down the original line in the Vasco to make way for Los Vaqueros Reservoir. New utility poles were added all the way down to the Levy, so that now the electric power lines follow Morgan Territory Road from the Livermore side up to Morgan Territory Regional Preserve at the ridgetop summit.

The ranch went through many owners after the Smiths; most of them used the land for running cattle. The Rasmussen family from Highland Road owned it for a while. The current owners lived for a time in the deteriorating little two-story redwood house recalled by Omery Smith, but finally tore it down after building a modern home.

1 Omery Smith, telephone interview, 18 Sep 1996.

2 Hugh Beirne was not literate, and he signed his name with an X on documents. His surname is often spelled Beirne, but just as often Byrne. He invented a middle initial of "L" because another person named Hugh Beirne was picking up his mail. Details on purchasing from San Francisco General Land Office, Cash Entry 4090, National Archives, DC.

3 Richard Lawrence, phone interview, 25 July 1996.

4 Omery Smith, phone interview, 18 Sep 1996.

5 Lawrence, phone interview.

6 Omery Smith, phone interview, 9 Oct 1996.

7 Edward Jablonski, *America in the Air War* (Alexandria, VA: Time-Life, 1982) 131.

8 Maurer Maurer, *Combat Squadrons of the Air Force, World War II* (DC: US Government Printing Office, 1969) 755.

9 "35 Missions," *The Livermore Herald* 4 May 1945: 1.

10 "Livermore Men and Women in the Armed Forces," *The Livermore Herald* 15 Dec 1944: 1.

11 Lawrence, personal interview, 23 Feb 1999.

a Omery Smith, letter, 15 Oct 1996.

John Gleese Sr. (standing) and brother-in-law Charles Hardiman, in the 1930s. Courtesy of Carol Hardiman.

Irish Vaquero

The six-year-old grabbed the worn rope handle of the wooden bucket his mother handed him and followed the path to the side yard of the cottage, where the potato pit had been dug. Whistling, he swung the bucket back and forth as he walked, as high as he could stretch, like a pendulum gone amok. He knelt to peel back the straw covering the pit, reached in, and stirred the loose dirt, feeling for a potato. He pulled one out, but instead of dropping it in the bucket, he remained stock still, blue eyes staring at the stinking black mass that melted in his hand. Disgusted, he threw it on the ground and reached in the dirt several more times, only to find more of the same rotting substance.

WITH A PARTIAL crop failure in 1845, the nightmarish saga of the invasion of Ireland by potato blight began. By 1846 the disease had affected the potato crop of the entire country, and the results were catastrophic. The potato, introduced from South America 200 years earlier, had become the mainstay of the Irish diet. Potato blight is caused by a fungus with tiny spores that can quickly and imperceptibly infect an entire healthy field of growing potatoes. Often the harvested potatoes appeared fine when first stored in the pits; only later did the rotting effects of the disease appear. Scholar Cecil Woodham-Smith maintains: "The soft, warm climate of Ireland, particularly in the west, with its perpetual light rains and mild breezes, provides ideal conditions for the spread of the fungus, and has been truly described as a forcing-house for blight."[1] To make matters worse, the winter of 1846–47 proved to be the coldest and most prolonged that Ireland had known. Then the blight struck again in 1848. The toll: More than a million and a half people in a country of eight million died of starvation or from problems exacerbated by lack of nourishing food. Another million chose to emigrate between 1845 and 1851, many to the United States.[2]

Patrick Gleese[3] was born in 1840 in Loughrea, a small farming town on the two-mile lake of that name in County Galway, western Ireland. He must have been hardy indeed to survive. He did not emigrate until 1866, but the drastic effects of famine and the confiscation of Irish property, justified by the English on the basis of the famine, had not disappeared.[4] Largely rural and far from cosmopolitan Dublin, County Galway was among only four Irish counties that were not a part of the English plantation system, which displaced Irish owners and confiscated their property, without recompense, for new owners from Scotland or England.[5] But Patrick's family was Roman Catholic and therefore consistently under restrictions from the English government.

Patrick Gleese worked as a hod carrier in New York City after his arrival in the United States, but he soon made his way west, helping to build the transcontinental railway. By 1868 he had arrived in the Livermore area. His future wife, Mary E. Coppinger, also from County Galway, had sailed around the Horn to San Francisco in 1868. By 1872 Patrick had acquired the NE¼ of section 14 and the SE¼ of section 11 at the head of Collier Canyon Road in the Tassajara district in T2S/R1E. Married in 1875, he and Mary had three children, Joseph, John, and Mary. The family farmed and raised Norman cob horses, and by all reports earned affection and respect from many friends and neighbors. In 1879 Patrick planted 160 acres in wheat, 55 in barley, and 60 in hay. Their cow produced 150 pounds of butter. He built a large barn in 1879 and a large addition to the family home in 1897. The 1885 tax assessment showed that, besides land and improvements, Patrick owned three wagons, seven horses and seven colts, two cows, one calf, numerous hogs and poultry. In March 1897 the *Livermore Echo* reported that Patrick Gleese had recently received good prices for three Norman cob horses that he had shipped to San Francisco.

At his funeral in March 1901, *The Livermore Herald* reported, "The church was thronged and the funeral cortege was one of the longest ever seen in this valley. When the head of the procession was at the grave the last vehicle had not passed First Street, over half a mile away."[6] Mary Gleese sold the farm to Thomas D. Carneal in 1911, and later Carneal willed it to his tenants, the Vargas family.

Soon after Patrick's death in 1901, Mary Gleese and her sons purchased some Black Hills property to run cattle. At first, son John lived in a small cabin on the site. Joseph died in 1910. After the sale of the Collier Canyon ranch in 1911 and their subsequent additional land purchases along Morgan Territory Road, John Gleese and his mother moved to section 30 T1S/R2E on the ridgetop, where an earlier owner had already built a house with a truncated pyramidal hip roof. John paid a carpenter cousin to add a redwood porch all around as well as indoor plumbing.

The house, just over the hills to the east and not visible from the road, is the last remaining century-old dwelling along Morgan Territory Road. At the height of his property ownership in the Black Hills, John Gleese, in partnership with his mother and brother-in-law, Charles

Hardiman, possessed sections 19, 29, and 30, plus the east halves of sections 31 and 32, all in T1S/R2E—a total of 2,560 acres.

Charles Hardiman had married John Gleese's sister, Mary, and John married Charles's sister Ethel. Before their marriages, Mary Gleese and Ethel Hardiman lived in San Francisco, where Mary worked as a hospital nurse and Ethel taught kindergarten. William Joseph Hardiman, father of Ethel and Charles, had emigrated from County Galway more than 10 years before Patrick Gleese, in March of 1854, but did not arrive in San Francisco until after the Civil War. He met and married Mary Hosmer Smith in San Francisco, and the couple moved to Idaho, probably seeking a drier climate for relief from his asthma. Their son Charles, one of six children, was born in Silver City, Idaho—now a ghost town—in 1876. Ethel was born in San Francisco in 1887.

Charles and Mary Hardiman had three children, Dorothy, Claire, and Charles Jr. They lived up on Morgan Territory Road from about 1924 to 1937, then moved to Danville so the children could attend school there after the Emergency Summit School closed in 1937 for lack of students. Charles Jr.—nicknamed "Buster"—married the niece of a Danville rancher and moved back up to the Black Hills in 1967.

John and Ethel Gleese also had three children, John Jr., Marie, and Eugene. Although John Gleese Sr. was called Jack by most of his family and acquaintances, for the sake of clarity this narrative will refer to him as John, and his older son as Jack. Jack Gleese lived on Morgan Territory Road—or as the southern half was called then, the Black Hills Road—from just after his birth in 1919 until he left the hill in 1939. These accounts would have had considerably less flavor as well as fewer facts without his ready humor and excellent memory. Jack patiently shared details and personal experiences that a researcher of dusty public records can never unearth. His wife, Rose Stanley Gleese, was also of great help, especially urging that the role of women on the ranches in those years should not be neglected.[7]

John Gleese would become very irritated if anyone chanced to call him a farmer. His son Jack said, "That name would raise him out of his chair!"[8] He was a rancher and used his property for grazing. As western movie fans know, if a rancher designated himself a cattleman, he was supposed to be ready to fight to the death with other ranchers who preferred to raise sheep. John Gleese, however, believed that the two animals could be raised in perfect harmony on the same ranch. After all, he reasoned, cattle and sheep have no prejudice toward each other.

At first Gleese raised polled Angus, then Herefords, usually running anywhere between 150 and 200 head. He placed the cattle in a fenced pasture until they had grazed the grass down to about 15 inches. Next he moved them out and released sheep into the same area until they had grazed the grass down to about two inches—always careful never to allow the sheep to denude the pasture. When the animals had grazed enough in one area, he would shift them to still another fenced pasture. Usually he ran about 250 head of merino sheep.

This system of raising both cattle and sheep had several advantages. The price of beef fluctuated in those days, but the price of wool remained constant. Also, John could sell about 75 lambs each year. In the spring, hired shearers working by hand removed the pelt from each sheep. Rolled in a ball and tied with twine, the fleece was stuffed in burlap wool sacks measuring three by eight feet.

Local rancher Michael Murray remembered that his job as a child was to stomp the balls down in the sacks. The lanolin from the wool gave his boots a long-lasting shine. When filled and tamped down, the sacks were so heavy that they required two men to lift even one. Wool buyers drove their wagons up the road to the Gleese ranch and made competitive bids.

Trucks were not used in the '20s to transport cattle; cattle were herded everywhere by riders on horseback. One southern route to market for Gleese cattle was down Morgan Territory Road to Beck Road (now Manning and North Livermore), down May School Road, and over to Vasco Road. "Our biggest job at this point was the crossing of Highway 50. We had to stop traffic in both directions in order to cross," Jack Gleese recalled.[9] Their destination was the McComber feed lots, located on property now occupied by the Lawrence Livermore National Laboratory. This drive lasted from dawn to dusk. In later years, southbound drives for the Gleeses sometimes ended at the Morris ranch, where the cattle were loaded on trucks. Even today's travelers are occasionally caught in slow traffic as local ranchers move cattle from one field to another along the byroads north of Livermore.

Northbound drives down Morgan Territory Road toward Clayton stopped at the Correa ranch, where the cattle were loaded into trucks and trailers. When a new shipment of cattle arrived, the Gleeses would pick them up in the railroad corrals located near the Cowell cement plant midway between Concord and Clayton. "The big difference was these cattle were wild and very spooky. Also the climb up to 2,100 feet in four miles was very slow and troublesome," Jack noted.[10]

First they drove the cattle to the ranch of their friend Joe Stockfleth, where they branded and vaccinated them, using Stockfleth's modern corrals and cattle chutes. That was one day's work. Beginning at five the next morning, they drove the cattle along the Concord-Clayton Road, down Marsh Creek Road to Morgan Territory Road and up to the Gleese ranch, arriving at about three or four o'clock in the afternoon. Auto traffic, stray stock, dogs, and unfenced land were problems that added to the relentless uphill climb. "It was sure good to see the home ranch after making this long dusty hot drive."[11]

Top: John Gleese Sr., in portrait at right (courtesy of Jack Gleese) and with his wife, Ethel Hardiman Gleese, his mother, Mary Coppinger Gleese, and his son, John Jr. (Jack). Group photo courtesy of Carol Hardiman. Below: John Gleese Sr. with his granddaughter Jackie—son Jack's daughter. When Jack Gleese was growing up, he and John Sr. were considered "the two hardest-riding cowboys" in the area. Photo courtesy of Jack Gleese.

Top: Mothers and daughters (l. to r.) Mary Coppinger Gleese, Mary Smith Hardiman, Ethel Hardiman Gleese, and Mary Gleese Hardiman, with Ethel's son Jack, who referrred to this group as "some of the women who made things work." Courtesy of Jack Gleese. Below: Mary Coppinger Gleese and a flock of her chickens. Courtesy of Carol Hardiman.

Jack Gleese remembers 'going straight downhill'

"When I was about 12 or 14 years old, my father and I had the name of the 'two hardest riding cowboys' in the area. And my father was a wonderful man and a great father. I respected him greatly. But when I went out with him, you had to ride. And if an animal broke loose going down ... one of those big hills, you were expected to go down full gallop. And if I didn't, he'd say, 'What in the h— is the matter with you! What are you going to do? Sit there all day!' ... He'd go right straight down one of those hills, he didn't mind putting a lariat on a bull or steer or a cow or anything, going straight downhill. I've seen him do it. And I've done it with him. To the point where the saddle would lift up in back, clean off the horse's back, and you'd be looking down his neck...." [a]

Cattle drives and roundups were shared events, with many hill families and friends involved. Often they ended with a community barbecue, sometimes at the Nunez or Cardoza ranch. Several days earlier, eager helpers would dig a pit about four feet deep by 16 feet long, fill it part way with rocks and start an oakwood fire. On roundup day, a steer and a lamb or two were killed, cut up, and placed over the slow fire on a grate improvised from a barn gate. Volunteers turned meat with a pitchfork and applied sauce with a paintbrush tied to a broom handle. Over the voices the clanging of a game of horseshoes and an occasional shout of triumph rang out. Someone would play a fiddle, squeeze box, or guitar while tired riders relaxed and enjoyed their meal and fellowship by a smoky fire under the stars.

Besides cattle and sheep, John Gleese ran 20 to 25 horses, including six head of heavy workhorses. On some 60 acres of open meadowland near the road, he raised red oat hay that was used mostly as feed for their horses. Jack recounted the steps in the process: "In the fall of the year we would work [the soil] up. And we would sow it in red oat hay. Red oats. And we'd cut that with horses and mowers when it ripened in the spring. And we'd rake it to windrows and then we'd use what you call a "buncher" with two horses on it, and we'd put it in bunches. And then we'd go out with a four-horse team and a wagon and we'd load the wagons with it and bring it in and put the hay in the barn for the horses and for what we might have to feed in the wintertime."[12]

Jack Gleese rode his first horse as an infant, with his father. "He couldn't wait to get me on board horse, so before I was a year old ... he used to put me on the horse in front of him and then we'd go out and look at the cows...."[13] By the time Jack became a teenager, he was a bruising rider. "I've ploughed up a lot of land with my body," he said dryly, years later, about some of his rougher rides with his father.

Jack's mother, Ethel, was also an excellent rider. Before she met John, she had ridden side-saddle, "lady" style, but her new husband informed her that that method was "out the window—we ride cowboy."[14]

Actually, the word John Gleese most often used to describe himself was not cowboy but "vaquero," the term surviving from Mexican land grant days. Jack recalled his father as having "big blue laughing eyes, and he was always laughing. He was always happy. But don't cross him. If you ever crossed him it would be just like crossing a bulldog. He could get real hard if he was pushed. But it took a lot to push him."[15] John Gleese was about six feet one, very powerful, with broad shoulders and a heavy chest that tapered to narrow hips. As Fred Mourterot, who lived down on Vasco Road, described him: "He was really a roper, that guy. He used to carry a 60-foot riata and he'd maybe wrap a steer at 50 feet away from him with it."[16]

The going pay for ranch hands was $30 a month, but John Gleese paid double that for good hands when he could afford it, his son said. He also provided their room, board and tobacco. Itinerant skilled workmen traveled from ranch to ranch—Jack remembered George Davis, a harness and saddle maker, as well as the riata maker Henry Hughes. Usually in the spring Davis showed up with his horse and the cart that contained all his tools. He remained at the ranch for two to three months, repairing and replacing the leather work for another year. He could strip a saddle down to the tree and re-leather it entirely. A dead shot, he was a great storyteller of the wild days in Leadville, Colorado, Jack said, but he was very shy around the ladies. Hughes wove riatas with strips of three-eighths-inch leather into which he had worked tallow to make the strips soft and pliable. Much better than lariats made of plant materials, these riatas did not break, and they were not as susceptible to changes in the weather. John Gleese favored a rawhide lariat, sometimes using one 70 feet long.

Jack and his dad broke horses together in their corral, but not in traditional western movie style by hanging on until the horse stopped bucking. Rather than "breaking" the horse, John called his method "training," gradually allowing the horse to adjust calmly to harness and saddle, attempting in the process to prevent the horse from bucking. "If you can keep a horse from buckin', it never learns to buck, it's a dependable horse."[17]

Jack carried his 30–30 Winchester rifle with him everywhere he went in the hill country. "In those days I was a pretty tough hombre!" He used it for protection against beast and man. If some flatlanders came riding up to the ridgetop in their car and began to give him trouble, "as soon as I turned the horse around and they saw that Winchester stuck in the scabbard in my saddle, why [they'd decide] it might be well not to push this guy too far."[18]

Start with a medium size potato . . .

"Bread was made in a large preserving kettle which was aluminum. The kettle was used because it was very large so it could hold a large amount of wheat flour. . . . The yeast culture was kept on the back of the stove so that the temperature was pretty constant. The day before the bread was to be made Mother would grate a medium size potato and add it to the quart jar containing part of the culture. The jar was set in a dish in a warm spot on the stove . . . to work. The next morning it would be foaming over the top. This would then be added to the flour in the kettle along with warm water enough to mix to a heavy dough. This then would be covered with a cloth. The dough would rise up into a dome and would be punched down several times before it was made into loaves and biscuits. These items were then put in their pans and left to rise before going into the oven to bake. The loaves were very large, about 14" long by 6" high. About six or eight loaves would last about one or two weeks as I remember. The stove had to be kept at a near constant heat so that the bread would brown and not burn." [b]

The Gleese family acquired their first radio in 1925, a Guilfillen Nutridine bought at Sherman Clay in San Francisco. It sported three dials, had four dry-cell batteries and operated on one six-volt wet-cell battery. "We had an antenna strung across the canyon and we could get stations from all over the world. . . ."[19] The next milestone came in 1938 when they purchased a Norge refrigerator, along with a generator that powered not only the refrigerator but also lights in each room and outside on the porch. "And when you turned too many of them on, . . . the generator . . . would start to labor, why then you knew you had to shut off something. . . . It was our first power and that was a big deal."[20]

Sheep were herded along Morgan Territory Road, January 1939. Photo courtesy of Bob and Irene Justice.

Jack's mother, Ethel Hardiman Gleese, had traveled extensively by train throughout the United States and Canada with her mother, Mary Hosmer Smith Hardiman, and the two women were very close all their lives. Her mother's family came from traditional Boston society, Jack said, and this influenced both women. "My grandmother wore . . . one of those lace collars . . . buttoned up just so. When she got up in the morning, she was fully dressed, my mother the same way. She never came to the kitchen in a robe. Nooo, she was fully dressed."[21] Ethel Gleese emphasized the qualities of honesty and cleanliness. "My mother could not stand a liar. If you lied to her, you were really in trouble. . . . She believed in honesty. Even if it hurt, she said tell the

truth." One of her favorite axioms was "cleanliness is next to godliness." "She would say, 'I don't care how worn, how patched, or how many holes are in the trousers or the shirts, but if they're clean, that's fine by me.'"[22]

Fred Mourterot remembered Jack's other grandmother, Mary Gleese, as a "terrific cook. And boy, she'd bake the best bread, had the best meat. Anytime you went, there was always a meal ready for you."[23] Jack agreed that his grandmother Gleese was "a very fine Irish cook," who made a marvelous Irish stew and potato soup.

On the Idaho ranch where Jack's mother lived as a girl, the family had a Chinese cook who brought meals in from a separate kitchen outbuilding on a wheeled cart. However, after her marriage to John Gleese, Ethel learned to cook from her mother-in-law, Mary Gleese, and became a good cook herself.

Both women made wonderful cakes and puddings. "The fellas that worked for us, their eyes'd bug out when they set those big bowls of pudding on the table. . . . We always had dessert after dinner."[24] Jack's mother never became quite as good at baking pies as her mother-in-law, he said, but in any case the champion pie maker in the family was his aunt, Mary Gleese Hardiman. "I can hear her whistling away, and she's just fluffing things together, and while you're saying, 'What's goin' on?' she had a pie in the oven."[25]

Although Jack loved his family and the freedom of living on the ridgetop, he decided as a young man that ranching was not the life for him. "I told my dad when I was 21: 'I slept on the ground enough, I've eaten enough dust and I don't want any more of it.'"[26] His father understood and never questioned Jack's choice. In order to attend Alhambra High School, Jack had boarded with family friends in Martinez, driving home on weekends in the car his mother had bought for him. He graduated from high school in 1939 and left the Black Hills for college, although he didn't finish. After a variety of jobs as machinist, truck driver, and pattern maker, he settled into the position of salesman for a number of firms. He married Rose Stanley, whose family still farms along North Livermore Avenue, and after his retirement they moved into the Sierra foothills, where Jack enjoys gardening but does not raise cattle or sheep.

In 1949, after having helped a neighbor rope and brand cattle, John Gleese returned home feeling unusually tired for him, even at the age of 71. The next morning he awoke to discover a lack of feeling on his right side, the result of a small stroke. Despite a good recovery, he and Ethel decided to retire to Danville, where he died in 1951.

1 Cecil Woodham-Smith, *The Great Hunger* (NY: Harper and Row, 1962) 98.
2 Woodham-Smith 411.
3 Old Loughrea records do not list the name Gleese, but rather Gleeson. Most likely, Patrick shortened his name. He was illiterate, but he could sign his name.
4 Between 1848 and 1864, immigrants in the U.S. sent £13 million to their Irish relatives and friends for boat passage to this country. Woodham-Smith 412.
5 Terence de Vere White, *Ireland* (NY: Walker, 1968) 32.
6 Page 1.
7 Jack and Rose Gleese, personal interviews, 18 July 1995, 26 Nov 1996.
8 Jack Gleese, July interview.
9 Jack Gleese, letter, 2 Aug 1995.
10 Gleese letter.
11 Gleese letter.
12 Karana Hattersley-Drayton, "Interview with Jack Gleese," Sonoma State U Anthropological Studies Center, for the Contra Costa Water District, 9 Sep 1995: 24.
13 Hattersley-Drayton, Interview 2.
14 Hattersley-Drayton, Interview 2.
15 Hattersley-Drayton, Interview 42.
16 Karana Hattersley-Drayton, *Report on Oral History Completed Under the Historic Property Treatment Plan for Construction of the Los Vaqueros Dam and Reservoir and Related Requirements, Los Vaqueros Project* (Rohnert Park, CA: Sonoma State U Academic Foundation, 1996) 23.
17 Hattersley-Drayton, Interview 5.
18 Hattersley-Drayton, Interview 27.
19 Hattersley-Drayton, Interview 40.
20 Hattersley-Drayton, Interview 41.
21 Jack Gleese, Nov interview.
22 Jack Gleese, Nov interview.
23 Hattersley-Drayton, *Report* 23.
24 Jack Gleese, Nov interview.
25 Jack Gleese, Nov interview.
26 Hattersley-Drayton, Interview 41.

a Hattersley-Drayton, Interview 4.
b Jack Gleese, letter, 29 Oct 1996.

Fog in the Vasco (present site of Los Vaqueros Reservoir), under a rising moon. Photo by Don Homan.

A Hermit's Aerie

ONE DEFINITION OF "hermit" is "a person who lives by himself in a lonely or secluded spot." The southwest quarter of section 20 T1S/R2E is certainly such a location, accessible as it is only by dirt roads through neighboring ranch lands off Morgan Territory Road or up from Vasco Road. Andrew Lindholm, remembered locally only by the soubriquet "Andrew the Swede," made his home in this beautiful secluded place for about 50 years.

Barely above the chaparral and into oak woodland, the site is rocky in places and overlooks a steep descent into the Vasco, the valley that used to be part of the Mexican land grant *Rancho Cañada de los Vaqueros*. Gradually the valley acquired the name Vasco because of Basque sheepmen and farmers who settled there in the 1800s. Today part of the older Spanish name has been given to the Los Vaqueros Reservoir that has inundated the valley. This quarter section is surrounded by high country and is an excellent viewing site for majestic golden eagles, which often soar above their nesting spots on nearby cliffs. Jack Gleese, who lived on a neighboring ranch, imagined that his father would evaluate the land on section 20 as "worthless" because, with all the rocks and trees, it made poor pastureland. "You couldn't raise *goats* on it."[1]

Obviously, Andrew Lindholm had a different basis for property evaluation. Since Andrew raised neither sheep nor cattle, he did not desire grazing land. The 1910 U.S. census for Contra Costa County listed him as a farmer, age 55, who had emigrated from Sweden in 1885. His death certificate listed his father's name as Andrew Lindholm also; his mother was Christina Olson. During the 1880s, Sweden went through an agricultural depression; 325,000 Swedes out of a total of 4.5 million immigrated to the United States. They came predominantly from the southern and western portions of Sweden—landless younger sons and daughters.[2] Andrew Lindholm was a bachelor and a tenant of Louis Grunauer, a dry-goods store owner in Byron. He made his living by trapping and cutting wood for neighboring ranchers. Several stone-terraced roads run through the property, but narrow trails he carved out in the chaparral were just wide enough for his horse to pull a log. Andrew lived in a rundown gable-roofed cabin that he had built himself; its one room contained two bunks, one on each side.[3] Later, he added a storage area at the back. Richard Lawrence, then a young neighbor, remembered three or four antique rifles, several with octagon barrels. Various traps hung on the house walls outside.

Lindholm's barn was impressive, described by visitors as meticulously handmade of redwood. Jack Gleese recalled with admiration: "The craftsmanship, it was beautiful. There wasn't a warp in it anywhere."[4] The barn door hinges were hand-forged. The barn had three bays: one for a horse stall, one for storage of a sled and wagon, and the middle one for hay storage. Andrew had other skills, too. "He'd put up fruit, he put his own fruit up and his vegetables and things like that in jars."[5] His fruit cellar, built into the side of a hill, had a base of hand-hewn sandstone blocks, each about 12 by 16 inches, put together without mortar. According to Jack, Andrew cut the stones himself from sandstone formations in the trail cuts that he made. To keep the fruit cool, he probably diverted a spring; he "had a little ditching system in the floor of his cellar. . . . And the water would run through there. . . . It just kept everything nice and cool. You go in there, the hottest day in summer, and it would be as cool as could be."[6] He also kept his cart in this structure. "Because it was damp it kept the wheels nice and tight. . . . But all the side of it

Andrew the Swede's craftsmanship

Jack Gleese remembered Andrew Lindholm's wheel sled, used for hauling firewood before the era of truck beds. Andrew had a sled of his own and made several for neighboring ranchers, among them John Gleese. The sled had two wheels on the back and hinged runners on the front that turned so the sled could be steered. A cord of wood would fit on it. "And he made those sleds all out of walnut. The runners and all of the support timbers were all made of black walnut. So they were very fancy." [a]

was lined with shelves and that's where he kept his fruits and things that he canned."[7] Andrew stored homemade wine on the shelves as well. The barn still remains on the property although the roof is gone. Recently someone stole most of the sandstone blocks left of the fruit cellar, but the Park District has recovered them.

Both Richard Lawrence and Jack Gleese described Andrew as a man of five feet six, about 140 or 150 pounds. Jack added, "He was strong as an ox. He was like my father: wide shoulders and tapered down to narrow hips." Jack also noted that the Swede had a broad chest and could "carry a hundred-pound sack of grain on his back all the way down to his place."[8] He had gray hair by the time they knew him in the 1920s and 1930s, with light blue eyes and a ruddy complexion. Richard called him a typical "mountain man" who wore beat-up jeans and shirts. At times "he could be a contemptuous old son-of-a-gun," but on other occasions he was hospitable.[9] In Swedish-accented English, he entertained young Richard or Jack, when they happened by, with his tales of skating for miles in Sweden or of sailing around Cape Horn. "He sailed around the

Horn, many many times, and around Africa and into the Orient and all that. He was a sailor. Yes, he was."[10] Sometimes if he was in the mood, he served a meal to his guest with his tales, always an unvarying menu of fried potatoes and eggs. Andrew also baked bread in loaves "about a foot long and eight inches square. He usually put a number of eggs in his bread and sometimes he would make some of the loaves sweet."[11]

Down near a spring was his small vegetable patch, and he planted several fruit trees, including apple, apricot, and plum, and a Ponderosa lemon. "He had phenomenal lemons," Jack Gleese remembered. "He had a lemon tree there that would—each lemon would make a cup of juice. They were huge lemons."[12] Interviewed by Karana Hattersley-Drayton, one Vasco neighbor, Joe Vallerga, recalled the lemons from a visit to the Swede's place as a schoolchild. Vallerga had never seen a lemon tree before: "That lemon tree just sits in my mind today."[13] Andrew also raised chickens. He hunted deer and brought what he could not eat to share with the Gleeses. Huge coveys of quail lived at his place, and he would occasionally kill one or two for himself. All told, he was an independent and self-reliant man who enjoyed a simple life and appreciated the beauty of the hills. Two large short-hair cats were his only constant companions. "They must have weighed 18 pounds apiece. They were huge big gray cats with great huge big yellow eyes."[14]

As Andrew got older, however, many physical tasks grew more difficult, and John Gleese arranged for him to receive a small county pension. Richard Lawrence remembered that on some nights Andrew would help himself to hay for his horse from the Bettencourts' barn, but neighbor Jerry Bettencourt did not begrudge the old man that small portion. Andrew also reportedly had a problem sometimes with drinking. "On one occasion, one of the Greuninger brothers found Andrew passed out drunk in a water trough in Byron. The farmer pulled the old man out and revived him."[15] However, Jack Gleese insisted that Andrew was not an alcoholic. "Andrew really did not have a drinking problem as such. I knew him all my young life and the only time that he would get to being jolly would be at Christmas time at our house when we had Christmas cheer and everyone was in a festive mood. As for the occasions in Byron those people thought that it was a big joke to pass the bottle around to get the poor man drunk. This was a common thing in those times. But he was not a drinking man as such, just on an occasion a little happiness."[16] One day John Gleese discovered Andrew incapacitated and ill at his cabin and drove him to the county hospital in Martinez, where he died of heart disease several days later on 10 July 1938 at age 82.

Though fond of solitude, and with much of his life matching the usual notion of hermit, Andrew Lindholm still remained a part of the Morgan Territory Road community. He engaged in the system of barter and trading work. "He was our neighbor. We took care of him, and he worked for us and he did things for us."[17] Once in a while, George Davis, the harness and saddle maker, would spend the night with him on George's way to or from Byron. On Christmas and holidays, Andrew inevitably would "find his way up" and join the Gleese family around their table for the celebratory meal.[18] Sometimes he brought loaves of his homemade bread wrapped in clean flour sacks as gifts. "We always thought that it was his way of saying thank you for the dinners that he had at our house as I do not remember him thanking Mother for the dinner. If he did, it was not very often. He was a man of peculiar ways."[19]

Most Scandinavian immigrants of the late 1800s migrated to the northern midwestern states where the climate closely resembles that of their native countries. Andrew Lindholm instead chose the Black Hills, perhaps at first because of their proximity to San Francisco Bay and the world of ships. Perhaps he enjoyed watching the fog that frequently covers the Central Valley and the Vasco area like billowing ocean waves. At these times Brushy Peak becomes an island, and the teeth of the Sierra are another coast silhouetted 160 miles away.

1 Karana Hattersley-Drayton, "Interview with Jack Gleese," Sonoma State U Anthropological Studies Center, for the Contra Costa Water District, 9 Sep 1995, 34.

2 Stuart Oakley, *A Short History of Sweden* (NY: Praeger, 1966) 210.

3 Hattersley-Drayton 19, 21.

4 Hattersley-Drayton 22.

5 Hattersley-Drayton 23.

6 Hattersley-Drayton 23.

7 Hattersley-Drayton 33.

8 Hattersley-Drayton 16, 24.

9 Hattersley-Drayton 17.

10 Hattersley-Drayton 19.

11 Jack Gleese, letter, 14 Dec 1996.

12 Hattersley-Drayton 21.

13 Karana Hattersley-Drayton, *Report on Oral History Completed Under the Historic Property Treatment Plan for Construction of the Los Vaqueros Dam and Reservoir and Related Requirements for the Los Vaqueros Project* (Rohnert Park, CA: Sonoma State U Academic Foundation, 1996) 31.

14 Jack Gleese, personal interview, 26 Nov 1996.

15 Hattersley-Drayton, *Report* 31.

16 Jack Gleese, letter, 14 Dec 1996.

17 Hattersley-Drayton, Interview 16.

18 Hattersley-Drayton, Interview 18.

19 Jack Gleese, letter, 14 Dec 1996.

a Hattersley-Drayton, Interview 19.

May School, 1915. Courtesy Alameda County Schools.

School Days, School Days . . .

CHILDREN LIVING on Morgan Territory Road in the second half of the 1800s and the first part of the 1900s attended one of six one-room schools: Tassajara, Highland, May, Summit, Summit Emergency, or Morgan Territory.

At first, students living in the Black Hills area attended **Tassajara School**, built in 1865 on land owned by Albert G. Wilkes near the old Tassajara post office.[1] Around 1882, when Tassajara School became too crowded, the county formed Highland School District to serve students in the southeastern section of the Tassajara Valley.[2] The two structures that exist today, Tassajara School and Highland School, are not the original buildings. In 1888, six years after the Black Hills students had been shifted to Highland School, citizens erected the current Tassajara School building on Finley Road.

The first **Highland School** in Contra Costa County was located just north of the county line near the intersection of Highland and Manning roads. Today the site is marked by a eucalyptus grove to the west side of Highland Road. In 1882 Highland School boasted 44 pupils with one teacher, who was paid a monthly salary of $60. When rancher Thomas D. Carneal built the section of Highland Road from its intersection with Collier Canyon to its dead end at Manning Road in 1916, the new road came through the schoolhouse plot, and Carneal offered to erect a modern schoolhouse elsewhere on his property. In August 1922 the first classes were held in the new fireproof concrete building donated to the district by Carneal.[3] The initial estimated cost of the schoolhouse had been $7,000, but Carneal continued to add amenities, and his final costs probably came closer to $10,000.

This schoolhouse, now used as a private residence, still stands today at the corner of Carneal and Highland roads. Hugging the northwest fence corner next to the two roads, a restored tank house on the property once sported a windmill that powered the school's gravity-fed water system. Older students carted coal for the school stove from the tank house, which had a chute for coal delivery cut on the north side. Jack Gleese recalled riding horseback across the hills from the ridgetop of Morgan Territory Road to pick up his friend Johnny Robles on their way to Highland School in the 1920s. At the closing exercises of Highland in June 1924, Johnny played a harmonica accompaniment for a chorus singing "Old Black Joe."[4] The last students attended in 1953, and the school served as a community center until sold to private owners.[5]

After 1966, children in the Black Hills, despite living in Contra Costa County, came under the jurisdiction of the Livermore Valley Joint Unified School District and attended one-room **May School** on the road of the same name three-quarters of a mile east of its intersection with North Livermore Avenue. May School was named for George May, an Irish rancher in the district who, when Alameda County first established May School District in 1869, supplied most of the student body from his seven children.[6] Some years after May School closed, arsonists burned it down in 1979. Pupils now attend multi-grade schools in the city of Livermore.

Along the highest elevation of Morgan Territory Road, early tax maps showed **Summit School District**. Possibly this school has been neglected by local historians because the Altamont Pass area east of Livermore also had a one-room "Summit School." The Altamont school had more students and served a district not so isolated as the Black Hills. When people mentioned "Summit School," most everyone assumed they meant the Altamont school in Alameda County.

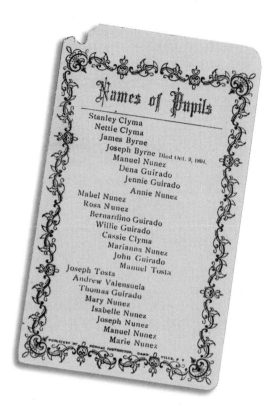

Summit School souvenir from teacher Nina McPherson. Courtesy of Mary Butterfield.

On 28 May 1886 Contra Costa County bought the title from Hugh L. Beirne for half an acre of land that already contained a schoolhouse building mentioned by the surveyors in describing the plot. This half-acre lies west of Morgan Territory Road at the highest point of the road. A creek bed borders one side of what is empty grassland now, with no hint of the little schoolhouse. Although the land is well within Contra Costa County boundaries, Livermore Valley Joint Unified School District of Alameda County currently owns it. Summit School's first year was from September 1884 to June 1885. Local property owners had agreed to tax themselves in order to raise $200 to build the school.[7] For an anticipated 23 pupils, the Contra Costa County School Board Ledger on 26 May 1884 showed that

Summit School had been apportioned $36.92, part of the budget of Highland School. By 1890, 17 students were in attendance. The teacher listed for that year was Sabra S. Brite; she also had been the teacher in 1889. The *Contra Costa Gazette* on 24 June 1905 announced that an average daily attendance at Summit School for the past year had been 14.

Sabra Simpson Brite and her husband, James, leased a Tassajara ranch for a share of the profits. The U.S. agricultural census shows that in 1880 they raised 80 tons of hay, 2,800 bushels of wheat, and 1,000 bushels of barley. In addition, they produced 400 dozen eggs and 200 pounds of butter. James B. Brite was born in Louisiana and died at his Tassajara ranch on 18 October 1906 at age 65 of pulmonary tuberculosis. He had come to California about 1858. Sabra arrived in Mariposa County, California, with her family in 1855 and married James on 3 October 1868.[8] Her parents, William H. and Maria L. Simpson, farmed along Tassajara Road. Before her marriage, Sabra taught at Tassajara School soon after it was first built in 1865.[9]

After California granted women suffrage in 1911, Sabra Simpson Brite proudly voted in every state election. Although some school districts forbade teachers to be involved, she may have attended the women's suffrage meeting held in Livermore at the Farmers' Union Theatre in May 1896, for which the room had been "neatly decorated for the occasion with flags, drapery . . . by the committee of the Ladies League of Progress."[10] Possibly she attended and even helped to plan the open-air meeting of suffragists on the evening of 30 September 1911 at the Livermore flagpole. Several downtown merchants kindly turned on their electric light arches, and a large audience turned out to hear well-known speakers from Berkeley and New York. Sabra Simpson Brite died in 1923, late enough to know that Amendment 19 to the U.S. Constitution, granting nationwide suffrage to women, had passed in 1920.

In 1890 six-year-old Beatrice Brite was a student in the lowest grade (then called the eighth grade) at Summit School while her mother was teaching there.[11] Usually teachers were single women or men who boarded with families near the school, their room and board being counted part of their salary. Sabra Brite was a married woman whose journey home from Summit School included five miles down Morgan Territory Road and several more miles west to the Brite ranch in Tassajara, not an easy trip. In 1895 and 1897 the *Livermore Echo* was critical of women appearing on the city streets wearing "articles of dress supposed to be used exclusively by men."[12] However, it seems unlikely that Sabra would ride sidesaddle up a muddy dirt road in a

blowing wind in typical 1890s dress. How did she manage? Did she huddle under a slicker, riding horseback with her little daughter? Did she sometimes have to stay overnight with the Beirnes or the Clymas? Each family supplied two of her pupils, and their homes were not far from the schoolhouse. Was James Brite an unusually enlightened husband of the Victorian era who allowed his wife to work outside the home and perhaps hired a housekeeper to prepare meals for him and their other three children?

Sabra Brite taught at Summit from 1889 through 1891. Beatrice graduated from Livermore High School in 1902, then attended Stockton Normal School and taught at schools in Contra Costa and Yolo counties. Like her mother, she became a dedicated teacher. Before her marriage to Charles Bright of Bloomington, Indiana, in 1909, she was teaching at Knight's Landing. A week before her death at age 69 in 1953, she was at work in her Bloomington classroom.

Summit School is dim in the memories of surviving hill residents, and few details remain. The front door inside a small porch faced to the north, the back door to the east; there would have been a small belfry and, of course, the requisite two outhouses. Probably its exterior walls were painted white and the windows trimmed with dark green shutters. All three of the Clyma children attended Summit School, and Stanley Clyma returned as teacher. Albert Morris's aunt Mary Nunez Bloching walked with her sister and their teacher Stanley Clyma in the morning southward up Morgan Territory Road to school at the summit, and stopped after school at the Cardoza homestead to help Lucy Cardoza by babysitting.[13] Nina McPherson became teacher after Stanley Clyma and promoted his younger sister, Catherine, from second to third grade. Catherine graduated from Summit School in 1903.

Summit School District evidently had some difficulties. In 1885, soon after the opening of

'The most dangerous of roads'

In 1900, Summit School trustees were in such disagreement that, in order to have enough students to keep the school open and avoid a threatened lawsuit, School Superintendent Phalin had to negotiate with a trustee who lived up near the school. As darkness fell, the argument had still not been settled, "So back we went, dark and threatening rain, down a dark canyon, having the most dangerous of roads." The next morning when they had to repeat the drive, Phalin no longer trusted the driving of his friend "off and on the road . . . [which had] embankments ten, twenty and thirty feet high. . . ." When at last the matter was settled satisfactorily, Phalin swore that "he would not make that trip again after dark for the whole State of California, let alone doing it in order to save a school district." [a]

the school, two trustees selected Miss Johnson as the teacher, but one trustee insisted that Miss Colehan was the rightful teacher. The *Contra Costa Gazette* reported: "The latter at present has possession of the school house and how the matter will end it is difficult to conjecture."[14]

The final paperwork clue to the original Summit School in Contra Costa County is a short note stating that the school had been suspended for lack of attendance. The County Board of Supervisors took this action 7 August 1911 because an average of only four pupils had attended the previous year; an average of eight was necessary for a school to continue.[15]

When families on the hill petitioned Contra Costa County in 1932 for an "emergency" school, nine pupils were enough for the county to grant the petition, especially since the original Summit School District was already a precedent. The old schoolhouse by this time was a scattered pile of a few small boards because—as was typical—most lumber had been removed to build something elsewhere. The county created a schoolroom by partitioning off one side of John Gleese's porch. With its nine pupils—Omery and Ormond Smith; Richard Lawrence; Dorothy, Claire and Buster Hardiman; Marie, Jack, and Eugene Gleese—**Summit Emergency School** remained open from 1932 to 1937. Jack remembered three teachers who boarded at his home: Miss Morehouse, Miss Alma Beman from Byron, and Miss Miller from Martinez.

Claire Miller, fresh from her San Francisco Normal School graduation at age 21, taught at Summit Emergency during the 1935–36 school year. "I was the biggest kid of all," she said years later.[16] She certainly needed that youthful energy and sense of fun because her nine pupils spanned six different grades from first to eighth. From her $1,400 yearly salary she paid the Gleeses $45 per month for room and board. When she first arrived at the Gleese ranch from Martinez, Claire automatically felt on her bedroom wall for the electric switch. "First time I reached for the switch to turn on the light, they said, 'No lights.' I couldn't believe it."[17] Electricity had not arrived yet on the hill; the Gleeses used kerosene lamps. The school district did not supply Claire with any sort of curriculum guide, only textbooks to follow. Eighth-graders had to pass a test on the Constitution. She "worried about whether I was getting across" to all of her students. Being with most of the children she taught not just during school hours but "morning, noon, and night" made her feel "antsy."[18] Teachers who, like Claire, boarded with families of their students had little privacy.

Despite never having been on a horse before, Claire soon learned to ride Molly, a wooly brown mare that always had a little colt running alongside. One of Claire's favorite free-time activities was riding down to the Correa ranch to meet new livestock and helping to drive them uphill to the

Gleese ranch. At school, Claire especially liked Friday afternoons when she taught her students ballroom dancing, often to their favorite Victrola tune, "Cheek to Cheek." She also taught tumbling and acrobatic stunts. On "play days" when different one-room schools met for a picnic, entertainment, and competitions, the Summit students wore red bandannas, white shirts, and jeans and performed their acrobatics.

Occasionally on warm evenings, John Gleese piled all the children and Claire into his car and drove them down to Marsh Creek Springs for a swim. Oakland firefighter Ormond C. Smith stopped by the school on some of his vacation days to treat the students to ice cream or watermelon. Once in a while, Superintendent White visited to observe.

Claire had no car, the Gleeses had no telephone, the road became a mess in any rain, and mail usually was picked up only once a week at the post office, so making arrangements to travel between the Gleese ranch and her home in Martinez for holidays was no simple matter. The next year, Claire managed to find a job teaching first grade in Martinez so that she could stay with her parents. When Summit Emergency School closed in 1937 for lack of students, those left in the Black Hills first attended Highland School and later May School.

Early tax maps label the northern end of the road as the **Morgan Territory School District**. Here the settlers in 1858 built a small schoolhouse east of the road on the NE¼ of section 4 T1S/R1E, and hired William Ellis as their first teacher.[19] Eventually, the building began to deteriorate and the teachers objected in rhyme: "But the shanty in time grew old and very poor,/And the sun shone through the cracks in the old worn floor./Then came teachers who complained, and said 'twas bad,/To teach in such an old schoolhouse made them feel sad."[20] The school building sat on a foundation of rocks, which led to a favorite schoolboy trick. "The kids would pull a

Edith Olofson Wright remembers Morgan Territory School as a student and as a teacher in the '20s:

"*It was a pretty school on top of a hill, white with green shutters. . . . We kids had a good time there. Most of us walked or rode the family plow horses to school through rain or shine. There were never more than 16 pupils in that room, but they covered every grade from first through the eighth. We had to pass state tests to receive our diplomas.*

"*The teacher was supposed to do everything. I lived at my family's farm a mile or so from the school. Every morning I packed my lunch and saddled my horse before riding to school. When I arrived there I swept out the place and brought in a bucket of water from the well. It was placed in the vestibule with a metal drinking cup. At nine, I'd ring the bell and the students would line up to march in. This was the custom in schools in the early part of the century. We sang a few songs from a school songbook, accompanied by our foot-pumped organ. After that, we'd settle down to study. I'd take one class at a time, completing lessons in all the basics. When the students weren't reciting they were expected to be quiet and study. We had no discipline problems. Parents taught their children to behave in those days. And, surprisingly, we had few health problems in spite of the community drinking cup.*"[b]

bunch of rocks out from one side, and when the teacher walked over that way, the school would tip."[21] In 1880, on land purchased for $25 from Robert Howard near the original site but on the west side of the road, local residents helped construct a new school consisting of one large room, a vestibule, and a bell tower. The architect and main carpenter on the job was Louis Steingrandt.

Morgan Territory School, 1947. Courtesy of Contra Costa County Historical Society.

To help pay for building expenses, the school district raised $100 at a dinner and dance at the Clayton Town Hall on Thanksgiving Eve 1881.[22]

A *Contra Costa Gazette* article written in 1899, when Ellen A. Riley was teacher, praised the little school: "A visit to Morgan Territory School while in session makes a favorable impression on the visitors and they leave it in doubt as to whether the pupils or the teacher should be credited with the perfect harmony that exists within the school room. The village and country school teachers are the masons who have laid the foundation of education in ninety percent of our renowned men in this republic, and we are certain that one of the Morgan Territory pupils with half a chance will prove that the labors of his teacher will by no means prove in vain. So we congratulate the people of Morgan Territory"[23]

Howard Morgan attended the school from 1914 until 1924. He received $3 a year to care for the teacher's horse and the pot-bellied stove. "One evening he removed the ashes from the stove and placed them in a cardboard box. He was called to another task and the ashes were forgotten. When he returned to school the next morning to start the fire, he found that a large hole had been burnt through the floor. . . ."[24]

Although Jack Gleese had started elementary school at Highland, in 1928 Morgan Territory School trustees pleaded with his parents to allow him to attend there because they were short of pupils. For the next several years, until the Summit Emergency School was opened, Jack rode 15 miles each day to school and back, with his black lunch box in a burlap sack tied to his saddle. The school bell rang at nine, lunch recess was from noon to one, and classes were over at three.

"My mother made sure that I had a good lunch . . .," Jack recalled. "Three sandwiches roast meat, peanut butter and jelly, tuna, or maybe one of each. Fresh fruit that was in season, a piece of cake or pie. There was usually a candy bar for the afternoon recess. It is well to note here that the school children had a family-like relationship. So we would trade our lunches with the less fortunate members for a part of their lunch. It was a wonderful uncomplicated time that sad to say is gone forever."[25]

Jack noted that he was lucky to be from a working ranch, which provided him with a horse to ride; using the cow trails through the hills from Marsh Creek Springs, the Silva children walked nine miles round-trip. One of the more exciting moments in Jack's young life occurred on his way home from school. His horse was loafing along at a trot about halfway on the route. From the top of a bank along the road came the distinctive scream of a mountain lion. Jack's horse immediately doubled up in a knot and took off like a skyrocket, after abruptly dumping Jack, with no apology, in the middle of the road. Jack stayed absolutely still where he had fallen, listening intently with heart thumping to the lion rustling in the leaves overhead until the sound disappeared. Slowly, bruised but not seriously injured, he rose to resume the uphill trek to the

ranch. Meanwhile, the horse arrived home riderless to the distress of his mother, who sent his father down in the car to look for him. His hike turned out to be shorter than he had expected.

Ray Blomberg, a student in the '30s, remembered that the Morgan Territory School bell was so large as to render it unusable. "You couldn't ring the bell 'cause it would shake the school so much. Really."[26] The school trustees purchased the bell in 1904 and asserted that "its ringing tones will be heard in every part of the district."[27] The bronze bell is 34 inches high counting its handle and 133 inches in circumference at the bottom—much larger than the traditional school bell or even ship's bell, which one might have surmised to be its original use. Probably it had been a mounted fog warning bell. Someone managed to steal the bell from the school, and it was missing for years. A lack of pupils closed Morgan Territory School in 1947, and in 1949 the building burned down. Its bell, however, mysteriously reappeared and now has been mounted at the entrance of the central administration building of the Mount Diablo Unified School District. Unfortunately, it was mounted on a cement slab, which prevents anyone from hearing its historic sound, and its weathered bronze has been covered with garish gold paint. Mount Diablo Unified School District recently sold the 0.9-acre lot on the hill just north of the Curry Creek turnoff where the second Morgan Territory School used to be, and a new home has been built on the site.

Carole Cardoza Murray, who attended May School, believed that the best part of the one-room school experience was that the students taught each other. Having to teach a concept is one surefire way to learn it. She emphasized that no one felt put down or superior; the feelings in the schoolroom were of cooperation and caring. Her teacher for all of Carole's elementary grades at May School was Verna Ladd, a tall young woman with long brown hair. "She was beautiful to me."[28] Dorothy Reinstein Lamee summed up

Highland School student body, 1931-32: front row, l. to r., Bob Bettencourt, Edward Vargas, Bill Bettencourt, Bernice Vargas, Ann Murillo, Minnie Medina, Frank Marciel, Peter Banke, Bill Lusareta; back row, l. to r., Clarence Bettencourt, Ernie Vargas, Frank Murillo, Albert Dias, teacher Emma Luttrell, Harold Mitchell, Warren Reinstein, Herman Vargas, Art Reinstein. Photo courtesy of Tom Vargas. The 1922 building is now a private residence (below); 1999 photo by Anne Homan.

Above: Morgan Territory School, c. 1929: front row, l. to r., Verna Baeta, Olivia Silva, Evelyn Baeta, Mary Silva, Vernon Baeta, Albert Morgan; back row, l. to r., Ralph Rosenblatt, Ray Blomberg, Harold Blomberg, Jack Gleese, teacher Marie Rosenblatt (later married to Michael Morgan), Angelina Silva. Photo courtesy of Ray Blomberg.

Below: Summit School, June 11, 1936: back row, l. to r., Dorothy Hardiman, teacher Claire Miller, Richard Lawrence, Jack Gleese; middle row, Ormond Smith, Omery Smith, Eugene (Bud) Gleese, Sheriff Veale, Claire Hardiman, Marie Gleese; in front, Charlie (Buster) Hardiman. Photo courtesy of Jack Gleese.

117

Readying a one-room school for a community dance

"When a dance was held in the May School . . . the desks were unscrewed from the floor and placed around the walls with the seats facing the dance floor for the spectators. To smooth the floor for dancing, the men would pull a bale of hay across it. Then a pure wax candle was shredded and scattered over the surface. The musicians sat up front on the teacher's platform." c

her experience at Highland School: "We were all one big family."[29]

Besides being a place for education of the young, the local schoolhouse was a public building in a central location ideal for community get-togethers. "The schoolhouse was . . . the recreation center for the settlers. Once a month, desks would be pushed back, a violinist and organist enlisted for dancing, and the grownups filed in."[30] Edith Wright remembered such times at Morgan Territory School: "We ladies sat on one side of the room—men on the other. We'd all bring cakes and Ike Morgan would make a big kettle of coffee in the school yard. We'd dance almost all night, returning home in buggies and wagons during the early morning hours."[31] A popular violin player at Morgan Territory School dances was the Austrian musician Joseph Schwendel, who lived off Marsh Creek Road; Jake Ackerman played the organ.[32] Edith and her friends learned square dancing, the waltz, the two-step, and the schottische. Amelia Colldeweih Smith had reminisced to her daughter, Dorothy Smith Bennett, about attending similar dances. "She and her sister, and later on her beau, would drive over unlighted roads of north Livermore in an open buggy," Bennett recalled. "Sometimes lanterns were hung in the trees to guide the trav-

elers to the dance location. Remember, there were no street signs, no street lights, and some of the roads did not deserve the name. After dancing all night, with time out for food about midnight, the dancers would return home at dawn just in time to change clothes and swing into the day's chores."[33] The entry fee for each woman was a cake; for a man 50 cents to pay the musicians.

Two local musicians who often played at May School dances were John Stanley, a north Livermore farmer who played the fiddle across his knees, and Sama Sorenson, an accordionist.[34] In 1895 when the Brite family held a special neighborhood farewell dance for a friend at Highland School, the Livermore String Band supplied the music, and Robert Armstrong acted as floor manager.[35]

James D. Smith, headmaster at Livermore College in the 1880s and early 1890s, remembered another social function of the one-room schoolhouse—evening spelling tournaments. With their well-studied *Webster's Spellers* clutched in their hands, young and old would assemble on a Saturday night to compete in spelling contests by candlelight. Two previously selected captains would choose teams that lined up on two sides of the schoolroom. One person called out the words, and whenever contestants were guilty of a misspelling, they had to sit down. The team with one player left standing was declared the winner. Often the crowd held two or three contests on the same evening, with different captains choosing their own teams. "When one would miss a word there would be great cheering and when the misspelled word was taken to the contesting side, the word might be missed again, and then there would be more cheering."[36] One of the two best spellers, according to Smith, was Sabra Simpson, who rode eight miles on horseback to take part in the spelling contest.

At the end of the school year, the community gathered to honor graduates and to enjoy enter-

Richard Lawrence, sole member of the Summit Emergency School graduating class of 1936. Asked about the cast on his arm, he said, "I was playing Johnie Schneider." (See "A Pair of Rodeo Cowboys.") Photo courtesy of Richard Lawrence.

tainment provided by students. At Summit Emergency School in the '30s, Jack Gleese remembered "at graduation time we always put on a play to a packed schoolroom of family and friends followed by a wonderful pot luck."[37] Carole Murray recalled that "our graduation exercises at May School were the hit of the neighborhood in 1955." They included pantomimes, songs, recitations, even acrobatics.

One big advantage to attending a small school, Richard Lawrence pointed out, is how simple planning a reunion is. He can have one anytime he wants—he was the only graduate in his 1936 class from Summit Emergency School.

1 Virgie V. Jones, *Historical Persons and Places . . . in San Ramon Valley* (Alamo, CA: Morris-Burt, 1977) 154.

2 In the *Contra Costa County School Catalogue for 1882*, "Highland" is the subtitle for the school designated "Tassajara #2." By the 1884 catalog, the listing is simply "Highland School."

3 "Schools of Highland and May Districts Will Start," *The Livermore Herald* 5 Aug 1922: 1.

4 "Highland School Exercises on 14th," *The Livermore Herald* 6 June 1924: 4.

5 Dennis Harvey, "8200 Highland Road, Livermore Country Living on 3 Acres" (San Ramon, CA: Prudential California Realty, March 1997).

6 Action was taken at the Board of Supervisors' meeting on 3 May 1869, Minutes, vol. 3: 121. *Alameda Schools' Map Book #4*.

7 "Summit School District," *Contra Costa Gazette* 8 March 1884: 3.

8 In several public records her name is spelled "Sabrina." Contra Costa County index to marriages, microfilm 1294354, item 6, Family History Library, Oakland.

9 Jones, *Historical Persons* 154.

10 "For Woman Suffrage," *Livermore Echo* 28 May 1896: 3.

11 The current school grade numbering system, with the first grade being the first grade of attendance, did not begin in Contra Costa County until 24 Dec 1890. "Board of Education," *Contra Costa Gazette* 24 Dec 1890: 3.

12 "Local Echoes," *Livermore Echo* 11 Apr 1895: 3.

13 Antoinette Morris, personal interview, 9 Sep 1996.

14 "A School Squabble," *Contra Costa Gazette* 3 Oct 1885: 3.

15 Minutes of Contra Costa County Supervisors' Meetings, Vol. 17: 200.

16 Claire Miller Hubbell, personal interview, 20 Oct 1998. Claire continued teaching until her retirement in 1972, but she never again taught in a one-room school. After her year at Summit, she taught only first grade.

17 Hubbell interview.

18 Hubbell interview.

19 Mae Fisher Purcell, *History of Contra Costa County* (Berkeley: Gillick, 1940) 495.

20 "Advancement," *Contra Costa Gazette* 10 Dec 1881: 3.

21 Raymond Blomberg, personal interview, 30 July 1997.

22 "Advancement."

23 "Clayton Dots," *Contra Costa Gazette* 15 Aug 1899: 2.

24 Wallis Bruce Alexander Jr., "The Historical Development of the Mt. Diablo Unified School District," MA thesis, Cal State U, Hayward, 1968, 38.

25 Jack Gleese, letter, 2 Aug 1995.

26 Blomberg interview.

27 "Clayton Dots," *Contra Costa Gazette* 13 Feb 1903: 2.

28 Carole Cardoza Murray, personal interview, 1995.

29 Dorothy Reinstein Lamee, personal interview, 29 Aug 1996.

30 Sara Maloney, "A History of Morgan Territory Road," *The Tri-Valley Herald, Brightside* 8 July 1979: 2.

31 Maloney 2.

32 Joseph Schwendel's grandson Leland had the violin restored by an expert recommended by the Smithsonian. It is now being played in the Pittsburgh Symphony in Pennsylvania. Leland Schwendel, letter, 18 Oct 1996.

33 Virginia Smith Bennett, *Dublin Reflections* (Dublin, CA: Dublin Historical Preservation Assoc., 1991) 191.

34 Bennett 192.

35 "Highland," *Contra Costa Gazette* 7 Sep 1895: 2.

36 "'When the Gringo First Came,' Life History of Prof. J.D. Smith," *The Livermore Herald* 31 July 1925: 6.

37 Jack Gleese, letter, 29 Oct 1996.

a "Summit School Trustees," *Contra Costa Gazette* 24 Feb 1900: 8.

b Maloney 2.

c Bennett 192.

"Top-of-the-World" Park

COOL AND CLOUDY, the early morning held a threat of rain. Bright-colored fire trucks from various local districts sprawled over the staging area of Morgan Territory Regional Preserve near the summit of Morgan Territory Road. Hoses and equipment lay on the ground, and fire crews in turn-out gear wandered about, apparently aimlessly. By the door of the house next to the parking lot, however, an alert firefighter tersely signaled a waiting team of four to enter. All four wore breathing apparatus. After a period, the four exited and a new crew entered. Smoke curled silently from under the house eaves to merge with gray sky.

The East Bay Regional Park District had offered the 100-year-old house—too abused by time and the elements and too architecturally compromised by previous owners to save—to fire districts for a practice burn on 7 November 1996. This was a rare and valuable opportunity for fire personnel to enter and move around in a burning building, but in a controlled environment. All window, door, and chimney openings were boarded up to keep fresh air from encouraging flames. Straw bales placed inside provided a ready ignition source. Firefighters set these on fire, and parts of the structure began to burn, although a light spray of water from a fire hose kept the flames from blazing up uncontrollably. Ultimately, after all the crews had at least one turn and most two turns inside, fire took the upper hand, and everyone was pulled out. Flames soon followed the trails to the outside scouted earlier by smoke, and eventually the roof collapsed with a huge whoosh. The entire structure was quickly consumed; only hundreds of square nails mark the spot.

This pioneer house was probably built between 1888 and 1893, when the tax records of owner Benjamin Guirado showed that his improvements climbed in value from $100 to $800. The presence of so many square nails also attests to the age of the structure—by 1895 round nails were being used almost exclusively in this area. The 1888 tax records revealed that Guirado was running several horses and 22 calves up in the Black Hills. He bought the NW¼ of section 30 T1S/R2E with agricultural college scrip in 1872 for $222.43,[1] and in 1886 bought the NW¼ of section 30 from Chilean sheepherder Juan Luna Castillo for $1,200. At the time, Guirado's home was at Bird's Landing in Solano County, across the San Joaquin River from Contra Costa, where he farmed on gently rolling hills and with his wife raised a family of 15 children. He had married Maria Burton—a native of Livermore and granddaughter of San Jose alcalde John Burton—about 1868 when she was approximately 15 years old. Their first home was on Grizzly Island in the San Joaquin Delta. Benjamin Guirado was born in 1844 in California; his parents were from Mexico. At six feet, he was a tall man for his era.

Someone had moved a small building from another location and attached it to the northeast corner of the house that was burned by volunteers in 1996. Although used as a chicken house, the attached building was more than the usual outbuilding, with several glass windows as well as an interior redwood ceiling. It could have been an earlier dwelling required by pre-emption rules before the large house for the entire Guirado family was needed when they moved permanently into the Black Hills from Solano County. Farther to the northeast in the preserve is an area with a family orchard of several walnut trees and three fruit trees. Possibly the site of that original house was here. The architect who examined the large Guirado home and recommended condemnation did not look closely enough at the little added structure to give an expert opinion.

The Benjamin Guirado home, c. 1932. Courtesy of Carol Hardiman.

The Contra Costa County voting register of 1892 listed Benjamin Guirado at age 47 as a Black Hills stock raiser, and the family apparently had moved over from Solano County by that time. Guirado had a dark complexion, brown eyes, and grayish hair. Literate, he signed his tax records with neatly formed handwriting. By 1893 he probably had also built a large barn to the northeast. The Park District razed the barn in 1982 soon after buying the property. Guirado most likely also dug the rock-lined well found east of the house. In tax records for the Black Hills ranch in 1893, he declared three wagons, nine horses, nine colts, 10 cows, 12 calves, 33 stock cattle, two hogs, and a cream separator.[2] A Summit School souvenir presented by teacher Nina McPherson listed six Guirado students between 1893 and 1896.

Benjamin Guirado died of a heart attack on 22 July 1903. Several months later, Maria Guirado and her daughter Mary Chaves had a bad accident on Morgan Territory Road. As they were driving, a wheel came off the axle of their buggy. Both women were thrown out and received cuts and scrapes on their heads. After taking another rig down to Livermore, they needed 27 stitches between them.[3] Still later that year, on 5 November 1903, the youngest daughter, Secundina, married Rosendo Cruz at the Guirado ranch "near the summit school house."[4] On 4 November 1911, Endeavor Hall in Clayton was lit for the first time by electric lights at the wedding dance of Ben Guirado Jr. and Marian Nunez.[5]

In the county probate record, the Guirado improvements included a house, barn, blacksmith shop, windmill, and water tank.[6] Benjamin

Guirado had been using the land not only for grazing purposes but also for harvesting wood. At the time of his death, 85 cords of cut wood were on the property; in 1905 Maria Guirado sold an additional 50 cords, perhaps cut by her sons. The family had a creamery business and 49 head of meat cattle in Solano County, which Maria sold in 1904 for $535. In 1905 she sold livestock from the Black Hills ranch, including 71 head of cattle and 27 horses. Maria signed her mark to a deed of sale for the Black Hills property—320 acres—in 1911. A.S. Edwards of San Francisco was the buyer, for $3,500. Maria Guirado died in 1915; she and her husband are buried at St. Michael's Cemetery in Livermore. Of nine children who survived them, several, including Secundina, lived locally in Byron, Clayton, and Livermore.

The land went through several changes of ownership, including the Collins and Hardiman families, and ended in 1948 as property of Stanley and Genevieve Smith.

The quiet rural atmosphere of Morgan Territory Road was first challenged at the southern end of the road in the summer of 1970. Two men wanted to buy 425 acres to the east of the Doubletree development—Tomás Robles's original property—to create an off-road motorcycle park. Picnicking was to be allowed along Cayetano Creek and in "spectator areas." One site would be reserved for racing events, and the remainder of the park would be unimproved, "used as open riding areas where an individual may ride over any terrain he chooses."[7] For an admission fee of $2.50 apiece, a maximum of 600 motorcyclists was expected daily. Local residents quickly acted to gather opposition to the proposal. Roger and Suzanne Lake drove to Carnegie State Vehicular Recreation Area on Corral Hollow Road to the east of Livermore, where they photographed the damage from fires and erosion caused by off-road motorcycles. Carol Hardiman spoke strongly against the plan in a newspaper

interview with the *Independent*.[8] A number of Morgan Territory Road property owners attended the Contra Costa County Planning Commission meeting on September 15 to protest the planned park. The Lakes presented their slides, and Tassajara Fire Chief Warren Reinstein told of the fire danger at such a park, situated on a one-lane road crowded with motorcycles and the cars of spectators. The proposal was defeated, and the property is still for sale.

In 1971 some landowners on the northern end of Morgan Territory Road about two miles south of Marsh Creek Road decided to develop 832 acres into a luxury residential project designed especially for horse owners. Besides 471 single-family homes and 100 townhouses, the developers planned stables and extensive riding trails. This proposal to the east of the road included a small piece of section 4 and most of section 3 T1S/R1E as well as portions of sections 33 and 34 T1N/R1E.

Marsh Creek closely follows Morgan Territory Road along this area, but the creek was not indicated at all on the subdivision map. The rich corridor of riparian habitat would apparently have been eliminated. All planned roads of the "Morgan Territory Estates" subdivision dumped into one main road that ended at Morgan Territory Road. Such poor road access was almost an invitation for fire to roar down its familiar route on the east slope of Mount Diablo. The closest school was seven miles away. No provisions had been made for sewage or water. When the city of Concord refused to supply these necessary public services, the developer said he would build his own sewage system and discharge the treated effluent into Marsh Creek. Clayton and the Contra Costa County Planning Department voted against the project, which was in violation of the county master plan for development. However, although the area was also indicated as planned open space by the Association of Bay Area Governments (ABAG), the County Planning Com-

Bill Dickinson, president of the Contra Costa Park Council, responded to the 1971 plan for 'Morgan Territory Estates':

"We believe this development, if allowed to proceed, will not only destroy an area that has been previously designated for open space because of its remoteness, its accessibility to proposed expansion of Mt. Diablo State Park and its own natural scenic beauty, but . . . it deceives an unsuspecting public. Buildings are planned to be built on unstable soil and the area currently lacks adequate water, sewage treatment and roads compatible with such a project. To impose the expense of providing such utilities on the ultimate purchasers or the local taxpayer should not be tolerated." [a]

mission, a separate body, voted on 21 December 1971 in favor of the development. A small local private organization, the Contra Costa Park Council, was the "only organized body that showed any consciousness of openness and park space in the county" at that time, according to member Manfred Lindner.[9] The Park Council brought the decision of the commission to public attention and organized an informational meeting to air ideas about the proposed subdivision.

At its meeting on 8 February, the commission reversed its decision and denied the application for development. Since then, most of this area has gradually been developed into 5-acre "ranchettes."

The Contra Costa Park Council and other organizations concerned about open space in the Black Hills and Morgan Territory had had a wake-up call with the issue of Morgan Territory Estates. Manfred Lindner had become especially fond of the area. He hiked on the old Guirado property, now owned by the Smith family and called Hilltop Ranch. Bill McMillan was leasing the place and gave Lindner permission.

Lindner took photographs and presented a slide show to the Board of Directors of the East Bay Regional Park District in 1974. Morgan Territory "is such a beautiful place. I've been enchanted by it," he told the board.[10] In the spring of 1974 he led hikes on the Smiths' Hilltop Ranch, publicizing its appeal and continuing to press for the creation of a park. One of his organized hikes attracted close to 70 people.

In the summer of 1975, heirs of the Smiths' estate sold the ranch plus section 19 T1S/R2E—969.48 acres in all—to the East Bay Regional Park District for $400,000.[11] This became the nucleus for Morgan Territory Regional Preserve, which by 1996 had grown to 4,147 acres.[12] Sandy Joyce and her father, Bob, who worked at Tilden Park, lived in the old Guirado home at this time, acting as caretakers for the newly created Morgan Territory Land Bank. Sandy and her father enjoyed the primitive conditions: "You got to live in an older time."[13] Because the electricity often went out, kerosene lamps and candles had to be kept handy. During an emergency, well water had to be dipped out by hand and boiled on the wood stove. A claw-foot tub had pride of place in the bathroom. When the wind blew, which was often, they could feel it coming through the house walls. Sandy claimed with a smile, "I didn't need a hair dryer. I'd just bundle up and stand by the window."[14]

Oaks are the main tree species at the preserve, with coast live oak and blue oak predominant. The year 1996 was a bumper year for acorns, because of good rains during the previous two seasons. Acorn woodpeckers are abundant in the preserve and use standing dead valley oaks for granaries. A writer for *The Valley Times* noted that the numerous black-tailed deer also like acorns. "In a good acorn year, deer will grow very fat, and more twin fawns will be born the next spring. Given a chance, deer will eat about 90 percent acorns, if they're readily available."[15] The California laurel, or bay tree, with its glossy, pungent leaves, also occurs commonly. The preserve itself contains no pine trees, although gray pines flow down the east flank of Mount Diablo's North Peak to meet Morgan Territory Road at its northern end. The other major tree species in the preserve is the buckeye, with its vivid white candelabra and sweet odor in the spring. Bright-colored butterflies such as the California sister pollinate the buckeye's blossoms. To conserve water, this deciduous tree sheds leaves in late summer, leaving its bronze fruit to dangle unprotected in the wind. An unusually large grove of buckeyes is on the Upper Mollok Trail.

The preserve is a place of infinite variety, with rolling sandstone hills—some wooded, some open—against tree-framed vistas of Mount Diablo to the west, the Sierra and Central Valley to the east, and Suisun Bay and the Sacramento/San Joaquin Delta to the north. Bay Area natural historian Malcolm Margolin commented, "With most of the park more than 2,000 feet above sea level, it has an airy, top-of-the-world feeling to it."[16] In springtime more than 90 species of wildflowers bloom here; some are found only in this area. Spring displays rival the brightest of Persian carpets, especially the hundreds of gold fields sprinkled with purple-blue larkspur. Coyote, bobcat, fox, and an occasional mountain lion still roam, although grizzly bears are long gone. Raptors soar overhead, among them the golden eagle and prairie falcon. Morgan Territory Preserve, the neighboring Contra Costa Water District property around Los Vaqueros Reservoir, and the nearby Altamont Pass area have a large population of nesting golden eagles. The working list of birds maintained by park rangers in the isolated preserve contains 112 species. On the many sandstone boulders—which sometimes contain Indian mortars—colorful lichens and mosses create an intricate tactile network.

Three-hundred-foot cliffs line the east side of

Manfred Lindner warned in 1972 that time for preserving open space was running out:

"It is my understanding that the Park District has long-range plans which will ultimately include a regional park somewhere in the Morgan Territory area. It is also my impression . . . that for the obvious reasons of other commitments, such plans for Morgan Territory would be of low or moderate priority. . . . In view of the recent events which have occurred in that area, I should like to urge the Board to give the highest possible priority to Morgan Territory before land prices outpace the financial resources and ability of the District to pay." [b]

the canyon carved by Marsh Creek. The stream meanders down through steep hillsides covered by a dense riparian forest of the trees already mentioned as well as others that require more moisture, notably big-leaf maples and sycamores. Wild grapevines often link them all.

Prairie Falcon Trail travels from woodland to chaparral habitat. Red-barked manzanita, sage, wild lilac, coffeeberry, and toyon are dominant inhabitants in this plant community, along with the narrow green needles of chamise. In an 1861–62 survey of the area, the maps and notes of E.H. Dyer showed areas of "chamisal," a now rarely used word for the impenetrable thickets formed by chamise. Dense shrubbery along this trail surrounds hikers—claustrophobics be warned!—until the abrupt edge of the cliff, where again unfolds the panoramic view of the forest below and the hillside grasslands above.

The Bob Walker Trail and Ridge memorialize the landscape photographer and activist who in the 1980s and until his untimely death in 1992 promoted Morgan Territory Preserve, "the place where he felt the deepest emotional and spiritual resonance,"[17] as well as the preservation of other open space in the Bay Area. At an interview several months before he died, Walker spoke about his work: "I've really felt evangelical about making people stop and realize that they're in the middle of a very stunning landscape. It's all around them, and so accessible, but often they've overlooked it because California is loaded with so many superlatives."[18] He served on the board of Save Mount Diablo and chaired the San Francisco Bay Chapter of the Sierra Club. Walker's photographs capture not only the beauty of light on the lush East Bay hills but also the encroachment of development. He gave slide lectures and exhibits, led hikes to educate the public, and encouraged hikers to write letters to park officials. As one of his friends noted, he was "magnetic and exuberant and he loved the land unequivocally."[19] Susan Watson, president of Save Mount Diablo at the time of Walker's death, praised "his boundless enthusiasm, his gentle and humorous ways, and his persistent but non-aggressive work for the land he loved."[20]

The Morgan Territory Estates proposal was one of the factors that led to the organization of Save Mount Diablo, co-founded in 1971 by Art Bonwell and Dr. Mary Bowerman. Early members included representatives from the Clayton Planning Commission and the Contra Costa Park Council. Bowerman wrote, "My dream is that the whole of Mount Diablo, including its foothills, will remain open space . . . that the visual and natural integrity will be sustained."[21]

Save Mount Diablo has worked vigorously to carry out her vision. Its members, now numbering 6,000, have helped to raise money to preserve open space. "They have become the most effective citizen lobbying group in Contra Costa County," according to Jim Cutler, Assistant Director of Comprehensive Planning for the county.[22] The open space acquired by Save Mount Diablo and various park districts adds up to

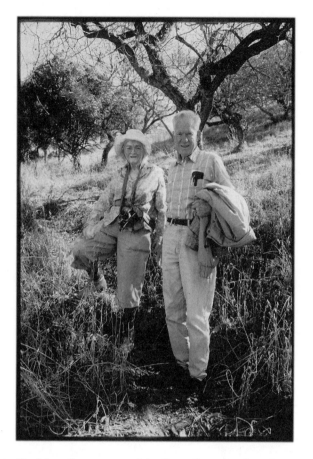

Dr. Mary Bowerman and Art Bonwell, co-founders of Save Mount Diablo. Photo by Stephen Joseph.

roughly 64,000 acres—100 square miles—that will never hold a subdivision or a shopping mall.

Another sort of acquisition accompanied construction of Los Vaqueros Reservoir. The Contra Costa Water District wanted control of all real estate within its watershed, and some landowners along Morgan Territory Road were forced to sell to the district. Denny Mallory had to sell not only all his property but also his houses. He and his son have moved to Grass Valley. The water district also proposed liens and restrictions that would have devalued other properties. Through a number of "town hall" meetings with water district personnel, residents have so far avoided any property restrictions and have maintained a good-neighbor policy. Quarterly meetings at the firehouse continue to update water district staff and Morgan Territory residents.

In 1989 Malcolm Margolin believed that the land along Morgan Territory Road should be bought up for public parkland within the following 10 years or it would be gone, and with it the opportunity to preserve wildlife habitats. "The areas near Livermore and Clayton are poised for growth, explosive growth. They'll be rolling out tract home developments. You need several thousand continuous acres for certain species to survive, such as foxes, which roam for food."[23] Already Clayton has grown from a sleepy country town to a slick suburban community. Around Brentwood, bulldozers are razing orchards and preparing for concrete foundations. Livermore, in spite of the defeat of similar designs at the polls in 1984 and 2000, is still considering dense development along North Livermore Avenue in Las Positas Valley, the flat farming area that stretches from Interstate 580 to Manning Road. The pressure on Morgan Territory Road increases every day.

This area is a unique, irreplaceable piece of wilderness in the midst of the heavily populated Bay Area. Seth Adams, Save Mount Diablo's Director of Land Programs, tells of his vision: "If we're successful, despite waves of new residents and a sea of development, Mount Diablo will never be an island.

"Public lands already stretch from the mountain southeast to Morgan Territory, Los Vaqueros, and Brushy Peak. My hope is that our parks, along with recreational routes such as the Diablo Trail and conservation easements on private lands, will someday extend like a peninsula down the Diablo range. They'll cross Altamont Pass through the windmill lands and on to the Park District's Del Valle and Ohlone Wilderness preserves and still farther to Mount Hamilton and

Henry Coe State Park. Hikers, cyclists, and equestrians will join eagles and mountain lions."[24]

1 San Francisco General Land Office, Agricultural College Scrip, VA, Entry 348, National Archives, DC.
2 1893 Contra Costa County Tax Assessment.
3 "Clayton Dots," *Contra Costa Gazette* 31 Oct 1903: 2.
4 "Clayton Dots," *Contra Costa Gazette* 14 Nov 1903: 2.
5 "Crisp News from Town of Clayton," *Contra Costa Gazette* 4 Nov 1911: 5.
6 Contra Costa County Probate Record 002751.
7 Letter sent to the Contra Costa County Planning Commission 17 Aug 1970 by Donald A. Stewart and William J. Grandberg.
8 "Motorcycle Proposal Outrages Ranchers," *The Independent* 30 August 1970.
9 Manfred Lindner, personal interview, 8 Jan 1999.
10 Lindner interview.
11 "Morgan Territory to Be Park," *The Independent* 22 June 1975: 1.
12 James Bruggers, "Maintaining the Mountain," *The Valley Times* 1 Dec 1996: 4A.
13 Sandy Joyce, personal interview, 19 Jan 1998.
14 Joyce interview.
15 Judie Marks, "In a Nutshell, Acorns Are Manna for Many Critters," *The Valley Times* 6 Nov 1996: 18A.
16 Malcolm Margolin, *The East Bay Out* (Berkeley: Heyday Books, 1988) 52.
17 Sarah Pollock, "Paradise Saved," *Diablo*, December 1992: 52.
18 Pollock 54.
19 "After the Storm; Bob Walker and the Art of Environmental Photography," text panel at the Lindsay Museum exhibit, Walnut Creek, CA: 24 Mar-30 July 2000.
20 Susan Watson, "Bill Mott and Bob Walker Will Be Sorely Missed," *Diablo Watch*, Fall/Winter 1992: 4.
21 Seth Adams, "A History of Mt. Diablo and Surrounding Open Space," Save Mount Diablo Internal Documents: 1999.
22 "Maintaining the Mountain" 1A, 4A.
23 Linda Davis, "Time Doesn't Spare Morgan Territory," *The Valley Times* 3 Dec 1989: 2C.
24 Seth Adams, letter, 5 Oct 2000.

a Tom Debley, "Group Aims to Block Diablo Development," *Concord Transcript* 28 Jan 1972: n.p.
b Manfred Lindner, letter to Board of Directors, East Bay Regional Park District, 24 March 1972.

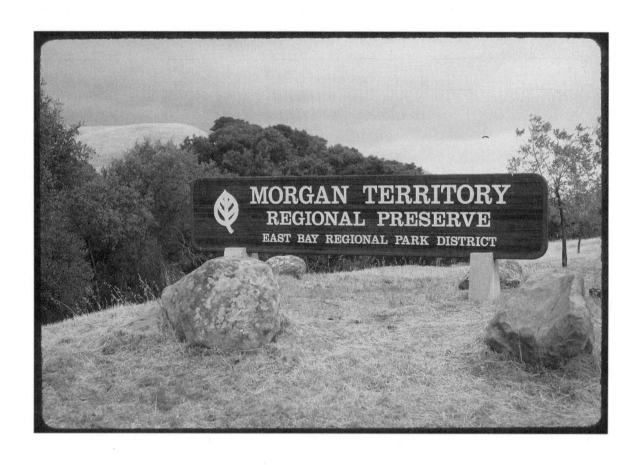

Sign at the staging area for Morgan Territory Preserve. Photo by Anne Homan.

Fire and Rescue Volunteers

THE DAY BEFORE had been rainy, but 15 January 1995 dawned a sunny Northern California Sunday. Three college-age friends, Erik Smith, Erin Scurran, and Beth Steiner, decided to enjoy the midwinter weather in Morgan Territory Preserve. Erik had previously been rock climbing at the preserve, and he led the young women along Prairie Falcon Trail to show them the cliffs. Erin was afraid of heights, so she and Beth stayed well back from the drop-off, enjoying some hot chocolate from a thermos, while Erik climbed down a short way. After he came back up, Beth wanted a closer look and attempted to reach a rock ledge about three feet below. Wary of her footing, she sat down and scooted over to the edge. Later, she related vividly, "I don't know how it happened, but I lost my balance and I slid down like a toboggan, like just right over the ledge, and I just went whoosh, right off the cliff. From what they told me I hit four different cliffs. ... I remember the tumbling—I remember thinking to myself, 'When am I going to stop falling?'"[1]

Her friends watched in horror as she slipped over the edge. Erik ran around the cliff face and down into the ravine. After he found Beth conscious amid rocks and brush, he comforted her and covered her with his coat, trying to stave off shock by keeping her warm in the chilly, sunless ravine. Meanwhile, Erin raced to the parking lot to dial 911 on the emergency phone. The call came into San Ramon Valley Fire Station 37 on Morgan Territory Road at about two o'clock. The 10-minute wait for firefighters to respond felt like forever to Erin.[2]

Rescue workers estimate that Beth fell more than 300 feet. She lay in a very steep area, inaccessible to their equipment. Soggy ground caused by heavy rains the week before prevented fire trucks from getting anywhere near her. One

Beth Steiner awaits rescue after a 300-foot fall in the Preserve

"I was in so much pain. I was in excruciating pain. I never knew so much pain existed. They kept telling me—don't go to sleep." [a]

four-wheel-drive vehicle became stuck in mud up to its frame. Consequently, all rescue equipment had to be hand-carried down a narrow canyon trail to the site—about a mile from the parking lot. The crew from Fire Station 37 divided into two teams: one to administer first aid and stabilize Beth's condition, the other to prepare for her evacuation. Workers assisting Beth found that the portions of her body that hit the cliffs had absorbed the shock, and her head was not injured. She did not suffer a concussion, but doctors later diagnosed a torn spleen, a punctured lung, compound fracture of the elbow, three breaks in her pelvis, and an H-shaped fracture of her sacrum, the large bone near the end of the spine. The fire crew talked to her nonstop, keeping her awake so that she could communicate about her injuries.

The other half of the crew went to work above the ravine where Beth had fallen. A regional parks helicopter arrived to help transport personnel and equipment to the top of the cliff. The crew decided that the fastest method to lift her from the ravine was in a stretcher guided directly up the cliff, so they set up necessary ropes and equipment.

Increasingly worried about Beth's condition as time raced by, fire personnel realized that the cliff rescue they were attempting could take many precious minutes—and then a crew would still have to carry her to the nearest possible heli-

Volunteer firefighter Don Homan describes his view of the evacuation:

"I was up on top of the cliff 'cause I was help-ing to pull her up on ropes if it became necessary. The helicopter flew down . . . way below where I was . . . maybe 200 feet. They got down to . . . where the helicopter blades were just about touch-ing the trees. . . . I didn't find out about it until later, but . . . when they get [the helicopter] in place, they have a system where they can turn the hovering over to a computer. They just push a button or lever or something and it does not move. It just sits there like a rock—it doesn't move forward or backward or up or down even with the wind blowing. It looked like it was sitting on the ground with the blade moving, meanwhile making a terrible racket. Then when they picked the gurney [holding Beth Steiner] up into the heli-copter, I guess the winch line was twisted because it went twirling round and round." [b]

copter landing site half a mile away. Senior Fire Captain Roger Lake decided that the better op-tion would be a helicopter with a cable and res-cue basket. Such a craft is available only through the U.S. Coast Guard. Lake received permission from Coast Guard headquarters in Virginia, and as luck would have it a crew and helicopter were standing by for emergencies at San Francisco Airport. The Coast Guard craft did not arrive until 4:15, just as daylight was fading; in a few more minutes, helicopter rescue would not have been possible.

Roger Lake summed up the events of that day, "It was one of those calls where everything went right. It was horribly complex."[3]

Usually, emergency personnel have little or no contact with the victims after a rescue. Beth, however, wrote thank-you notes and Christmas cards and even invited the Station 37 crew to a celebration at the nursing home where she was recuperating. About 18 months later she visited the Morgan Territory firehouse. She had a long recovery, including months in a wheelchair and painful physical therapy. In a television interview about her experiences, she reflected, "Sometimes it hurts so bad you just want to lie down and cry. But you can't do that. You can't do that unless you want to fail. And I certainly don't want to fail."[4] By April she was walking on her own, but with a pronounced limp. Two years later in 1997, she was walking well and had recovered almost 95 percent use of her fractured left arm. She now has a little son named Matthew and is attending nursing school.[5]

Approximately 25 people were involved in Beth Steiner's rescue, including personnel from San Ramon Valley Fire District, East Diablo Fire District, East Bay Regional Parks, and the U.S. Coast Guard.[6] The fire personnel from Station 37 on Morgan Territory Road who responded ini-tially to her friend Erin's frantic call were all vol-unteers. It comes as a surprise to most people to learn that more than 75 percent of firefighters in the United States are volunteers, not paid. Paid firefighters are found mainly in metropolitan areas. Many years ago, farmers and ranchers in this area as in others around the country simply responded in a neighborly fashion with wagons and water buckets whenever they smelled or saw smoke, or with first aid supplies in medical emer-gencies. Gradually, however, the desire for train-ing and better organization led to a more formal structure.

In July 1931 a severe fire, started by lightning on Mount Diablo, burned over 25,000 acres, west down into the Tassajara Valley and eastward all the way through the Black Hills to Morgan Territory. During the night exhausted firefighters somehow kept it from jumping Morgan Territory Road near the old Howard ranch. As it was, ranchers lost about 150 head of cattle in the Morgan Territory area; Sylvester Olofson lost 50 and Isaac Morgan another 50. For six days, more than 300 men battled the blaze, termed the worst in the history of the mountain.

Spurred by this fire, Gerry Gill, the Morgan family, and other residents in September 1931 formed the **Marsh Creek Fire Patrol and Improvement Association**, which covered the area from Marsh Creek up through Morgan Territory and the Black Hills south to the Alameda County line.[7] They held monthly training meetings and sponsored occasional family barbecues, both of which strengthened community ties. This organization was not a formally organized fire district, simply a local group that lobbied for equipment, for monies to train jail inmates in firefighting, for sufficient fire protection. At first Marsh Creek Fire Patrol maintained a fire truck and several pickups at Marsh Creek Springs Resort, but in 1959, the Contra Costa County Board of Supervisors gave permission for the vehicles to be kept at the Marsh Creek Detention Facility located off Marsh Creek Road about 1.5 miles east of Morgan Territory Road.

Denny Morgan, Gerry Gill, and Chet Anderson worked for the sheriff's department at this facility. They also were volunteer firefighters, and they enlisted the help of inmate volunteers in fighting fires. A plane crash started a particularly fierce fire on 17 July 1945.[8] For 38 hours six sheriff's personnel and 62 inmates fought the fire, which burned about 900 acres. Flames raged over property belonging to Jim Murphy, Vernon Cakebread, and the Pimentals. About a month later, another fire burned almost the same amount of acreage, starting in the Marsh Creek arroyo on the north side of Marsh Creek Road. Extinguishing this fire took the efforts of 103 inmate volunteers, several of whom were badly burned while trying to rescue horses.

One of the difficulties in mounting a successful firefighting operation in those years was a slow response time. No telephones existed in the area. World War II had gobbled up materials and personnel needed for new installations, so Pacific Telephone and Telegraph Co. could not bring in the first phone lines until 1947.

At regular intervals along Morgan Territory Road, the Marsh Creek Fire Patrol placed 55-gallon drums donated by the Shell Oil Co. Volunteers filled the drums with water in the dry season. The roadside drums supplied a ready source for wetting burlap grain sacks used to beat out fires—there were no convenient city fire hydrants, only wells and farm ponds, sometimes far from the road.

"All of us had sacks. In that day we actually put out fires with wet sacks," said Highland Road rancher Gordon Rasmussen.[9]

Jerry Bettencourt, Joe and George Cardoza, and Al Morris represented the Black Hills ranchers in the Marsh Creek Fire Patrol. During the early '40s Herb Reinstein, Stanley Anderson, E.C. Rasmussen (Gordon's father), and the Bettencourt brothers from Tassajara Valley came up the back way over the old Finley Road to meetings. Vernon Cakebread served as president in 1944, and at the December meeting that year, volunteers expressed a strong need for another fire truck as well as about 55 new water drums. High priority was given to finishing their project of grading fire trails. The members made final plans for a men's barbecue at their next meeting. Annual dues in 1947 were $3.50. That was the year the Marsh Creek Fire Patrol came under jurisdiction of the newly created **Eastern Contra Costa County Fire District**, which began at the eastern boundary of the county and extended west to Tunnel Road. Marsh Creek Fire Patrol received $4,000 to purchase two surplus fire trucks from the Army.

In 1953 the Marsh Creek Fire Patrol and Improvement Association listed 38 dues-paying

Gordon Rasmussen relished the volunteers' home advantage:

"We were pretty well trained in the hills. Where the other fire districts—we used to kind of laugh at 'em. They would come running out and the first thing they would do was radio back and say that their truck was stuck. In fact I remember seeing a lot of them going through a ditch and not knowing the overhang of their truck and not realizing that when they dropped those axles into a little bitty ditch that the back end loaded with water was going to just sit there. It tickles me when I think back on some of those things when they were coming to our aid." ᶜ

members; in October it had a bank account with $333.75.

In the late 1940s, Tassajara Valley too fell within the boundaries of the Eastern Fire District, whose headquarters were in Moraga. "The county shuffled us around to more or less whoever would take us. We were kind of the stepchild of the county fire district," Gordon Rassmussen said.[10] When Tassajara School closed in 1946, the Danville School District tried to sell the building, but the title to the site was not clear. Tassajara firefighters talked the county into giving the school to the Eastern Fire District, and local volunteers began to meet regularly at the school for training. "We got all these volunteers going. At that same time the old schoolhouse was just about destroyed. No windows hardly, the roof leaked, no foundation, sagging in the middle. So between our volunteers in the fire department we were meeting there every month and more. We started fixing on the old schoolhouse," Rassmussen said.[11] He emphasized that these meetings were "a lotta fun. We'd kinda have a

little party after every time. We'd sit around and visit and get a chance to really know our neighbors."[12] On each Fourth of July, the volunteers sponsored a community barbecue at the schoolhouse. The monthly training meetings and the schoolhouse restoration project in Tassajara essentially served the same function as the Marsh Creek Fire Patrol and Improvement Association. They focused local resources and created community feeling as well as improving local fire protection.

Weapons for fire protection at first were the ranchers' own tractors and disks, pickup trucks, axes, and burlap sacks. Finally in 1964, Tassajara acquired its first fire engine, a 1949 Dodge power wagon, about the size of a pickup. Part of the advantage for local volunteers in firefighting, naturally, was that they knew their own hills and the abilities of their own farming equipment. When fire trucks from Danville responded to Tassajara, their crews often had difficulties.

Besides being unfamiliar with the Tassajara Valley and Morgan Territory areas, firefighters from the Eastern Contra Costa County Fire Protection District had to drive a long way to respond to emergencies there. Interstate 680 did not exist; slow, narrow roads were the only routes available. Moreover, Moraga was a fairly wealthy community of large homes in contrast to the poorer farming communities farther east. Local ranchers shouldered the burden of the same fire district taxes as the richer folk in Moraga. The rapidly urbanizing Moraga-Orinda area gained more voting power than rural parts of the fire district. With all these factors in mind, Marsh Creek and Tassajara Valley volunteers decided to form their own localized fire districts.

Marsh Creek Fire Protection District split off from Eastern to become an official entity in August 1967. About a year later, however, the original Eastern District became Moraga Fire Protection District and the Marsh Creek organization's name was changed to **Eastern County**

Fire Protection District. A letter from the secretary of the Eastern Contra Costa County Fire Protection District to the Board of Supervisors reasoned: "The Moraga area of the District has always been known as the Moraga Division and is generally known in the area as the Moraga Fire Department. It was felt that this was a change in name to conform with the general usage. ... The area now in the Marsh Creek Fire District really encompasses a great deal more territory than just the Marsh Creek area. It was felt that it would be better to give the District a name which was more representative of the area of the District."[13]

Providing strong local representation from the Morgan Territory area, residents Martin Wright, Bill Morgan, Dennis Sattler, and Ben Galvin all served on the Board of Commissioners of Eastern County for a number of years. Gerry Gill, who ran Marsh Creek Springs Resort, was the first chief, soon followed by Ray Morgan, who guided the district through many changes. By the time of Ray's death in 1985, Eastern County had combined with Brentwood Fire District to become the current **East Diablo Fire Protection District**, which continues to provide fire protection for residents north of the summit on Morgan Territory Road.

Although Bill Morgan currently serves as an East Diablo commissioner, there are no volunteer firefighters left in the district. Fire Station #51, still maintained near the Marsh Creek Detention Facility on Marsh Creek Road, has a paid firefighting staff.

Tassajara Fire Protection District—encompassing the old F-2 county service area—split off from Moraga Fire Protection District and was activated on 30 January 1970, with Warren Reinstein as chief and Gordon Rasmussen as chairman of the Board of Commissioners. Dean G. Watts acted as secretary; the other commissioners were Hank Bettencourt, Albert Hansen, and Jørgen Clausen. Their new district encompassed 42 square miles, including Morgan Terri-

tory Road in the Black Hills, from section 31 near the summit and south to the Alameda County line. Much-needed support in training as well as general encouragement came from Phil Phillips of the Dublin-San Ramon Services District. He helped give Tassajara volunteers specialized training in fighting house fires, loaned training films, sponsored first aid training sessions, and attended every meeting. Moraga Fire District turned over the Tassajara School building to the newly formed district, and firefighters continued their campaign to restore the old school.

In 1970 Tassajara District managed to buy their first new fire truck, a one-ton Dodge. The firefighters built a truck bed to carry the pump and water tank. The district slowly acquired more used trucks, which were kept in local barns. Gordon Rasmussen explained the hand-me-down status of equipment for the Tassajara District: "Those other fire districts loved the chrome. ... They had all the bells and whistles, and when they had some old jeep or something, why then we would get it."[14]

At that time the 911 system was not yet in place. In an emergency, a person dialed the fire department number. An answering service in Livermore called the first volunteer on the telephone tree, and housewives played an essential role as dispatchers via the telephone lines as the tree system went into effect. Busy party lines sometimes interfered with contacting volunteers. For a while Warren Reinstein and Roger Lake were on the same party line, which also made rounding up personnel difficult. Warren had a handi-talkie, which he left on all night just in case.

In 1975, after much bureaucratic red tape, the county allowed Jørgen Clausen to sell the Tassajara Fire District an acre of land on Tassajara Road just north of its intersection with Highland for a fire station. The Tassajara District borrowed $20,000 from the county and soon erected a new metal building. Volunteers dug a well in 1977 so they could keep an oil tank car donated by Southern Pacific Railroad filled with water. The tank stores up to 12,000 gallons.

"We were overtaxed, and we decided to do something about it, and we did, and we had fun doing it," Gordon Rasmussen mused. "That's what I think about the most, when I think about all the effort and the hours we put into it—it's the fun we had. It was just a great, great group of guys who would show up."[15] To share in the fun, the district invited the community twice a year to a barn dance held in the new fire station. In summer they also hosted a picnic on the Tassajara School grounds. Both of these events included a moneymaking raffle that helped purchase needed equipment not available with the tight funding of the district. The official budget for Tassajara Fire District's first year was $7,000.

The volunteers got plenty of experience after Tassajara District joined Twin Valley Mutual Aid in 1976, sometimes traveling as far as Mines Road, Altamont Pass, Sunol, and the Dublin hills to put out fires during the summer fire season. In 1977 the district was serving 280 residents spread over 42 square miles. Volunteers responded to 18 calls that year. The district owned one fire engine, a tanker, two patrol trucks, and one heavy patrol vehicle. In this same year Lawrence Livermore Laboratory became the radio dispatcher for the district.

With his monthly salary of $100, Tassajara Fire District Chief Warren Reinstein was the only paid firefighter. According to Gordon Rasmussen, Warren was a generous, hard-working rancher, always ready to work for someone else more than for himself. However, he also enjoyed socializing with neighbors and friends. Gordon commented, "He always had time to come by and visit. The time would just go by and you didn't care."[16] "He missed his calling," Warren's widow, Vera, added. "He belonged in public relations."[17]

Meanwhile, up on the ridgetop of Morgan Territory Road, Roger and Suzanne Lake had bought 10 acres on section 31 T1S/R2E from Mary Gleese in 1969. Roger reflected about their first experience on the road: "We wanted to live in the country, and we were looking for places to live. We drove the road for the first time and thought nobody in their right mind would live up here. Almost got hit on the Levy."[18] Despite their initial reaction, they fell in love with the view from the Black Hills and managed to negotiate the land sale. "We didn't want to be too far from town, but we didn't want to be in an area that was gonna develop. This seemed like an ideal place."[19] Before building their house in the summer of 1970, Suzie and Roger hired a well witcher to find water on their property. They laugh to think about their backward planning. If they had not found water, they "would have been in the soup."[20] At this time only five other families lived nearby on the ridgetop: Harry and Brigette Gim, Denny and June Mallory, Charles and Carol Hardiman, the Schells, and the Johnsons.

The Lakes worked hard at developing their site, taking on many of the chores themselves in order to save money. They bought shares in a cable tool drill rig and drilled their own well. From a local landowner they bought an old hay storage shed that stood near a corral about a mile downhill toward Livermore. "We had that old drilling truck. We're nuts. We drove the truck into the building, lifted the building up, actually lifted it up, and drove the thing up the hill one foggy morning. If anybody had come flying over [in a vehicle], they woulda—" Here Roger shakes his head. "And then we started bringing it up the driveway and got stuck in the trees, so we had to take off the roof."[21] With its roof replaced, the shed now houses a boat. The Lakes quickly learned that winter on the ridge brings fierce winds, so they added an underground anchor to the west, which they hook to their house with a cable during the storm season.

Another natural difficulty of living in the Black Hills is the high fire danger, and the Lakes soon took an interest in fire protection. Tassajara Fire Station lies a good 30 minutes away from the top of Morgan Territory Road, so the Lakes as well as other local residents wanted more immediate protection. In 1968 the Hexcel Corporation in Livermore gave George Cardoza a 1942 GMC urban pumper, the first fire engine specifically for use on Morgan Territory Road. The Morris family stored the pumper in a shed on their property for about seven years. By 1972 Roger and Suzie Lake had joined the Tassajara Fire District as volunteers. Many mice lived in the Morris shed, Suzie said, and when Roger drove the fire truck up the hill, she saw mice bailing out and rolling all over the road.

In June 1972 Tassajara sent over another vehicle, the 1949 Dodge power wagon, to help service the Black Hills. Since the main volunteer force at the time lived along the ridgetop on Morgan Territory Road, the Gims offered to keep this engine in their garage. Several months later, the Tassajara District sent the power wagon to auction and replaced it with a used four-wheel drive California Department of Forestry fire truck. The drawback with this truck was its small gas tank. It held only 10 gallons, so the volunteers had to carry extra cans of gas. Just to drive up to Gims from the Tassajara fire station used up half the gas in the tank, Roger said. "It was so slow you could walk faster up the Levy."[22]

In 1973 the Lakes built a new garage to house the fire engine. The Morgan Territory Road contingent now became known officially as Fire Station 2, while the original building on Tassajara Road was called Fire Station 1. With fewer residents to serve, Station 2 always had to work harder to scrounge resources. "It was always a hassle to get equipment, any kind of equipment," Roger complained.[23] At one point Tassajara District bought some new hose. They gave Roger three lengths (about 150 feet) of the hose,

Suzanne Lake recalls the first fire engine assigned specifically to Morgan Territory Road:

"They had the [practice] burn going, and we came rolling in, you know [in a 30-year-old, hand-me-down urban pumper], and Roger turned on the pump, and I jumped out, and I grabbed the hose, and no water came out. They spent the rest of the drill lying under the truck trying to figure out what was the matter with it. That was so funny."[d] *(Roger Lake summed up dryly, "Go to a drill to fix the truck."*[e])

but told him that "we'll keep the rest of the hose on another rig, and we'll bring it up to you [in case of a fire]."[24] At this time Station 2 was averaging about four calls a year. When Hank Bettencourt resigned from the Board of Commissioners in 1974, Roger Lake took his place. In 1975 Station 2 received its beloved used CDF 1959 GMC, fire truck #5, and volunteers stored this vehicle in the Lakes' garage and used it until 1990. Suzie speaks for all the volunteers: "We loved it. It was a good truck—versatile, easy to work."[25] From 1976 until 1990, Roger served as assistant fire chief for Tassajara.

Suzanne Lake, in spite of being 4 feet 11 inches tall and weighing no more than 100 pounds, is not content to leave firefighting to the men. There was some talk when she first came on the scene, Suzie said, of forming a ladies' auxiliary for the Tassajara District. She added, laughing, "They chose the wrong lady for that." One time in the early '70s, "Roger sent me off with a backpack, and some men thought that was awful. It was an acceptance thing—the ranchers were not used to women doing this."[26]

'My wife's just as much a volunteer as I am'

"The women have been great for the program," said Roger Lake in 1978. "Everyone meets formally once a month, but during one stretch last summer the women met for about 10 weeks in a row. They'd get some of the chiefs to help them practice on the trucks, and really took a personal interest in the whole thing. There's no discrimination—my wife's just as much a volunteer as I am. Out here the women are equal with the men— we're all volunteers. They're really appreciated, and have helped out tremendously by taking such an active interest in the program." [f]

Assistant Fire Chief Steve Eppler especially encouraged participation by women. Besides Suzie, Helen Phinney, Linda Harriman, Renée Parker, and Pat Johnson were particularly faithful women volunteers. Finally, at one drill, Suzie recollected, "All the old guys were there, and we women showed them how to work their trucks— there were no problems after that." [27] Another internal struggle involved the institution of first aid training. Roger remarked, "Even getting them to start handling medical calls was like pulling teeth." [28] The volunteers were afraid that they would be held liable if they did something wrong. Medical training is now an integral part of their regimen.

By 1978 the Tassajara Fire Protection District ran on a yearly budget of just under $25,000. The district responded to 44 emergency calls that year. They owned five fire engines, four at Station 1 and one at Station 2: a 400-gallon 1949 White urban 1000-gallon pumper, a 250-gallon 1969 Dodge wildland patrol, a 250-gallon 1973 Chevrolet wildland patrol, a 1000-gallon 1942 GMC six-wheel tanker, and a 500-gallon 1959 GMC heavy wildland patrol. [29] In 1979, after the death of Warren Reinstein, Steve Eppler took over as chief, a position he held until 1990. Gordon Rasmussen retired in 1981, to be replaced by Vera Reinstein. Steve Morgan, who lives on Morgan Territory Road, has been a faithful member of the Board of Commissioners since 1983.

An arson-ignited blaze broke out on 14 July 1981 and burned 2,400 acres from Blackhawk Ridge to Finley Road to Curry Canyon. It raged for three days until it was contained. Burning chaparral sent up huge columns of flame fanned by erratic winds in areas too steep for fire engines to maneuver. The main attacks had to come on foot and by air. Ben Stewart of the California Division of Forestry said appreciatively of the assembled firefighters, "It's a direct attack. Hot, smoky and dirty, with hand tools. It's the only way to do it, and they're doing a tremendous job. These guys are the real heroes." [30] CDF set up their command post at Tassajara Fire Station 1 to coordinate firefighting efforts. Forestry had jurisdiction because of the threat to Mount Diablo State Park. They called in reinforcements to mount an air attack to coordinate with the ground efforts. *The Valley Times* reported, "Again Wednesday, aerial tankers bombarded the brush and grass fire with chemical retardant while helicopters swept over the rises and canyons of Blackhawk Ridge, dumping water on flames which shot as high as 150 feet." [31]

Roger Lake told of the volunteers from Tassajara being caught in the middle of an aerial drop of bentonite: "We were up on a ridge. We were getting 40- or 50-foot columns of flame coming up through the brush. There were air drops on us, behind us, in front of us, to keep sparks away. I wanted the photographers to get behind the trucks, but they wouldn't go. I grabbed the reporter and threw her out of the way of a chemical drop. One photographer had his camera pushed into his face—he was lucky he didn't get his neck broken." [32]

At one point, Helen Phinney had driven a patrol truck to a ridge saddle to deliver sandwiches to a fire crew. "All of a sudden, the fire blew up. She put her turn-out gear over her head and followed another truck out. Personnel in other fire trucks had to turn on their pumps and shower themselves with water," Roger Lake said.[33] John Clary, currently assistant chief for East Diablo Fire District, found himself in the same situation that day. "We were trying to contain one of the flanks. It blew up in the brush. We were in a bad location; I got everybody out but me. We didn't have the protective gear required today, and I got burned on my hands, legs and ears. It hurt."[34] A firefighter who had been bulldozing hillsides for a day and night "had a face smudged with dirt and his bright yellow fire retardant clothes were a dull gray." He commented to a reporter, "You get used to it. But it does get a little hard when the 'dozer' starts going sideways."[35]

That Wednesday evening, 32 hours into the battle, all Tassajara units, except for Morgan Territory Patrol 5, which was providing protection on Morgan Territory Road, were stationed at houses on the west side of Finley Road with instructions to protect them from the approaching fire. The wind came up after dark, gusted up to 25 miles an hour, and sent flames scurrying into more brush. As chaparral that had been holding back the rocks on the hillside burned, rocks came tumbling down the hill toward the firefighters. "We could hear and feel them whistling past in the dark. One hit a CDF fire truck and put it out of commission."[36] Tassajara truck #6, the 1942 GMC tanker, was used as a mobile reserve. When the fire neared a structure or the road, the tanker with its great water capacity knocked the fire down and then moved to the next hot spot, leaving mop-up to hand crews or other engines. Although the flames came close, no structures were lost, and no one died. Almost 1,000 firefighters from all over the state fought the blaze, using 54 fire trucks, 10 bulldozers, five airplane tankers, and helicopters equipped with buckets.[37] Not that long ago, the main weapon against fires had been wet burlap sacks. The public cost from this act of arson was over $500,000, which did not include estimates for the value of destroyed grazing land.[38]

A record 76 emergency calls came through for Tassajara District in 1982, the year after the Blackhawk Ridge fire. By 1986 Fire Station 1 had 23 volunteers and Station 2 had 12. At this time Suzanne Lake and Bob Geil were co-captains of Station 2, making Suzie the highest-ranking woman engaged in firefighting in Contra Costa County. The district also had two paid personnel and six interns, with a yearly budget of $70,000. Up on Morgan Territory Road, Station 2 at first handled emergency medical calls involving mostly car accidents. Then bicycle riders discovered the challenges of the winding road. A biker who fell recently had been riding in a thick fog. Medical calls also involve accidents to hikers or mountain bikers in Morgan Territory Preserve.

To the northwest of Tassajara Fire District, **San Ramon Valley Fire Protection District** served 70 square miles in the '80s—from Rudgear Road south to and including Bishop Ranch, Las Trampas Ridge on the west, and Mount Diablo on the east—with a paid staff of 74 firefighters at five stations. This area included Danville, Blackhawk, and northern San Ramon. In 1990 Tassajara Fire District decided to merge with San Ramon Valley. This merger with a larger district has had advantages and disadvantages. One very obvious plus is the spacious new metal building, now known as Fire Station 37, erected in 1992 near the summit on Morgan Territory Road. Volunteer Don Homan especially appreciated this amenity. When the firefighters kept their engine in the Lakes' garage, parking it after a call, often in the dark, was a difficult maneuver. The garage had originally been built to house the four-wheel-drive truck with the small gas tank. Engine #5 was much larger.

Engine #5's old home was the Lakes' garage:

"We always had to back the truck in so that it could come out quick. There were only about two inches on each side of the engine, making it very difficult to judge and back it in. It always went in a little bit cockeyed—that was always the problem. There's a four-by-four post in the center of the garage that holds up the garage essentially; this is what everyone would hit. I would repair it, but it happened again and again. When you backed the engine up, the aerial would clang and bang against the roof. You'd panic thinking you'd hit something, but it was only the aerial. Then it would usually smash the side running lights. So you would ruin two things at once—the fire truck and the post. . . . The momentum of a fire truck with 500 gallons of water in it is just a little more than a car." [g]

Other advantages of the consolidation with San Ramon Valley are the engines housed inside the new fire station: a 1,000-gallon truck, a 600-gallon truck, and a one-ton patrol. Down at Doubletree—the housing tract on the site of the old Robles Ranch—San Ramon Valley Fire Station 37 also houses a one-ton patrol truck that holds 250 gallons of water. Still a further benefit is San Ramon Valley Fire District's strong support of additional training. The district sends specialists and videos as well as allowing Station 37 to use the tower at Pleasanton to practice fighting house fires. An abundance of excellent quality uniforms and personal equipment for each volunteer is still another advantage.

However, the merger with San Ramon Valley also entails some difficulties. The fire district wants Station 37 to have the best vehicles they can afford, so fire trucks are replaced often with more up-to-date models. To paid firefighters who have time to peruse instruction manuals and familiarize themselves daily with the many different dials and all the equipment on a new truck, replacement is a blessing. The firefighters build up confidence in their ability to use the vehicles through frequent practice. But to volunteers who meet semi-monthly, it is a problem. Nevertheless, the volunteers persevere, and Station 37 is proud of its record.

At 11 o'clock on the evening of 18 January 1992, an emergency call alerted Station 37 firefighters. Roger Lake noted, "We got this call . . . saying a truck has slipped over the edge of the road. Didn't tell us the magnitude of it. We drove up to find all these kids . . . ."[39] A mini-pickup with a camper shell had indeed gone off the road at one of its steepest overlooks. Ten young people, all under the age of 16, had been inside. Driving around for a lark, the teenagers from Berkeley and San Francisco had no idea of their location. Two were riding in the cab; eight were in the truck bed. The driver failed to negotiate a turn and lost control. The truck rolled over and over down the hill, demolishing the camper shell and scattering kids as it went, until it reached the bottom of the canyon 200 feet below.

To keep track of so many victims, the firefighters resorted to putting numbers on their heads. Some firefighters were assigned to search the steep slope. Worried that in the dark and confusion and steep terrain volunteers might have missed someone, Roger said, "We kept asking them how many were in the truck."[40] After the volunteers had treated minor injuries, a line of ambulances arrived to take the teenagers to local hospitals for checkups. This emergency call was particularly poignant for the Lakes; their only son, Matthew, had died recently in a vehicle accident. They were grateful for this apparent miracle in which all the young people survived.

Left to right, volunteer firefighters Don Homan, Roger Lake, Suzanne Lake, Burt Weiss, Robert Geil and Sue Geil, with Engine #5, about 1985. Courtesy of Roger and Suzanne Lake.

Roger followed up the incident with a personal letter urging the parents to help their children realize that they had been given a second chance at life and "to understand how precious life is, to be careful, and to make the most out of their opportunities."

Since the merger of Tassajara Fire District and San Ramon Valley Fire District, the old Tassajara Fire Station 1, now San Ramon Valley Fire Station 36, has mostly paid firefighters, with only two volunteers. However, community members have still been working on Tassajara School. Vera Reinstein led the Old School Foundation from 1979 to 1998. The wooden floor of the school is beautifully restored, and third-grade classes in the San Ramon Valley School District take part in a living-history program every year that gives students a one-room learning experience at the old schoolhouse.

Station 37 is now the only station in the San Ramon Valley Fire District with an all-volunteer staff. Roger Lake is senior captain, while Suzie Lake and Steve Morgan function as co-captains for the 19 firefighters. Steve Morgan continues as the representative for Morgan Territory on the Board of Commissioners.

Black Hills volunteers continue to work hard to study confusing dials and hose connections, to practice drills even as the wind and fog freeze their faces, and to struggle with administering CPR to a dummy named Resusci Annie. They want to protect their families and their community, and they enjoy the feeling of a job well done, but they also have fun together. Their reliance upon one another engenders a special camaraderie. Fire Station 37 continues its tradition of Fourth of July community barbecues at the station house. In 1999 and 2000, station firefighters sponsored a Halloween party. Sue Geil commented, "I would say the fire department is the cohesive part of the community feeling up here. It has brought the neighborhood . . . closer together. Whether it's an emergency or [another] problem, we call on each other. This is a caring group up here . . . ."[41]

1 Joe Krebs, "News at 6," NBC, WRC, Washington, DC, c. 27 Feb 1996.

2 Erin Scurran, telephone interview, 14 Oct 1997.

3 Roger Lake, personal interview, 5 Oct 1997.

4 Krebs.

5 Beth Steiner, telephone interview, 7 Oct 1997.

6 Catherine Hedgecock, "Copter Rescues Hiker Injured in 200-Foot Fall," The Valley Times 16 Jan 1995: 3A.

7 Jack Gleese, letter, 15 April 1997.

8 The old minutes and various memorabilia from the Marsh Creek Fire and Improvement Association are kept by the secretary of the organization. Bill Morgan is the current secretary and graciously allowed the author to consult them.

9 Gordon Rasmussen, personal interview, 9 Sep 1997.

10 Rasmussen interview.

11 Rasmussen interview.

12 Rasmussen interview.

13 Letter on file at Board of Supervisors' Martinez office dated 2 July 1986.

14 Rasmussen interview.

15 Rasmussen interview.

16 Rasmussen interview.

17 Vera Reinstein, personal interview, 9 Sep 1997.

18 Roger Lake, personal interview, 20 Mar 1997.

19 Roger Lake, Mar interview.

20 Roger Lake, Mar interview.

21 Roger Lake, Mar interview.

22 Roger Lake, "Tassajara Good-by Dinner," 8 June 1990.

23 Roger Lake, Mar interview.

24 Roger Lake, Mar interview.

25 Suzanne Lake, personal interview, 5 Oct 1997.

26 Suzanne Lake, personal interview, 20 Mar 1997.

27 Suzie Lake, Mar interview.

28 Roger Lake, Mar interview.

29 Tom Beaudin, "A Practical Approach to Fighting Tassajara Fires," The Valley Pioneer 10 May 1978: 21.

30 Carla Marinucci, "Tassajara Families Remain Calm While Firefighters Swelter," The Valley Times 16 July 1981: 3A.

31 Erin Hallissy, "Firefighters Slowing Diablo Blaze," The Valley Times 16 July 1981: 1A.

32 Roger Lake, Oct interview.

33 Roger Lake, Oct interview.

34 John Clary, telephone interview, 7 Oct 1997.

35 Marinucci 3A.

36 Roger Lake, Oct interview.

37 "Mt. Diablo Fire Under Control," The Livermore Herald 17 July 1981: 1.

38 Erin Hallissy, "Fire Stopped After Burning 2,400 Acres," The Valley Times 17 July 1981: 1.

39 Roger Lake, Oct interview.

40 Roger Lake, Oct interview.

41 Ken Leiser, "If They Don't, No One Will," The Valley Times 6 Nov 1986: 4B.

a Krebs.

b Don Homan, personal interview, 6 Oct 1997.

c Rasmussen interview.

d Suzanne Lake, Mar interview.

e Roger Lake, Mar interview.

f Beaudin 21.

g Don Homan, Oct interview.

Apples and Almonds

ALONG THE WEST side of Morgan Territory Road, at 6.9 miles from the Livermore end and soon after the 7.5-mile road marker from the Clayton side, an untended orchard still lightly perfumes the green hillside with white and pink blossoms in the spring. The rows of trees occupy a northeast-facing meadow probably at least partly wrested from adjoining woods. On this section of the road, the meadow creates a break in the thick tree canopy. Although early local residents recall the apples, the majority of the remaining orchard now is in almonds. The apple trees have barely survived, with about five still flowering and the rest stumps. The apples were

smaller in size than today's Gravenstein, but their color, texture, and taste were reportedly similar. The original orchard also contained plum and apricot trees. A 1998 arson fire singed the remaining fruit trees and a few of the almonds, and walking through the orchard now is a challenge: Industrious ground squirrels have been digging unchecked for many years.

The family who lived here, the Clymas, took butter, eggs, fruit, and truck garden produce down to Livermore almost every Saturday to sell to customers or barter with merchants.[1] Their grocery account book from December 1921 to December 1922 shows a total of 344 dozen eggs

William and Phillippa Clyma, probably late 1800s. Courtesy of Mary Butterfield.

L. DEMARTINI. SR.   JOS. F. DEMARTINI   L. DEMARTINI. JR.

THE L. DEMARTINI SUPPLY CO.

THE CONFECTIONERS SUPPLY HOUSE
PROPRIETORS WESTERN NUTMEAT AND SHELLING CO.

CABLE ADDRESS
"DEMARTINI"
"LDSCO"

CODES
A B C 5TH
BENTLEY

CONFECTIONERS,' ICE CREAM
MAKERS' AND BAKERS'
SUPPLIES OF EVERY
DESCRIPTION

TOOLS, MACHINERY, RAW
MATERIALS. NUT MEATS.
EXTRACTS. CAKE OR-
NAMENTS. ETC.

PHONE KEARNY 354

125-127-129 TO 135 CLAY STREET

SAN FRANCISCO,
Jan. 26th, 1924.

Mr. William Clyma,
Livermore, Calif.

Dear Sir:

   We received 14 Sacks of Almonds, that you
shipped us, and we find, that we received 119 pounds
more than what you claim you shipped us, which is as
follows.

   We received 14 Sacks,

     Gross 679 lbs.
     Tare 14 "
     Net 665 "

as follows:

 13 Sacks of Languedocs & Commercial Net 621 # @ 07¢ $43.47
 1 "   " Nonpariels   ·Net 44 # @ 12¢ 5.28
               Total $48.75

as per enclosed check.

   With many thanks and good wishes, Compliments
of the Season.

     Yours respectfully,

     L. DEMARTINI SUPPLY COMPANY.

     Per- *L. Demartini*

LD/SR:FG
Encl.1.

P. S. ----- Received 679 pounds, your shipping weight
560 pounds, over 119 pounds.

Courtesy of Mary Butterfield.

and 54 squares of butter for $131.50 credit. William Clyma made the trip to town weekly if road conditions permitted. His wife, Phillippa, wrote to their daughter Catherine ("Cassie"), "Pap is going to town tomorrow. I have 9 doz eggs to send since last Saturday. . . . I made 2 squares of butter today. The snow is most gone, but it is very soft and muddy."[2] Mrs. John Beck received five boxes of fruit from the Clymas in 1910 for $2.50. The almonds they sold commercially for cash to the L. Demartini Supply Co. in San Francisco. In 1924 William Clyma shipped 14 sacks of almonds weighing 679 pounds to Demartini, for which he was paid $48.75.

The Clymas' property, the east half of the SE¼ of section 24 T1S/R1E, overlooks a magnificent panorama of Mount Diablo, a view that surely lightened the task of weeding a garden or watering an orchard. No evidence of a building is visible on the property. However, just over the fence line, two large pear trees grow on the east side of the dirt track that leads to the Cardoza homestead. On the west side of the track, where the land has the typical corrugated topography achieved when it has covered old excavations, a rock-lined well still exists. Placement of the Clyma home on Cardoza property remains a mystery, but Ida Cardoza Taylor definitely identified this area as the Clymas' home site.[3] The Clyma ranch was the farthest south in both the tax collection district and the census district designated "Morgan Territory." Iola Murchio Christy accompanied her friend Elodia Keller when Elodia was the local census taker. "In 1920, Elodia took the United States census for the whole Clayton area. I went with her in the one horse cart, the greatest distance being the Clymer ranch on the Livermore Road. It was January, the roads almost unpassable."[4]

William Clyma was born on 9 August 1848 in the village of Callestock in Cornwall, England. His father was a lead miner; his mother signed William's birth certificate with her mark. On 2

June 1874 William Clyma, by then a miner himself, married Phillippa Jane Kitto near Truro, Cornwall. Probably because of the widespread depression affecting the mining of tin and copper, then the principal industries of that county, the Clymas decided to emigrate. In the late 1800s, more than 30 percent of the miners and their families emigrated from Cornwall, lending plausibility to someone's jest that at the bottom of every hole the world over, a Cornish miner could be found.

Before the end of 1874, the Clymas had settled in Austin City, Nevada, a mining town that sprang up overnight, local legend has it, after a Pony Express horse in 1862 accidentally kicked over a rock that had concealed a cavern of silver. Although the 1880 U.S. census of Austin City listed William Clyma generically as a laborer, presumably he was laboring in the mining industry. William claimed U.S. citizenship in Lander County, Nevada, in 1880, and the couple's first three children were born in Nevada.[5] The oldest, John, born in 1875, died at 18 months. Next came Stanley, born in 1878. Their first daughter, Lillian—often called Lily or Nettie—was born in 1879. William Clyma was described as five feet seven, with a fair complexion, gray eyes, and light brown hair.[6] There is some suggestion that he may have developed weak lungs from working in the mines in Cornwall and Nevada; perhaps this contributed to the decision to travel farther west to California. Another son, Carl, lived not quite a year in California, dying in July 1886. The couple's younger daughter, Catherine ("Cassie"), was born at their new ranch "near Mount Diablo" on 1 May 1888.

On 11 October 1884 the Clymas bought Ferdinand Keller's 80-acre property for $3,000.[7] This was an unusually high price for land in the Black Hills, but the original homesteader, Jacob W. Harlan, had testified in 1882 to many improvements, including a house approximately 14 by 28 feet with a 15-by 17-foot addition, a large

A letter from home, 1913:

"Pap caught a big wild cat down by the pool. Sunday morning. He put a coop and a dead chicken in it down there—and keep the traps there all the time. Manuel Bent [Nunez] was hear Sunday and wanted one of the pups, so I gave him Duke—it took to much to feed three. . . . Pap is going to town tomorrow I have 5 squares of Butter —and 18 doz eggs—and sold two dozen eggs and 1 square of butter since he was in town last. My reds are laying all the eggs. The others are not laying hardly any. We have a big chunk of fruit cake yet—we eat some for supper. It is as good as it was at Christmas." [a]

barn, a stone milk house, a chicken house, and 46 fruit trees.[8] The 1887 Contra Costa County tax assessment showed that farmer William Clyma, living in the Summit School District, owned two wagons, two horses with two colts, two cows, and three stock cattle as well as some poultry. By 1892 the tax assessment listed two acres of orchard and six acres of vines on the Clymas' property; the orchard had grown to three acres by 1898. William worked on the local Republican election board and was active in the Masons.

Morgan Territory weather patterns have not changed much over the years. Phillippa wrote to daughter Cassie in January 1913, "It have been north wind and every thing froze up hear for days —it have been blowing a fright. I don't think it was ever so cold here before—but to night it is calm and cloudy. Rain is needed very much." In the same letter two days later she added, "it is a white world this morning it has snowed a little most of the day little fine stuff like white sugar and freezing as it is coming down. . . ." Taking care of her chickens with their golden eggs was important. William set up a permanent trap for predators. "We got a coon in the trap down by the pool this morning. Teddy and Duke [young dogs] had a big fight over him and Teddy drove of Duke. And eat of his front leg. So you see what a fine dog he is. Freeda [mother dog] is still trying to teach them to play with poor success."[9] On several occasions the trap caught wild cats, probably bobcats rather than mountain lions.

The Clymas encouraged their children to take advantage of educational opportunities. Stanley graduated in 1894 from Summit School at the top of Morgan Territory Road. He enrolled for teacher training at Stockton Business College, Telegraph Institute & Normal School. He wrote home to his family from Stockton, "I have got quite a number of new books. Now that I have the books and find how much work I have to go over, I doubt whether I can get over the required work in time. Algebra, Latin and Geometry are the three worst. . . .

"The only place I could room here was with a boy who had the mumps. I didn't like that so they put me over in the girls' building where I now am. There are forty or more girls on the same floor with me and no other boy. . . . The first night the girls piled trunks and chairs against my door and they also tangled up the bed-clothes while I was out."[10]

Stanley earned his grammar school teaching certificate and returned to teach at Summit School from 1897 through 1899. He taught at the coal mining town of Somersville during the 1903–04 school year and later became teacher and principal at Crockett School as well as a member of the Contra Costa County Board of Education.

William and Phillippa Clyma lost two grown children to tuberculosis. On 10 June 1904 Stanley married Elsie F. McPherson, daughter of Tassajara rancher Daniel R. McPherson. He was elected president of the Contra Costa County Board of Education in September 1906 and was chosen for the position of Richmond principal.

His obituary in *The Livermore Herald* on 29 August 1908, shortly after his 30th birthday, described his hopeful visit to New Mexico in May to seek relief for his illness in a drier climate, "but the disease was too deep-seated and he went into a steady decline."[11] His young wife helped him make the desperate journey home to Livermore. For part of the way he fell unconscious, but rallied enough to make his farewells at home. The *Contra Costa Gazette* obituary stated that "he was considered one of the most capable teachers in the State."[12]

Catherine Clyma died even younger, at age 25. Also a graduate of Summit School, she had studied to be a manicurist and received her diploma from the California School of Hair Dressing and Beauty College of San Francisco in February 1913. She worked as a cook at a private home to earn her room and board while attending beauty college. To encourage her daughter, Phillippa wrote frequently to San Francisco with homely news and advice. An excerpt from her letter of 31 January 1913 is typical: "Pap have been plowing again up above the vineyard. It was very weedy and he sowed wheat that Joe [Cardoza] brought up Christmas it was too good to give to the chickens. I am glad to see that you can go to church so often. Yes you will meet nice people thare and learn more good then you could in any other way . . . that will bring you peace at the last."

About a month before Cassie's death in December of that year, she moved to her sister's home rather than to her parents' because the site on Morgan Territory Road was so remote and her health so perilous. Tuberculosis was the scourge of the 1800s. Stanley's form of the disease was probably "galloping consumption," so called because of its sudden and virulent onset.

The Clymas' daughter Lillian married local businessman Joseph Laughlin, had three children, and lived out a normal life span on their ranch near Brushy Peak. She, too, studied to be a teacher and was an independent woman for her day. At the time of her wedding, she was teaching at Green School in Alameda County. Her wedding dress revealed her talent as a seamstress. Lillian and Joseph were married under a wedding bell at the Clymas' Morgan Territory home on 21 October 1903. The Livermore Presbyterian minister, the Reverend James B. Stone, officiated. The house was "tastefully decorated with evergreens," and a "scrumptious" dinner for 20 people followed the ceremony.[13] Despite being only five feet tall and weighing about 100 pounds, Lillian worked hard physically not only at traditional women's roles but also in the fields at haying time. After her marriage, Lillian and her parents usually exchanged a letter per week through the Livermore Post Office. In these letters they shared everyday life on a ranch or farm—the weather, canning fruit, growing ferns in the garden, caring for children, setting chickens and turkeys, butchering meat.[14] On 5 June 1926 Lily wrote, "Dear Ma, Well, it surely is awful hot again today. The old north wind is blowing too drying everything up. I suppose it will burn the fruit and make it drop off. I have a lot of little chickens now, so many I can't count them. . . . I baked bread yesterday. I never would have done it if I knew it was going to turn out so hot."[15] Phillippa's grandniece Mary Butterfield recollected her Aunt Lily's beautiful flowing handwriting and her aunt's encouraging her in the practice of calligraphy. Mary saved a number of photographs and keepsakes from this family.[16]

Neighbor Jack Gleese recalled William Clyma as a person of varying moods, sometimes gruff, other times amiable. "His wife, on the other hand, was always friendly, always with bread and jelly or cake and cookies for us kids."[17] Ida Cardoza Taylor also remembered Phillippa Clyma's cheerful hospitality.

Mail has been delivered in the rural Livermore Valley as far north as May School Road since 1911, but the post office did not extend the route

The Clyma orchard in 1996. Photo by Anne Homan.

farther north to Morgan Territory Road until the early 1960s. So neighbors in the Black Hills helped each other by taking letters to town and delivering letters on return. The Clymas and the Gleeses used this arrangement. Both families maintained wooden mailboxes along the road, but for neighborly pickup and delivery rather than for U.S. mail service.

William lived to age 80 and Phillippa to 85. Four years after her husband's death in 1928, when she was 76, Phillippa moved down from Morgan Territory Road to stay with her daughter Lillian. In an upstairs bedroom at the Laughlin home, Phillippa lived as an invalid for about eight years until her death on 4 November 1940.

She was buried beside her husband at Roselawn Memorial Park in Livermore. No other families have lived on their Morgan Territory Road property. Their house has disappeared. Only the orchard remains.[18]

1 Many long-time local residents pronounce this family's surname "Clymer." The family's Cornish accent added that extra "r" sound, and everyone who heard it assumed this spelling of the name. The family name, however, is "Clyma," on birth and marriage certificates as well as in census records and family correspondence. Nowhere did the family write their surname with an "r" on the end.

2 Phillippa Clyma, letter to daughter Cassie, 7 Jan 1913. I have retained the spelling and grammar of the letter writers.

3 Ada Cardoza Taylor, personal interview, 12 July 1996.

4 Iola J. Christy, "Clayton Stories," *Clayton Chronicles* Jan 1998: 5. Clayton residents sometimes referred to Morgan Territory Road as Livermore Road.

5 "Naturalizations," *Reese River Reveille* 20 Oct 1880: 3.

6 *Contra Costa County Great Register,* 1892.

7 *Contra Costa County Deed Book* 47: 26.

8 San Francisco General Land Office, Homestead Entry 2023, National Archives, DC.

9 Phillippa Clyma, letter, 7 Jan 1913.

10 Stanley Clyma, letter to the family at home, n.d.

11 Page 1.

12 "Death of Stanley Clyma," *Contra Costa Gazette* 29 Aug 1908: 2.

13 "Laughlin-Clyma," *Contra Costa Gazette* 31 Oct 1903: 5.

14 Mary Butterfield, personal interview, 20 May 1996.

15 Lillian Laughlin, letter to Phillippa Clyma, 5 June 1926.

16 Mary donated these papers and memorabilia to the Contra Costa County Historical Society.

17 Jack Gleese, letter, 20 May 1996.

18 The Clymas' property is now owned by Morgan Territory Road residents Harry and Brigette Gim.

a Phillippa Clyma, letter to daughter Cassie, 24 Jan 1913.

Thornton K. Taylor and Ida Cardoza, 1931. Courtesy of Antoinette Morris.

George Cardoza and Beatrice Vargas Pereira, 2 December 1928. Courtesy of Carole Murray.

A Holy Land

ISOLATED IN THE Atlantic Ocean about 814 miles west of Portugal are nine green jewels called the Azores Islands. Legend has it that the Azorean archipelago is the remnant of the lost island paradise Atlantis, which sank beneath the ocean after a natural cataclysm. The largest and most populous island, São Miguel, has an area of 288 square miles. The others, in order of size from large to small, are Pico, Terceira, São Jorge, Faial, Flores, Santa Maria, Graciosa and Corvo. In the late 1800s no one would have mistaken the Azores, regardless of their natural beauty, for a lost paradise. An aristocracy owned the land; its members forced the peasants to contribute a major share of their crop to the landlord as rent. Although officially the islands were under the rule of Portugal, the mainland "left the populace to their sad destiny—ignorant and illiterate, exploited by the self-imposed aristocracy. . . . "[1] Even by 1911, about 70 percent of the population remained illiterate. Compulsory school attendance was not the law until the 1960s, and then only four years of primary grades were required.[2] The once lush orange groves and vineyards of the islands had been ruined by an orange blight and a grape root louse that first invaded in the 1800s. Potato rot also wreaked havoc on the islands, destroying the principal subsistence crop.[3]

Many Azoreans saw emigration as the only way to surmount this misery. To avoid compulsory Portuguese military service, which started in 1800, thousands of young men emigrated illegally. Beginning in the late 1800s and continuing up to about 1920, when the United States passed stricter immigration laws, Azoreans came in large numbers to Massachusetts, Hawaii, and California, attracted by job opportunities, free public education, availability of land, and the overall possibility of improving their lives eco-

A new immigrant writes back to the Azores:

"Isto é uma terra santa que Deus abençoi sempre e a todos"—"*This is a holy land which may God bless always and for all.*"[a]

nomically and socially. This country was not a myth like Atlantis, lost in time, but a place where—with hard work—dreams could become reality. By 1915, 100,000 Portuguese had immigrated to California.[4]

The departure of Morgan Territory rancher Joseph Souza Cardoza from his native Azores is a family legend. About 1874, Antone Bent Nunez and his wife, Justina, were preparing to embark for California from São Jorge. Joseph Souza Cardoza, 17 years old at the time, just happened to be at the dock. Joe's son-in-law Thornton K. Taylor told the story: "He was standing on the dock and they asked him, 'Would you like to come to America?' He said 'Yes' and got on the boat and came with them . . . with only his shirt and pants and shoes."[5] Further drama in this dockside incident is that Justina Nunez was pregnant with her daughter Lucy, who would later become the wife of Joseph Cardoza. "She wasn't born yet," Thornton continued, "but the mother was pregnant. So, when they got over here and her [daughter] was born, Joe Cardoza used to carry her around in his arms 'cause he was friends with the Nunezes. And then he winds up marrying her."[6] Although this story of the abrupt leave-taking of Joseph Cardoza from his native São Jorge has come down through his family, there is another possible version. At age 17, he would soon be eligible for Portuguese conscrip-

Friday January 2nd A. D. 1891.

Present, Hon. *Joseph P. Jones*, Judge.

In the Matter of the Application of

Joseph Souza Cardoza
to be admitted a Citizen of the United
States of America.

Decree Admitting to Citizenship.

Joseph Souza Cardoza

a subject of *the King of Portugal* appeared this day in open Court and made application to be admitted a citizen of the United States of America. And it having appeared to the satisfaction of the Court, upon due proof and the production of a certified copy of the record, that the said applicant has heretofore, and more than two years previous to this date, declared on oath, before the Clerk of a Court of record having common law jurisdiction, that it was bona fide his intention to become a citizen of the United States of America, and to renounce forever all allegiance and fidelity to any foreign prince, potentate, state or sovereignty whatever, and particularly to *the King of Portugal* whereof he was a subject. And further proof having been made to the satisfaction of the Court by the testimony of *Charles Rhine* and *J. Bento Nunez,* two witnesses—citizens of the United States—who were sworn and examined in open Court; that said applicant has resided in the United States five years, and in this State one year, and that during that time he has behaved as a man of good moral character, attached to the principles of the Constitution of the United States, and well disposed to the good order and happiness of the same.

Thereupon said applicant declared on oath that he will support the Constitution of the United States, and that he doth absolutely and entirely renounce and abjure all allegiance and fidelity to every foreign prince, potentate, state or sovereignty whatever, and particularly to *the King of Portugal* whereof he was before a subject.

Now, Therefore, it appearing to the satisfaction of the Court from the foregoing proofs that the Naturalization Laws of the United States have in all respects been complied with in the matter of this application; the Court doth hereby ORDER, ADJUDGE AND DECREE that the said *Joseph Souza Cardoza* be, and he is hereby admitted and declared to be a CITIZEN OF THE UNITED STATES OF AMERICA.

Decree entered *January 2nd 1891*

J C Wittenmyer Clerk.

By *F L Hass* Deputy Clerk.

From the National Archives, Washington, D.C.

150

tion. In order to avoid military service, many strong young Azorean men swam through the surf to board foreign ships secretly. This could explain why Cardoza had no luggage for his journey.[7] Even by 1900, steamship steerage passage from the Azores to California cost only $10 to $15—a matter of wages for two to three weeks in the United States.[8]

Frederick Bohme wrote about the Azoreans: "Originating in a country with an agricultural economy, the Portuguese immigrants to California who were not fisherfolk came from the land, and in their new environment they turned to it again."[9] São Jorge Island is long and narrow, about 32 by five miles, with a range of mountains along its length; the tallest peak is about 3,500 feet. Lower fields are cultivated, and farmers use higher plateaus for pasturage. The island is well suited for raising cattle and famous for its dairy products, especially cheese.

The 1880 U.S. census for Contra Costa County shows Manwell Nunes, Joe Cardoza, and Joe Aenas laboring for Portuguese rancher John Silva in the Tassajara district. Before that they may have worked for Leland Stanford in Warm Springs at the vineyard Stanford and his older brother, Josiah, had begun in 1872. By 1876, "Stanford's Warm Springs property boasted 100,000 vines, more than 60,000 of which were bearing. With this grape crop he was able to produce about 50,000 gallons of wine per year. Besides grapes, the 660-acre farm produced various fruits, including oranges."[10] Obviously, such a large operation required many farm workers, and Azoreans were familiar with vineyards and oranges. The future father-in-law of Joseph Cardoza's son George worked at the Stanford winery for seven years, from 1892 to 1899, and family lore suggests that Joseph had worked there earlier.

The Azorean immigrants worked especially hard in California to buy property. "The practice among Portuguese-speaking people in California

was to acquire land and settle on it as rapidly as they could," Bohme noted, "with the result that, by 1920, about 15,000 first-generation Portuguese and Azoreans accounted . . . for some 10 percent of the farms owned by foreign-born whites in California."[11] In November 1882 Joseph S. Cardoza settled on the SW¼ of section 12 T1S/R1E and filed a pre-emption claim. Joseph B. Nunez and James McGrew testified to his house, barn, corral, and 150 feet of iron pipe from a spring to the house. In December 1884 Cardoza paid $400 for the land.[12]

By 1887 Cardoza had settled on an additional 80 acres in section 24 T1S/R1E, where he built his second home. The dirt access road winds up a steep hill from its entrance on Morgan Territory Road, past the home site of the Clymas and up into a more wooded area. At present the only evidence of the early ranch house is a rock-lined outline of the basement. Beneath a large spreading oak, the little one-story building, only 16 by 20 feet, had faced a marvelous view of both peaks of Mount Diablo. Antoinette Morris recalled hearing that the glass windows for the house were brought by ship from New York through the Panama Canal. At Martinez on 2 January 1891, Cardoza became a U.S. citizen. His witnesses were Charles Rhine and J. Bente Nunez.[13] By 1892 he had begun to run stock cattle on his range; by 1893 he was taxed for 50 calves and 115 head of cattle.

On 16 December 1895, at St. Catherine of Siena Catholic Church in Martinez, Joseph Souza Cardoza married Lucy Bent Nunez, and the census taker in 1900 found them living on section 24 with their first child, Mary. Lucy was 20 and Joseph 38 at the time of their marriage.

Joseph Cardoza had bought out his partner and friend Manuel Bent Nunez in 1896, and the 80 acres on section 24 were approved as a homestead for Cardoza on 16 January 1897. Besides the house, a barn and a bunkhouse were on the site. Water came from a spring higher on the hill, and a cattle trough is still kept filled from that same water source. One walnut tree remains of the family orchard, and their granddaughter Carole Cardoza Murray recalled some apple trees as well. Joseph and Lucy had 10 children; the only survivor today is the eighth child, Ida Cardoza Taylor, who with her husband, Thornton K. Taylor, kindly shared memories of old times.[14] Ida was born on 15 July 1911.

In addition to using his land for grazing, Joseph Cardoza cut oak wood to sell and barter in Livermore. In letters dated 30 December 1912 and 31 January 1913, Phillippa Clyma commented that Cardoza had a crew of "woodchoppers" at work on his section 24 property. When Cardoza and his crew had finished cutting and splitting the wood and loading it in a wagon, he would leave the hill about three in the morning, hauling the firewood down to Livermore with a four-horse team and returning late at night with an empty wagon. In 1903 a cord of white and live-oak wood sold for $6.00.[15] Some years later, John Gleese and his brother-in-law, Charley Hardiman, hauled four-cord loads of wood in the same way down to Livermore. John's son Jack Gleese recalled, "It . . . was a worrisome downhill trip which meant tying one of the rear wheels with a heavy chain so it was locked from turning with a larger knot of chain at a point in front of the wheel where it contacted the ground. Using this method and the very large brake blocks that were the brakes on the wagon, we went down the hill on Morgan Territory Road. I think you can visualize how this could be somewhat scary."[16]

The Cardoza family dealt mostly with Victor and Baughman's store in Livermore, where they bought clothing and shoes with the amount credited to their account for firewood. Baughman's still sells western wear in Livermore.

Cardoza also acquired 160 acres in section 20 T1S/R2E, an area now in Morgan Territory Regional Preserve. A stone corral is on this property. According to Ida Taylor, her father used the corral for branding and/or separating cattle. Since the walls seem too low to hold cattle, probably wooden rails were added to the top. Many of the stones are quite large and must have required great effort to drag into place, perhaps with horses. Maybe the corral had been made earlier by sheepmen from the Vasco area. Many rocks are scattered on the hillside here, some of which seem to have been purposely placed between trees—possibly by Native Americans to create a blind for shooting arrows at elk, deer, or antelope that could be chased down the gauntlet between two rock-studded natural ridges. A swath of clear grassy ground about 75 yards wide separates the two ridges from forested land. Several grinding holes overlook a nearby cattail-filled spring seep, also indicating Indian presence.

In 1908 Joseph Cardoza bought the large property that had belonged to John Beck, northeast of the junction of North Livermore and Manning Road—about 363 acres. Here on the "corner ranch" in section 16 T2S/R2E, the Cardoza family grew. Probably the oldest two children, Mary and George, had started at Summit School, but now that the family lived in Alameda County, they were in May School District. This property is much flatter than the other Cardoza sites in the Black Hills. Thornton Taylor commented, "They wanted farming land besides running the cattle. [Ida's] dad was a very progressive person, ambitious."[17] Now the family could plant hay and grain as well as use stubble fields for extra pasturage. They raised hogs, dairy cattle, and poultry including turkeys at this ranch, but still used their hill properties to run Hereford cattle and also to cut some firewood. Cardoza had so many different scattered properties that Jack Gleese's main memory of him was seeing him drive a horse and two-wheeled cart on the back dirt roads.

The Cardozas lost two of their 10 children at very young ages, one from burns and the other of severe colic; the rest survived into adulthood.

Tragedy struck again, however, with the flu epidemic. Their oldest daughter, Mary, had married Manuel Enos and had a baby, also Manuel, in 1917. The baby became an orphan when both parents died on the same day, 11 November 1918, from influenza. His Cardoza grandparents raised him as a foster child with their own brood. Young Manuel developed into a famous bronc rider on the rodeo circuit.

Of all the siblings, only Ida broke with tradition and married a non-Portuguese. Her husband's family—part Irish and part English—had moved to the Livermore Valley from San Francisco after the 1906 earthquake and fire. Thornton K. Taylor grew up on a Livermore ranch and worked for various ranchers in the area. He and Ida's brothers rode horseback in order to work cattle, but neither Ida nor any of the females in her family ever learned to ride. Her brothers' riding was never for pleasure, only for work. When Thornton Taylor bought a car, Joseph Cardoza would often call on his son-in-law to drive him around to his many properties. The vehicle was a touring car, certainly not the ideal vehicle for navigating dusty or muddy back roads, but Thornton never said no. By the time Ida married Thornton in 1931, the Cardozas had also bought an adjoining 160 acres along North Livermore Avenue that contains a large two-story house.

Joseph Cardoza had a powerfully sonorous voice. He never hit his children, but that voice was obeyed. He was good with animals, too. Even steers that were field animals would come up to the fence when he talked to them. Lucy Cardoza could seem forbidding at first, according to Antoinette Morris, but she was very kind. An excellent businesswoman, she involved herself in the financial part of ranching—unusual for a woman of her day and culture.[18]

The highlight of every Portuguese family's religious year was the Holy Ghost Festival on the weekend of Pentecost. Roots of these festivities

Thornton K. Taylor admired his wife Ida's parents, Joseph and Lucy Cardoza:

"Well, . . . [Joseph] had an 18-inch collar. He was about 5 feet 10. He weighed 260 pounds, all muscle. And the McCormick family were opposed to the Portuguese people in a way, they were not too friendly. And they caught [Ida's] dad, he had a long beard. And they caught her dad on saddle goin' up into the Black Hills. And the five McCormick brothers challenged him over a fence. So they grabbed him by the beard and jerked him off the horse and he whipped, singlehandedly, all five of them. That's how powerful he was. He never smoked or drank . . . but he would help everybody. And he and Ida's mother took in many many kids, [whose] parents couldn't support them. Move them in, send them to school, buy them clothes. That's the kind of parents they were." [b]

go back to the Middle Ages as a time of joy and feasting, especially for the poor—a celebration of the end of a famine in 13th-century Portugal and the perceived continued earthly presence of the Holy Ghost. The Don Carlos chapter of the fraternal order I.D.E.S. (*Irmandade do Divino Espirito Santo*, Brotherhood of the Divine Holy Spirit), which was organized on 12 April 1896, sponsored the yearly event in Livermore from 1907 until shortly after World War II. A square block in the Northern Addition of Livermore, bounded on one side by North Livermore Avenue, was the I.D.E.S. Park, which members had bought in 1907. They built a meeting hall, a dance hall, and a bandstand. The Fraternal Order of Eagles bought the property in 1947 and sev-

Carole Cardoza (Murray) and her dog "Fanny," about 1948. Courtesy of Carole Murray.

eral years later erected their current building on the old I.D.E.S. site.

Traditional Holy Ghost weekend celebrations in Livermore included a parade, bazaar, dinner, and dancing as well as church ceremonies. In 1915 Livermore streets were "gaily decorated with parti-colored streamers and welcome banners" along the parade route from I.D.E.S. Park to First Street and back.[19] A participant recalled the 1940 event: "On Saturday night before the

Sunday parade, the Livermore Band would escort the Queen with the crown and her attendants to the chapel at the Holy Ghost Grounds on North Livermore Avenue. . . . After the crown was placed in the chapel, there would be fireworks. The fire engine had to be close by, because there were hay fields across the street."[20] Ida Cardoza Taylor's first memory of the excitement and beauty of the fireworks is from when she was about seven years old. The dance followed the fireworks, and the next morning a large parade marched from I.D.E.S. Park to St. Michael's Catholic Church with all the little children dressed in white. After a Portuguese Mass, the congregation marched back to the park for a special meal of *carne e sopas*. Ida remembered that her dad used to contribute a steer every year toward this. "The meat would braise for hours in a flavorful sauce," said Madeline Henry, like Ida a granddaughter of Antone Bent Nunez. "Then it would be served over French bread with fresh mint. In the afternoon there would be dancing and visiting friends. And, of course, the carnival was there also."[21]

Ida recalled details of the family's Easter and Christmas celebrations. For the traditional Easter sweet bread, "I remember Mama used to braid the dough and then she'd put an egg in each braid and put it in the oven and you had bread and hard-boiled eggs."[22] She remembered Christmas at the corner ranch before the days of electricity. "We had a Christmas tree but we had to put on the tree lighted candles, you know, they would clip on. And then you'd light the candles. But it was so dangerous we were worried sick that we would set the place on fire, you know. So that didn't last very long."[23]

After Joseph Cardoza died in 1936, Lucy and her son George concentrated on the farming and business; her son Joe was in charge of the cattle. George had asthma and stayed away from horses because they aggravated his condition. In 1925 the Cardozas had bought the Levy ranch up on Morgan Territory Road, and George and his family moved there from his parents' "corner ranch." George had married Beatrice ("Nonnie") Vargas Pereira, daughter of a Portuguese rancher from Pleasanton, and by 1942 the couple had three sons and one daughter, Carole. Ten years later their last child, Russ, was born. The children loved life on the ranch in the hills, and Nonnie's role was easier than it had been down on the larger spread with her parents-in-law and their

many projects. The three older boys attended Highland School; Carole and her brother Russ attended May School.

A proud graduate in 1955, Carole is still enthusiastic about her one-room school experiences. She was 10 years younger than even the youngest of her three older brothers, and another 10 years went by before Russ was born, so she was often on her own at the ranch, playing with her best friend—a little dog named Fanny—or taking care of her sheep. Behind the barn was a vineyard, perhaps the remains of Samuel Levy's vines, although Carole thought her father had planted these. The children helped with the making of his red wine by stomping the grapes. Carole remembered sometimes on nippy winter mornings being given a little warmed-up sweet red wine. The full wine barrels were stored in the bunkhouse, and as teenagers her older brothers secretly siphoned off a jug occasionally to share with friends in town. To evade their parents' notice, they would push the car out of the driveway and then pile in as it headed downhill on the Levy grade before they turned on the ignition.

George died in 1969 and Nonnie in 1986. Before her death, Nonnie sold the property in section 20, and later—as partial settlement of her estate—her heirs sold more land, including the Cardoza homestead on section 24, to the East Bay Regional Park District, greatly enlarging the infant Morgan Territory Regional Preserve. An overnight backpacking campground is planned near the house site on section 24. At present George and Nonnie Cardoza's youngest son, Russ, and his family live at the Levy ranch. Carole married Michael Murray, descendant of one of the first Irish settlers in the nearby Dublin area. They recently built a modern home in the hills not far from the Levy. Four generations of Cardozas have lived and worked in the Black Hills surrounded by the beauty of this "*terra santa*," this holy land.

1 Carlos Almeida, *Portuguese Immigrants* (San Leandro, CA: U.P.E.C., 1978) 2.

2 Francis M. Rogers, *Atlantic Islanders of the Azores and Madeiros* (North Quincy, MA: Christopher Pub House, 1979) 345, 347.

3 Jerry R. Williams, *And Yet They Come* (NY: Center for Migration Studies, 1982) 67.

4 August M. Vaz, *The Portuguese in California* (Oakland, CA: I.D.E.S., 1965) 64.

5 Karana Hattersley-Drayton, "Morgan Territory: Interview with Ida (Cardoza) Taylor," for the East Bay Regional Park District, 2960 Peralta Oaks Ct., Oakland, CA 94605, 12 July 1996: 2.

6 Hattersley-Drayton 4.

7 The names used are the Americanized spellings. *Joseph* was originally *José*; *Cardoza* was *Cardoso*; *Bent* was *Bento*; *Nunez* was *Nunes*.

8 Robert L. Santos, *Azoreans to California* (Denair, CA: Alley-Cass, 1995) 38.

9 Frederick G. Bohme, "The Portuguese in California," *California Historical Society Quarterly* 35 (1956): 240.

10 Norman E. Tutorow, *Leland Stanford: Man of Many Careers* (Menlo Park, CA: Pacific Coast, 1971) 186.

11 Bohme 242.

12 San Francisco General Land Office, Cash Entry 10566, National Archives, DC.

13 Homestead and citizenship information in San Francisco General Land Office, Homestead File 5994 at National Archives, DC.

14 The 10 children of Joseph and Lucy Cardoza, from oldest to youngest, are Maria (Mary), George A., Joseph H., Margaret H., Henry F., Maria (Minnie), Adelina, Ida Isabel, Edward, and Rose C. Thornton K. Taylor died in Livermore 15 Oct 1998.

15 "Special Notices," *Livermore Echo* 11 June 1903: 3.

16 Jack Gleese, letter, 29 Oct 1996.

17 Hattersley-Drayton 14.

18 Antoinette Morris, personal interview, 9 Sep 1996.

19 "Holy Ghost Will Begin Tonight," *The Livermore Herald* 3 June 1915: 1.

20 Madeline Henry in *People, Bricks and Timbers: The Story of St. Michael's Parish*, 1978: 35.

21 Madeline Henry in *People, Bricks* 35.

22 Hattersley-Drayton 25.

23 Hattersley-Drayton 29.

a Rogers 329.

b Hattersley-Drayton 46.

Three Brothers

THE TIME-HONORED method for immigrants to surround themselves with familiar language and faces is to save money not merely for their own advancement but to bring relatives to the new land. The Bent Nunez family lived in the village of Velas, the largest settlement on São Jorge in the Azores, located near the island's northern tip.[1] Antone Bent Nunez[2] left his native São Jorge at about age 25 and according to census records settled in California in 1870. By 1874 he had evidently saved enough money to return to the Azores, marry Justina Candida,[3] and bring her—along with his two younger brothers and

Joseph Cardoza—back to California. On 26 December 1874 "Antone Bento" bought 90 acres of land in section 6 T2S/R2E from Absalom José. The 1885 tax assessor listed Antone Bent Nunes in Highland School District as owner of the NE¼ of section 6 and the possessor of one horse, a wagon, two colts, three cows, three calves, and 700 sheep. In the same year Antone registered his brand AB with the county.

Although Victorine Road is paved now, not so long ago it was a dirt track that continued farther than the present paved portion, weaving its way into the Black Hills and eventually intersecting

Manuel and Maria Bent Nunez, about 1891, with children (front row, l. to r.) Isabella, Marian, Mary; (back row, l. to r.) Mabel, Annie, Maria, Rose, and Manuel Jr. Photo courtesy of Fred Bloching.

with Morgan Territory Road. Antone Nunez and his family lived about 1.5 miles north on Victorine from its junction with Highland Road. His children attended Highland School; in 1890 Lucy, May, Rosa, and Tony were on the teacher's roll. Sometime during her childhood, Lucy was in a surrey accident up in the hills. Her daughter Ida had heard the story: "Oh, I remember Mama talking in the Black Hills, something frightened the horses and the surrey tipped over and she had a scar on her head . . . that she got at that time. Her head hit a rock and she had quite a scar on her head from that fall."[4]

Tax assessment for the Antone Bente Nunez family in 1903 listed among other items 45 stock cattle, six horses, and 25 calves as well as a sewing machine. Ida Cardoza Taylor remembered her grandfather as quite tall and a bit of a dandy on his trips into town, when he proudly wore a black coat and rode his beautiful black saddle horse.

In the traditional Azorean family the husband was dominant and the wife was kept secluded.[5] In the much freer American society, this archetype caused stress. Antone and his wife did not get along well, and Justina sued for divorce on the basis of cruelty, one of the few grounds for divorce at the time. Justina moved into Livermore but Antone stayed at the ranch. "Grandpa used to stop by and say hello but he didn't live with her. . . . I think he was kind of a rascal," Ida recalled with a little smile.[6]

In October 1911 Antone had 75 head of cattle grazing on pasture belonging to John Gleese, but the livestock disappeared. When his son Manuel came by to see his father, Antone accused him of taking his mother's side and stealing the cattle. Manuel, on the other hand, thought his father, in agreeing to the divorce settlement, had given away cattle and property belonging to Manuel.[7] The two men fought, and Manuel beat his father badly. John Gleese and another rancher happened by, stopped Manuel, and turned him over to Sheriff R.R. Veale, who booked him at the

Martinez jail for attempted murder.[8] On November 9 the court acquitted Manuel of the charge.

Antone had been gradually accruing more property; in 1901 he bought additional acreage in section 6 T2S/R2E from Henry Burton for $1,000, and in 1902 Rosa Azevedo sold him 80 acres in the NE¼ of section 8 T2S/R2E. He acquired 324 acres of the west half of section 5 from Mary Ives Crocker in 1903. In November 1911, not long after the fight with his son Manuel, Antone sold these properties to his wife for $8,000, presumably as part of their divorce settlement. He bought the Levy ranch in 1913 and probably moved there, but later sold it to Manuel Bettencourt.

The 1920 U.S. census listed Antone alone in Livermore at a house he owned on North K Street. Eventually he lived with his daughter Lucy on the Cardoza "corner ranch," where he died in 1939 at the age of 94. Justina had died 12 years before. His son Tony died very young, in 1911. The three daughters all married local ranchers.

The tax assessment of 1885 listed Antone as owner of 700 sheep, but by 1893 he was running cattle solely. Sheep require considerably more work than cattle. The fences must have extra wire, and sheep are more susceptible to attacks from coyotes and dogs. The predators do not bloody that many sheep; however, the flock panics easily, and the sheep will sometimes pile up against a fence and smother each other. They are tamer than cattle, but troublesome in lambing season when ranchers must be watchful, especially of yearlings frightened by their first experience of birth. Twins are a frequent occurrence; sometimes the ewe rejects one, which means the rejected lamb must be bottle-fed. Today no one in Morgan Territory raises large numbers of sheep. The local wool market is not very strong, so sheep are raised almost entirely for meat.

The second Nunez brother, Joseph Bent Nunez, was born on São Jorge about 1852. The

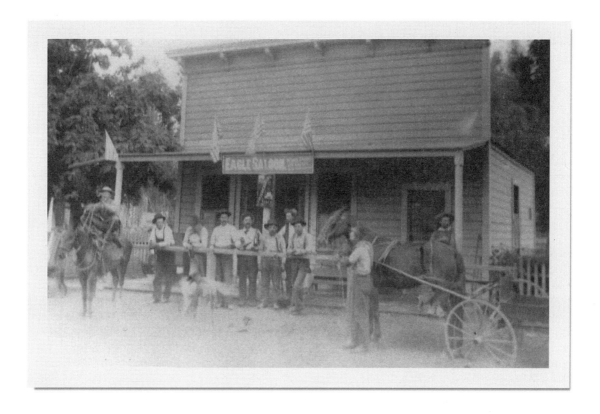

The Eagle Saloon, Clayton, c. 1909. William R. Bloching, son-in-law of Manuel Bent Nunez, is at far left in the group of men standing at the hitching post. Photo courtesy of Fred Bloching.

Contra Costa County Great Register of Voters of 1892 listed him as five feet four inches tall, with gray eyes and black hair. His first land record, following his probable 1874 arrival in Contra Costa County, was an 1877 deed, showing that he bought 160 acres in section 14 T1S/R1E from Jacob W. Harlan for $1,500. In 1897, however, this same acreage was set aside by the courts as a homestead for his brother Manuel Bent Nunez.[9] Joseph settled on the SE¼ of section 12 T1S/R1E. On his land office proof in December 1884, he listed improvements: a house, corral, well, and brush fence, and a quarter of a mile of graded road. The proof described the land as "rough and fit only for grazing." He paid $400 for the 160 acres. Joseph S. Cardoza, one of his witnesses, testified that he had known Joseph Bent Nunez "ever since I can remember."[10] Joseph Nunez and his brother Antone became U.S. citizens on 21 December 1882, signing their naturalization papers with their marks.[11] Probably Joseph Nunez returned to the Azores in 1887 to marry and bring back his wife, Barbara de Jesus, since no local evidence of their marriage is available. Joseph Cardoza sold Nunez the SW¼ of section 12 T1S/R1E in 1903.

Great-granddaughter Norma Bloching Dempsey had heard the story of Maria Joseph Nunez:

"When [my great-grandmother] sailed from the Azores . . . it was in an old sailing vessel and probably steerage. There were not many ships coming to the island and the seas were very rough. [Great] Grandma Nunez cried every time she told of how her mother would walk down to the docks to bring fresh straw for her bed when she was waiting to sail. She never saw her mother again." [a]

The tax assessor in 1892 listed Joseph Bente Nunez with a thriving ranch, including two wagons, five horses, two colts, seven cows, 12 calves, 24 stock cattle, 12 beef cattle, eight hogs, and poultry. Access to his property was possible from Marsh Creek Road along Sycamore Creek or from Morgan Territory Road through his brother's section 14. Under a large sheltering oak, the isolated cabin of the family stood near the bank of Sycamore Creek, about 1.5 miles east from Morgan Territory Road. Two rock cellar walls and a 10-foot well are still there, along with rusty water pipes and a structure damming the creek. The 1900 census listed Joseph and his wife and seven children in Morgan Territory. By 1908 tax assessments showed that he owned all of section 12 except the NW¼, which contains Sycamore Springs.

By 1912 the family had moved to Newman, a small farming town in the Central Valley near Modesto.[12] In November 1917 they sold their Contra Costa County property. The 1920 U.S. census listed the family plus a daughter-in-law and two grandchildren on a Holstein dairy farm that they owned near Newman. Their second son, Joseph Jr., left a will probated in November 1916 that showed he owned a dairy farm of 165 acres near Newman valued at $2,000, with probable yearly income of $200.[13] This branch of the family followed a major shift in Portuguese migration between 1900 and 1930 in California—from coastal settlement to dairy farms in the Central Valley.[14] Dairying had been an important industry on São Jorge, so probably Joseph Bent Nunez and his wife Barbara had learned the necessary skills early in life.

According to author Jerry R. Williams, the typical California-Azorean dairy farmer lived an isolated rural life: "Their inability to speak English made little difference in the daily life of running a dairy; tied to the farm by the necessity of milking the animals both morning and night, they seldom needed to communicate with anyone other than hired hands, who inevitably were Portuguese themselves, and the cows, who produced milk regardless of what language the dairymen spoke."[15] By 1923, 85 percent of the dairymen in Merced and Stanislaus County in the Central Valley were Portuguese.[16] Joseph died in Stanislaus County in 1926 at age 73. Dorenda Bloching Giovanni remembered visiting her cousins in Newman in the 1920s "in the dead of winter. And you know the cars didn't have heaters. So my mother used to heat up a brick and wrap it in a towel and put it in the back seat with me."[17]

After his arrival in this country about 1874, the third brother, Manuel Bent Nunez—three years younger than Joseph—first appeared in Contra Costa County records as the bridegroom of Maria Joseph at St. Catherine of Siena church in Martinez on 26 July 1879. Manuel's wife was the sister of Joseph Souza Cardoza. Manuel had saved enough money to pay for her passage by ship to America; Maria disembarked at New York City and rode by train to California. At the time of their marriage, Manuel was 25 and Maria was 30.[18]

With his friend Joseph Cardoza, Manuel

Nunez purchased property in 1885 on section 24 T1S/R1E, but he sold his interest in it to Cardoza in 1896. At first Manuel and his family lived in Clayton, but sometime before 1892 he had acquired property in section 14 T1S/R1E, north from the Cardozas on Morgan Territory Road. The tax assessment included one acre of vines, an acre and a half of fruit trees, three wagons, four horses, three colts, one cow, one hog, and chickens. Manuel was also running 130 stock cattle on section 24 with Joseph Cardoza, and on section 23, which Manuel was renting. During the years 1893 through 1896, the student body of Summit School included 10 children from the families of Joseph and Manuel Nunez.[19] The year 1902 must have been a very good one for Manuel. In September he bought an additional 480 acres of section 14 from Louisa and Jeremiah Morgan for $3,500; in November he bought eight town lots in Clayton from C. Rhine Company. His ranch home on section 14 was one-story, with a pitched roof and a front porch. It was destroyed by arsonists in 1945.

The Contra Costa County Great Register of Voters described Manuel as a little taller than Joseph at five feet six, also with gray eyes and black hair. He became a U.S. citizen on 28 April 1888. His two witnesses were Morgan Territory Road neighbors Alexander Norman and Jerry Morgan.[20] By the 1900 census, Manuel and Maria Nunez had eight children. Section 14 was in Summit School District, and their son Manuel graduated from Summit School in 1897.[21] Their daughters married local residents of Morgan Territory, Clayton, and Concord. Annie married John J. Morris; Marian married Benjamin Guirado Jr.; Mabel married Otto Schwartz, and Mary wed William R. Bloching. Isabel married Laurence V. Perry. Manuel and Maria Nunez's younger son, Tony, lived barely a year, and their older son, Manuel, died in his early thirties.

Manuel Bent Nunez and his son-in-law William R. Bloching ran the Eagle Saloon in

"My grandfather built all those bridges on that road"

Fred Bloching often drove his grandfather Manuel Nunez to the Morgan Territory ranch in the family buggy, fording the creek before the bridges were built. "There wasn't much of a road then—just a mud hole." Later he and his grandfather worked on the road for the county. "My grandfather built all those bridges on that road— he built them all. He was good at pilin' rocks. You know, he could stack rocks. . . . He could really make a rock wall good and not use any cement— stack 'em in there. They're still there in those bridges." [b]

One member of a pioneer Clayton family recalled that whenever his father needed a stone wall on his ranch, he would hire Manuel Nunez because of Manuel's expertise in placing the stones, a skill probably acquired on São Jorge, where farmers cleared and fenced their rocky fields by erecting stone walls. [c]

Clayton for a while, beginning about 1909. Fred Bloching has one particular vivid image of his father's management: "Those . . . miners used to raise hell in the saloon. I was just a kid about this big and a guy came in there one day and started raisin' Cain, and my dad told him to knock it off. He wouldn't do it, so my dad walked out around the bar and hit him like this [demonstrates an uppercut], threw him out the door, the double doors. The doors were going like this [flapping back and forth]."[22] At his Main Street butcher shop in Clayton, Manuel Nunez sold beef that he raised at his ranch property in Morgan Territory; also at times he supplied meat to the Rhine store. In 1912 he bought a town lot in Concord from F.W. Foskett and his wife, Alice, on the condition

Fred Bloching with his children Barbara and Dennis,
c. 1949, at the original Nunez house on section 14.
Photo courtesy of Fred Bloching.

that he not run a saloon business there. Manuel's great-granddaughter believed that he had an additional butcher shop in Concord; perhaps it was at this location.[23]

When their children were grown, Manuel and Maria Nunez moved into Clayton, where the census taker recorded them in 1920. The Blochings lived for a number of years with them at their home in Clayton, and the Blochings' children Fred and Dorenda have many fond memories of their grandparents. Manuel and Maria's first Clayton home burned in 1928, probably as a result of faulty wiring. Neighbors managed to save their rosewood piano, but nothing else. Dorenda had been in Oakland during the fire, and although only six years old at the time, she still remembers returning to Clayton to discover that the single identifiable item of her belongings was the handle of her wicker doll buggy "sticking up out of the ashes."[24] Manuel

immediately hired carpenters to rebuild. The family lived temporarily in the Eagle Saloon building; the saloon was not in business then.

In her later years Mary Nunez "suffered like Bernadette,"[25] from painful abscesses on her lower legs, but she nevertheless kept busy helping in the household—sewing clothes, carding wool, churning butter, and assisting with the cooking. Granddaughter Dorenda remembered her making traditional *morcela* (blood sausage) and *linguiça*. Mary enjoyed listening to the mandolin-accented strains of Portuguese music over the radio.

After he suffered a stroke, Manuel would often call Dorenda over to his corner of the living room. "He'd say 'C'mon, c'mon.' He'd want to play casino. He loved to play cards." When she was ill, her grandfather prescribed his special medicine. "I remember when I had a cold, my grandfather (they'd probably put him in jail now) would fix me a little glass of warm red wine, and he'd put cinnamon and lemon in it. And he'd make me drink it."[26] Manuel made his own wine from vineyards on his Morgan Territory ranch. "He had a cellar full of wine in wooden barrels."[27] In 1899 Manuel Nunez sued Charles Goethals for an unpaid bill of $65.50 owed for 3,588 bushels of wheat and 21 gallons of wine.[28] John Gleese leased Manuel's ranch for a while. Fred Bloching recalled, "I remember [John Gleese] comin' down [to Clayton] and talkin' to my grandfather. He'd come down and they'd talk for *hours*." Manuel died in Clayton in 1946 at age 91; his wife, Maria, had died in 1938.

The three Nunez brothers, Antone, Joseph, and Manuel, helped each other in tangible ways with immigration and naturalization, with land purchases, with mortgages, and probably with roundups and harvests. Impossible to measure, however, are the benefits of family emotional ties, mutual language, and inherited culture in a new and strange land.

1 Norma Bloching Dempsey, letter, 18 Dec 1996.

2 In California, the surnames are most often spelled *Bent* or *Bente Nunez*. Occasionally, the *Nunez* is dropped and the only surname used is *Bent*. Originally, however, the Azorean names were *Bento Nunes*.

3 In the birth records of her children at St. Michael's Catholic Church in Livermore, her surname is listed as *Candida*. On documents requiring her signature, it is often given as *Justina C. Nunes*. However, in her daughter's death record at St. Michael's, her name is listed as *Justine Texiera*.

4 Karana Hattersley-Drayton, "Morgan Territory: Interview with Ida (Cardoza) Taylor," for the East Bay Regional Park District, 2960 Peralta Oaks Ct., Oakland, CA 94605, 12 July 1996: 14.

5 Francis M. Rogers, *Atlantic Islanders of the Azores and Madeiras* (North Quincy, MA: Christopher Pub House, 1979) 54.

6 Hattersley-Drayton 7.

7 "Manuel Nunez Accused of Assaulting His Father," *Contra Costa Gazette* 21 Oct 1911: 1.

8 "Serious Ending to Family Quarrel," *The Livermore Herald* 21 Oct 1911: 1.

9 *Contra Costa County Deed Book* 78: 58.

10 San Francisco General Land Office, Cash Entry 10565, National Archives, DC.

11 Contra Costa County Superior Court Naturalizations, Book 1: 144, 145.

12 According to U.P.E.C. records. U.P.E.C. is a Portuguese fraternal organization based in San Leandro with 173 councils in 1978. They keep accurate records and offer insurance to their members. Carlos Almeida, *Portuguese Immigrants* (San Leandro, CA: U.P.E.C., 1978).

13 Stanislaus County Superior Court, Probate Record filed 2 Dec 1915.

14 Jerry R. Williams, *And Yet They Came* (N.Y.: Center for Immigration Studies, 1982) 42.

15 Williams 44.

16 Williams 44.

17 Dorenda Bloching Giovanni, personal interview, 21 Jan 1997.

18 Laurine Boissonon, letter, 12 Sep 1997.

19 Summit School District Souvenir, Nina McPherson, teacher.

20 Contra Costa County Superior Court Naturalizations, Book 2: 42.

21 Bernard Freedman, compiler, *Schools in Contra Costa County,* 1996.

22 Fred Bloching, personal interview, 21 Jan 1997.

23 Dempsey letter.

24 Dorenda Bloching Giovanni, phone conversation, 29 Jan 1997.

25 Giovanni interview.

26 Giovanni interview.

27 Bloching interview.

28 Contra Costa County Justice Court, Sixth Township, #2061, 21 Dec 1899.

a Dempsey letter.

b Bloching interview.

c George Frank, Oldtimers' Luncheon, 7 Oct 1996 at Clayton Museum, sponsored by the Clayton Historical Society.

Will Dias on Mighty Mouse, at the Livermore Rodeo, 1951. Courtesy of Marge and Will Dias.

A Pair of Rodeo Cowboys

RODEO TRADITIONS of the early California ranchos gradually developed into the western rodeo entertainment of today. Livermore sponsored its first official city rodeo in 1918, to meet its World War I assessment of $1,200 for the Red Cross. This first of a decades-long tradition was held on James Anderson's ranch, near what is now the Portola Avenue on-ramp to Interstate 580, "because there was a natural basin for holding stock and a rim that served as elevated seating for the spectators."[1] The Anderson ranch house had originally been the home of Robert Livermore on his *Rancho Las Positas*.

The first rodeo was so successful that local enthusiasts formed the Livermore Stockman's Rodeo Association, in April 1919. The founders sold shares at $25 each and purchased 15 acres in central Livermore, where they built a grandstand and bleachers. By 3 July 1919, 2,400 seats were ready, and the second rodeo took place on the site of what is now the Livermore City Hall and Police Station. Early rodeos in Livermore were celebrated near the Fourth of July holiday and had a definite Spanish influence. Later, because of the midsummer heat, sponsors changed the date to the second weekend in June.

On 4 July 1923 towheaded Johnie Schneider,[2] 19-year-old son of a Stockton area rancher, came in sixth in the saddle bronc contest at Livermore and started an amazing, versatile career in rodeo. For the next 10 years, he garnered a share of the money in every rodeo he entered. His numerous titles included World Champion All-around Cowboy in 1931, World Champion Bull Rider in 1929, 1930, and 1932, Best All-around Cowboy in Australia, 1935–36, and the Hawaiian Islands' Top Cowboy in 1939. Bronc riding, bareback riding, bull riding, steer decorating, relay races, pony express races, single and team roping, bull-dogging—he competed in every one. In the 1930

Livermore rodeo program, the name of Johnie Schneider appeared 24 times, and he placed in all but four events. Only five foot six, Johnie had a compact, quick, lithe body that helped him in the competitions. M.M. Hightower wrote in *Hoofs and Horns,* "At a rodeo he did just about everything but drive the water wagon and if they had made this a contest event he, undoubtedly, would have been up there, reins in hand and with the familiar gleam in his eye."[3] Johnie even competed in Roman racing, during which he rode standing on two horses at once. The *Prorodeo Sports News* reported that Johnie was "so strong he could do three chin-ups while holding the bar with only the middle finger of his right hand."[4] His son Tim agreed and recalled the unusually large hands and fingers of his father.[5]

In 1931, after marrying "the prettiest girl in Livermore"[6]—Julia Frates, daughter of Highland Road rancher Thomas Frates—Johnie rented a ranch house from the Morris family on the east half of section 14 T1S/R1E along Morgan Territory Road. Portuguese rancher Manuel Bent Nunez had bought the property in the 1890s and built the house. His daughter Annie Morris had inherited part of his property. Julia and Johnie's first child, John T. Schneider, born in 1932, remembers with fondness and considerable clarity of detail living in the old house until 1939.[7] He described the house as having no indoor plumbing. The family had to use the usual outhouse, and an outdoor faucet yielded cold spring water. Everyone took a bath in a big round washtub with water heated on the stove. A well was on the property; however, it wasn't used for water but for cooling purposes. John remembered his mother lowering Jell-O down into the well so that it would congeal. That memory offers a clue that no electricity existed at the site. Manuel Nunez had built the house near a hillside, which

In *Popular Science Monthly* Johnie Schneider wrote about what it took to compete in rodeo:

"All the cowboys are, of course, good riders. They have good wind, are well-knit, and strong. . . . Most of us train intensively a few weeks before the season opens in February and the work keeps us in shape until it closes the following December. We need plenty of reserve strength if we expect to rope a calf, milk a wild cow, ride a wild bronco without a bridle, ride a ranting Brahma steer without a saddle, ride a wild horse with neither saddle nor bridle and, for good measure, decorate or bull-dog a steer—all in one afternoon." [a]

meant that goats could and did jump from the hill onto the roof. Julia Schneider cooked on a wood stove in winter and a gas stove in summer. The house had wooden floors covered with Indian blankets. When Julia comforted her son in the rocking chair, floorboards creaked a loud lullaby. On visits to other homes, quiet floors did not seem natural to him.

When not traveling on the rodeo circuit, Johnie Schneider practiced every day. His son John hated that part of ranch living. His father and his father's partner got to ride horses, but John had to negotiate calves into the chute, and the men often yelled at him. Perhaps as a result of this early indoctrination, he never had the inclination to participate in rodeo. One important form of Johnie's physical training was jumping rope, even on all fours.

Johnie and his partner used a spring tooth harrow to break up the dirt clods in their roping arena. Raking yielded many obsidian arrowheads, some black, some light-colored, some with transparent stripes. A few were larger than the others—perhaps spear points. Mortars and pestles

were common finds. A mortar caught dripping water at the ranch for the chickens and dogs.

Although he did not care for rodeo practices, John loved living close to nature on the isolated ranch. Socializing by telephone was not possible—no wires had been strung in that section. Johnie Schneider kept a serviceable pickup truck because he had to haul horses, and on Sundays the family would drive down what was then a dirt and gravel road to Livermore to attend early Catholic mass at St. Michael's, to buy a *San Francisco Examiner,* and to visit relatives. As always, such a trip was no easy feat in the rainy season.

In 1934-35 Johnie Schneider introduced American-style rodeo to Australia, traveling to Sydney, Melbourne, and other cities on an eight-month tour. The highlight of the visit was participation of Johnie and other Americans in the Melbourne Royal Agriculture Show. Johnie transported not only his fellow riders but also horses from California because Aussie thoroughbreds were too light to push cattle around. With an instinct for more than entertainment, Johnie used the rodeo to promote the horse of the American West and later bought and sold horses that were shipped to Australia.[8] He followed up the Australian tour with a similar trip to Hawaii in 1939. And in the 1936 or 1937 rodeo season, according to neighbor Richard Lawrence, Johnie built a wind screen in his green Chevy half-ton truck and drove his horse all the way to Madison Square Garden to compete.[9]

When Johnie hung up his rodeo spurs in 1941, he had achieved his lifelong aim of being able to buy a ranch. Even during the Depression, he had managed to earn $7,000 to $8,000 yearly, more than enough to save up for his goal. "My real dream was to own my own ranch. I wanted a normal family life, a wife, daughters I could pamper and sons I could teach to ride and work good horses and cattle. That's what I wanted and those are the things rodeo gave me." [10]

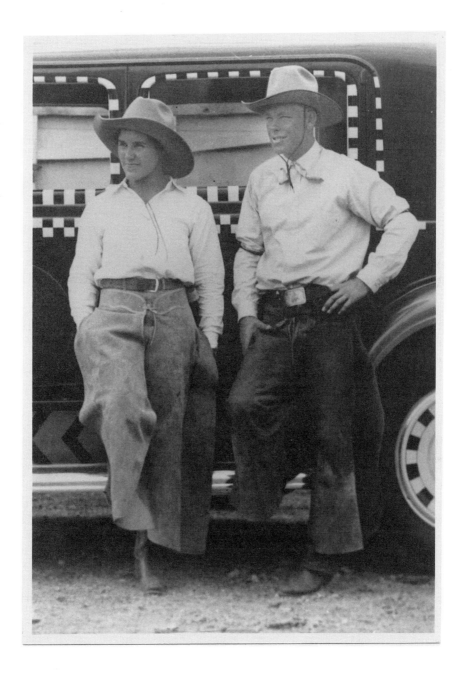

Johnie and Julia Frates Schneider. Courtesy of Livermore Heritage Guild.

The family's new property was at Elk Grove, near Sacramento. After the move Johnie qualified as a California state brand inspector and continued in this position until his retirement in 1969. Julia died at age 36 from cancer and was buried at St. Michael's Cemetery in Livermore. Later Johnie remarried, moved to a 30-acre ranch near Salinas, and had twin sons, Tim and Tom, in addition to John, James, and Mary, the three children by his first wife. He never gave up his interest in rodeo, however. His second wife, Bernice, recalled that on their wedding day, 23 June 1951, he was a judge at the Salinas rodeo.[11] He also continued his connection with the Livermore rodeo, visiting each year and serving as grand marshal of the rodeo parade in 1964.

Bernice and his friends described Johnie as a man with a wonderful outgoing personality who loved to tell stories and jokes, reminiscing about his rodeo days. "Many still consider him world class, but now his field is story telling," a reporter wrote about him in 1982.[12] He never fit the stereotypical rough, tough image of a lonesome cowboy but was a warm, sensitive person who enjoyed his family and even wrote poetry and short stories about his experiences.

Children seemed to be especially drawn to him and his rodeo career. The children of neighboring ranches along Morgan Territory Road were no exception. Omery Smith remembered as a child how thrilled he felt whenever he was allowed to watch Johnie practice at the Collins' corrals, now the parking lot of the Morgan Territory Preserve. Johnie took time to teach young Jack Gleese how to rope with the tied-hard-and-fast method used in rodeo calf-roping, with a short lariat tied to the saddle horn. Queried over the phone about his childhood memories of Johnie, Richard Lawrence replied that he was at that moment looking at the pair of spurs that Johnie had given him in 1934. They had been made for Johnie in Australia because his gear had been stolen.[13] In 1932 the city of

Livermore invited its youngsters to join the "Johnie Schneider Club" by paying a fee of one coin—it could be from a penny up to a quarter. Contributions totaled $115. The children participating rode in a wagon with Johnie in the rodeo parade, and the city presented him with a silver cup bought with the donations from the children. "The mob was so great that the parade watchers couldn't see Johnie because of the kids piled all over him."[14]

A statue of Johnie Schneider is at the new rodeo grounds at Robertson Park in Livermore, and he was elected to the Cowboy Hall of Fame in 1965. He died in 1982. At his request, he was buried in Livermore at St. Michael's Cemetery beside Julia, his first love. His plaque at the ProRodeo Hall of Fame in Colorado Springs reads: "Schneider had the soul of a poet and the heart of a cowboy."

Unlike Johnie Schneider, rodeo competitors today are more often specialists in one type of entry, just as the medical specialist has taken the place of the general practitioner. In *Popular Science Monthly,* Johnie noted, "Roping calves and steers may not excite the audiences as much as riding untamed horses, but I think it requires greater skill since we work against time."[15]

Besides doing some bronc riding, Morgan Territory cowboy Will Dias specialized in calf and team roping. Will's great-grandparents and one grandmother had immigrated to the Bay Area from São Jorge in the Azores, and Will's father continued the Azorean tradition of earning a living with farming and light dairying. Until 1929, Will's dad had a place near Dublin. Forced out by the Depression, he moved the family to Castro Valley but managed to rent grazing land on Crow Canyon Road.

The Dias family separated the milk they got from their cows, sold the cream to a creamery, and gave the skim milk to the hogs. Money from cream sales was the only cash they had in the winter. Times were hard, but Will recalled that the family ate well. "Nobody had any money, but nobody ate better than we did, I don't think. We had beef, we had chickens, we had ducks, and my dad used to kill two hogs ev'ry winter. They'd make four hams, four bacons, and then the part I didn't like. That was before they had freezers, so they put that meat in crocks, salted it, put another layer, put a little salt, a layer of salt. Oh God, I hated that salt pork. My poor mother, she'd take that pork out and then she'd put it in water, soak it, then she'd change the water the next day. She'd try to draw that salt out. It was terrible!"[16]

Finally, about 1936, the family bought a Kelvinator refrigerator, and Will's taste buds were no longer tortured with salt pork or warm milk. "Oh, that [cold milk] was good. I had a lotta people in my family they used to love to drink that milk warm from the cow, and I couldn't stand it. But after we got that 'frigerator, and we had cold milk, why then I started drinkin' milk."[17]

Will attended Hayward High, graduating in 1942. Students came from as far away as San Leandro and Niles, but the school still had only about 700 students. Here he met his future wife, Marge Wiles, when she was a freshman and he was a senior. "We've been goin' together ever since."[18] The first time Marge saw Will at Hayward High, he was on horseback.

"Well, heck, when I was just a high school kid," Will recalled, "I used to work on the threshing machines and hay presses from when I got outa school in June, for a dollar a day and board—and that was from five o'clock in the morning. We'd be comin' in an' havin' dinner at nine o'clock at night."[19]

Will's interest in rodeo developed naturally out of ranching and owning horses as he grew up. He practiced roping faithfully and kept his body in good shape with hard work. At age 77, he exercises daily with 100 push-ups and 25 chin-ups, and remains trim and wiry at five feet nine.

An early start

Will Dias recalled helping his father drive about 30 head of cattle plus six horses from Dublin through Norris Canyon to the property on Crow Canyon. While his father led the procession, blocking driveways in his 1926 Dodge, Will brought up the rear. He was six years old.

Never one for "boozin'," he has also been careful about his diet.

Will recalled that Harry Rowell, who owned a ranch along old Highway 50 (now Interstate 580), between Pleasanton and Castro Valley, bought horses from all over the West. As many as 50 railroad cars arrived in Livermore at once, Will said, filled with stock from as far away as Idaho and Oregon. After unloading the cars, Rowell's hands drove the assortment of mustangs and worn-out ranch horses 15 miles or so down Highway 50 to the ranch. The Calo dog food company bought many of the horses, but before that, Rowell tested them to find good buckers. He would phone young men—including Will— and invite them to ride the test horses for $2 a head. Rowell became one of the top rodeo stock suppliers in the country, while Will began to learn the art of bronc riding. When Will was about 17, former rider Perry Ivory took him in hand and gave him a number of pointers. However, Will never rode professionally until after his discharge from the Navy in 1946. "I started right after that, but I didn't have any money, so I hadda take it easy. It took money to get started, you know. I hadda buy horses and I hadda buy trailers."[20]

He and Morgan Territory neighbor Al Morris both were marked by growing up in the Depression era, Will said. "Al was just a plain guy. You know, he'd save two bits. He was like

After half a century, Will Dias still throws a wicked reata. *June 1999 photo by Don Homan.*

me, he was a Depression kid. Like I told myself, I says . . . when I get out of school and I get a job, I'm never goin' to be broke again!"[21] After his World War II service, Will went to work for the phone company at $30 a week and then in 1948 began to work for the East Bay Municipal Utility District, retiring in 1979. Remembering his Depression era lesson, he never quit his steady EBMUD job, but competed in rodeos on the side and saved his winnings. He entered about 25 or 30 rodeos a year along the West Coast all the way from Lakeview, Oregon, to Bakersfield, California. He was a consistent winner, but not of big money—he averaged $150 to $300 per rodeo. However, at a special roping event in King City in 1959, he and his partner won $1,800 apiece. They also won at Salinas that year.

In team roping Will always took on the more difficult role of the heeler, who has to rope the two hind feet of the steer. Usually, his header was his brother Melvin or his friend Leroy Gellerman. Telling of his bronc riding competition, Will remembered Hell Diver, a horse that no one was able to ride until Will stayed on him at the Sacramento rodeo in 1954. The ride was disappointing, though, Will said, because the horse did not buck very much that day. Another memorable rival, this time an excellent bucking horse, was Mighty Mouse. Will retired from bareback riding in 1959 but competed in roping until about 1990; he laughingly called roping "the old man's event."

Will and Marge were married soon after he left the Navy and lived in several places in the East Bay. They bought 60 acres in the Black Hills area from Joe Victorine in 1962. Part of their property includes the 20 acres that once belonged to the Androws family, and Will tore down their old barn and apple tree to make room for his and Marge's house. Will and Marge waited until 1984 to build the new house and moved in just before Christmas that year. Rarely sick, Will almost died of an aneurysm in 1995. Owing in part to quick and expert response from the volunteer fire company, which sent him flying off to the hospital in a helicopter, he survived. The Diases' daughter and son-in-law visit often, and Marge and Will enjoy babysitting their two grandchildren for several days at a time. Will usually trained his own quarter horses, and even now has a young horse that he has been working daily.

1 *Livermore Rodeo Program,* 1918-1993 Commemorative Issue: 26.

2 Johnie spelled his name with only one "n".

3 M.M. Hightower, "Former Champion Cowboy," *Hoofs and Horns* Nov 1953: 11.

4 *Prorodeo Sports News* 20 Apr 1992: 19.

5 Tim and Bernice Schneider, personal interview, 15 June 1996.

6 Hightower 11.

7 John T. Schneider, phone interview, 24 Sep 1995.

8 Bill Morgan, personal interview, 19 May 1997. "Pioneering Rodeos in Australia," *The Livermore Herald* 24 May 1935: 1,8.

9 Richard Lawrence, personal interview, 23 Feb 1999.

10 James Denison, "From the Arena to the Cowboy Hall of Fame," *The Sunday* [Monterey] *Peninsula Herald Weekend Magazine* 25 April 1982: 5.

11 Bernice Schneider, phone conversation, 21 April 1996.

12 Denison 3.

13 Lawrence, phone interview 23 Aug 1996; personal interview 23 Feb 1999.

14 *Livermore Rodeo Program* 40.

15 Johnie Schneider, "Ace Rodeo Rider Tells How He Tames Vicious Broncs," *Popular Science Monthly* Aug 1934: 26.

16 Will and Marge Dias, personal interview, 21 Sep 1996.

17 Dias interview.

18 Dias interview.

19 Dias interview.

20 Dias interview.

21 Dias interview.

a Schneider 107.

Lucy Correa Azevedo (Viera), proudly balanced on Grey Bob, c. 1915. Courtesy of Lucy Viera.

And What Are Little Girls Made Of?

MARIA THEREZA CARDOZA emigrated from the Azorean island of São Jorge to Boston in the late 1800s and then traveled cross-country to California, where she married Declusian "John" Silva, another Azorean.[1] He worked in Pleasanton as a paperhanger, but the couple lived on the old McGrew place on the north end of Morgan Territory Road, about six miles from Marsh Creek Road. Shortly before the birth of their second child in 1895, John died of pneumonia. The exact date is unknown, but his death occurred during the rainy season, and his body had to be brought down on a sled because the road was so muddy. Visiting physician Dr. George McKenzie declared, "Don't ever ask me up there again!"[2]

Left with two small daughters, Maria Thereza married Joseph Correa Azevedo, who had also emigrated from São Jorge. Their daughter Luzia (Lucy) described her father as a good, gentle man who was very strong physically and a hard worker, taking on the utmost exertion in order to become a property owner. A teenager who worked for him, amazed at his strength, asked Joseph how he could carry so many heavy fence posts at one time, and Joseph replied in his strongly accented English that they were "jus' pickets." Lucy remembered that her father bought cattle for $7 a head during a drought year when everyone wanted to sell. Natural grasses and sown crops had not sprouted, so he hauled hay—when he could find it—and feed by the wagonload. He made the feed himself by mixing straw, salt, molasses, and middlings (flour left over from milling). All the natural springs and creeks on the cattle range had dried up, so he also had to haul in water every day. When he finally sold the cattle, his profit was enough to pay $600 for the Haas ranch on section 20 T1N/R1E, on both sides of Marsh Creek Road.[3] The family soon included five girls and one boy. Their home

and barn were south of Marsh Creek Road, across from Rodie's Feed Store, but the buildings are gone now, destroyed by fire about 13 years ago.

Joseph Correa Azevedo died at age 47 in an accident near Martinez. His grandson, Everett Galvin, recalled hearing the story: "My grandfather was going down to Martinez driving two horses, pulling a wagon leading two other horses, going to deliver them to the Army. He raised lots of horses. Down by Muir Station, a train came around the bend, the horses spooked. The wagon overturned and went down the embankment."[4] A barrel of wine Joseph had been bringing to the station for shipment fell out of the wagon and struck him, fracturing his skull and breaking his neck.[5]

That evening, 4 March 1909, a Martinez undertaker named J.J. Hauser came to the Correa Azevedo ranch and—with the help of an interpreter—informed Maria Thereza of her husband's death. Since Hauser had possession of Joseph's body in Martinez, he insisted that he should be in charge of the funeral and attempted to coerce the widow into choosing a coffin.

Friends Manuel and Maria Bent Nunez came to the Correa Azevedo ranch to comfort the family and just missed Hauser. Maria Thereza told them of the encounter and asked Nunez to deal with Hauser because she wanted Henry Curry, a different Martinez undertaker whom she knew well, to be in charge of the funeral arrangements for her husband. Hauser refused to give up the body to Curry, however, and started back to the widow in Clayton with the body in his wagon. With the intervention of Nunez, Sheriff R.R. Veale, and Justice of the Peace Gus Goethals, Hauser was finally stopped, and Joseph Correa Azevedo's body was transferred to Curry's establishment. Hauser returned to the Correa Azevedo ranch the next day, stating his willingness to

Maria Thereza Correa Azevedo's court testimony was translated and published in the *Contra Costa Gazette*:

"I was prostrated with grief at the sudden news of the death of my husband, and told [the undertaker] Mr. Hauser that I did not know what to do but that I would wait until my brother-in-law, Antone C[orrea] Azevedo, came home before I could do anything. He told me that clothes would have to be placed upon my husband that night or they could not be placed upon him at all. . . . He brought out a book showing coffins and prices and told me to pick out one. I told him to wait, that I did not want to do anything until my brother-in-law came home. He asked me if I cared to spend $150 to bury my husband. I told him yes, that I would expend that amount of money. He asked me how I wanted my husband buried. I told him I wanted him decently buried in a nice suit of black clothes but I told him not to do anything until my brother-in-law would come. So he drove away."[a]

reduce the funeral price. When the Correa Azevedo family again refused his services, he insisted that they owed him $50.[6] Curry's Undertaking Parlors conducted the funeral. Joseph's tombstone at St. Stephen's Cemetery in Concord reads, "Closed are thy sweet eyes from this world of pain, but we trust in God to meet thee again."

The 1909 court-ordered inventory of the property belonging to Joseph Correa Azevedo showed that at his death he owned 1,045 acres of land, worth more than $6,000,[7] much of it along Morgan Territory Road.

Joseph's brother Antone had also immigrated and had been working with Joseph on their prop-

erties up in Morgan Territory. At the time of the death of his brother, Antone was a widower with four children. He had remarried, but that marriage had ended in divorce. Two years after Joseph's death, Maria Thereza married her brother-in-law, creating a combined family of 12 children, including two orphaned girls she had adopted. Lucy was not happy with this marital arrangement because her uncle, now her stepfather, was nothing like his gentle younger brother. Antone Correa Azevedo drank heavily, and his wife and children knew him as often cranky and mean. Before his divorce from his second wife, the local newspaper alleged, he had "frequently blackened her eyes and beat her. . . ."[8] Lucy said, "He was no angel, I tell you. I don't know whether he went to heaven or not."[9] Antone would drive into Concord in a cart pulled by a little white mule and, according to Fred Bloching, "get loaded to the gills. They'd take him and set him in the cart, hit the mule on the rump, and the mule would take him all the way to Clayton, just trottin' along on the right side of the road with the lines draggin' on the ground, take him right into the ranch and stop. He was drunker than a lord. I seen him."[10]

Lucy was the youngest and, at not quite five feet tall, the smallest of the 12 children, and although now in her late 90s, she is still eager to share stories of old days on the ranch. Lucy loved the outdoors and was permitted to spend every spare moment outside. With six older sisters helping her mother with the usual female tasks, Lucy was free to follow her inclination—which among other things meant she learned to ride at age five.

On a typical Saturday morning, Lucy rose before five o'clock. She helped one of her brothers milk the cows and feed the orphaned calves her stepfather had bought from a dairy. After eating a hearty breakfast with the family and four hired men, most likely syrup-covered pancakes and pinto beans flavored with ham, she headed with

The Correa Azevedo corral on section 10, in 1997. Photo by Anne Homan.

eager steps toward the horse barn. Warned by the creak of the barn door, the little bay mare Daisy greeted her with soft whinnies from the pungent darkness. The horse stood quietly as Lucy put on the well-worn western saddle. Trained by Lucy's brothers, the mare was an excellent cow pony.

Her brothers would already have saddled up and been talking to their father; now they called out to Lucy, "Hey, Shrimp, aren't you ready yet?" A miniature version of her brothers in her jeans and work shirt, Lucy led the mare outside and swung up into the saddle. The young cowpokes headed up Marsh Creek Road toward Morgan Territory to check on fences and the water situation for the cattle. Usually they ran about 500 head. In spite of his heavy drinking, Antone Correa Azevedo managed a successful cattle operation.

Lucy's daily chores involved the many animals raised on the farm: geese, turkeys, rabbits, chickens. "There was always somethin' to do—there was no time for just play."[11] Her son-in-law's nickname for Lucy is "Weasel." "He gave me that name 'cause . . . I weaseled out of a lotta things."[12] On school mornings, one of Lucy's chores was to let the mother hen and her half-dozen chicks out of their small shed and feed them. One morning she completely forgot to care for the birds: "That's all I could think about in school. When I got home I went right to see 'em, and they were all dead. It had been a hot, hot day. I cried. I must have been 10, 12 years old. I thought, I'm going to get a lickin.' So, I took and cut a little bit on each one's neck, just a little bit, and scattered them around like it had been a weasel that got 'em."[13] She took the hen and hooked it on a

Zebra Trick-or-Treat

Lucy Correa Viera remembers that her step-father never let the children go anywhere, and she was frequently bored. One Halloween she decided to create some fun on her own with the little white mule, Pancho. "There was a brand new bottle of black ink, and I made a little dauber of a little piece of cloth." She climbed out the window and very quietly picked her way to Pancho's stall, the last one in the barn.

"So I took the mule outside, waited till the moon came up, and I made a zebra out of him. Cutest thing you ever saw. Had eyelashes! Beautiful! I sat there and laughed, enjoyed doing it. Put it back in the barn. And in the morning I happened to stay in bed just a little later. They came and called me and said, "Come and see the old man's mule! You oughta see the old man's mule! He's so painted and he looks so cute." Well, I thought I'd better get up with the rest of them, 'cause if I wasn't there, he'd think I was up to somethin'. Put my hands in my pockets and sat and laughed with them. When he got up, well, the best part was, he blamed the saloonkeeper, old Berenson. And he also blamed Mrs. Keller, who was an artist. That's when I felt, well geez, I done real good.

"He hitched him up and took him to town [Concord] and the kids down there, they got the biggest kick out of him. They borrowed him to drive him up and down the street." [b]

board fence near a hole so that it seemed to have attempted escape from the weasel's attack. When her mother investigated and decided a weasel had done the damage, Lucy "didn't say anything. She never knew. I'd always get myself out of stuff."[14]

She even generously helped her siblings to weasel out of mischief. Her mother had warned the children not to climb the fig tree in August because the sap was down and the branches brittle. Nevertheless, Lucy's stepbrother Manuel did climb the tree, and a branch broke off. With a mixture of dirt and water, Lucy painted the torn spot so it did not look fresh. Then the two of them dragged the broken branch far away down to the creek, and no one ever suspected what had happened. Lucy's younger daughter, Mary, laughingly asserted, "We could never get away with anything 'cause she already did it!"[15]

Elementary schools in those days did not include kindergarten; however, Lucy begged so hard that school officials allowed her to begin first grade at age five. One day she was glad to catch a ride home in the buckboard of a neighbor, but when his horse fell, Lucy was thrown out and broke her arm. She could not finish the school term. Her arm healed after a fashion, but the next year it had to be rebroken and straightened. Although she loved school and had completed requirements by 1914 for her eighth-grade graduation from Mount Diablo School in Clayton, Lucy left to work on the family ranch without waiting for her diploma. "I had to help the boys and I never went back."[16]

She recalled that the school had two rooms—one for students grades five through eight and one for younger classes. Discipline included getting her hands whacked with a ruler for whispering and for putting her wrists down on her paper while writing. Her least favorite teacher was Miss Chapman in grade three. Spelling had always been Lucy's downfall, and she missed 18 out of 50 words on a big spelling test. Miss Chapman made her write the 18 words correctly 500 times each.[17] At a special celebration during the Camellia Tea sponsored by the Clayton Historical Society in February 1996, Lucy finally accepted her grammar school diploma. With the sense of humor that has kept her young in spirit, she commented, "It took me 80 years—I must be awful dumb."[18]

Frank Viera and Lucy Correa Azevedo, 16 June 1929. Lucy's veil was patterned after one worn by Anne Morrow Lindbergh. Courtesy of Lucy Viera.

Lucy Viera, May 1999. Photo by Anne Homan.

Lucy described her mother, Maria Thereza Cardoza Silva Correa Azevedo, as a calm person in the midst of the storm of this large integrated family. Maria Thereza and her daughters baked 16 to 20 loaves of bread every other day on their wood stove. They made cheese that had a flavor and texture similar to jack cheese today. Lucy remembered her mother's potato doughnuts and Portuguese sweet bread, made for special occasions. Another household chore was making lye soap. Despite her heart trouble, Maria Thereza worked very hard and had outlived her third husband by more than seven years when she died on 14 November 1936, one day before her 70th birthday.

Lucy married Frank B. Viera from Oakley in 1929, and they raised three children. She worked as a 4-H leader for 10 years and kept the family ranch running. A community activist, she served as a school trustee and on local committees for school unification and for extending city water to outlying ranches. Lucy, like her mother, has outlived her husband; Frank died in 1979. She has also outlived her 11 siblings. Although she lives today on section 20 T1N/R1E, she still owns part of section 10 T1S/R1E on both sides of Morgan Territory Road, which includes open meadows and a corral where her daughter Mary and son-in-law run cattle for themselves and for Lucy. She also owns property on the side of Mount Diablo above the mercury mines—where, she says, an old Indian lived, who paid for all his groceries with gold nuggets.[19]

1 The name "Declusian" has been spelled phonetically from Lucy Viera's pronunciation. Some Azoreans who came to this country with two surnames, such as Joseph Souza Cardoza and the Bent Nunez brothers, chose to use their second name most of the time. Others, including the Correa Azevedos, used their first surname. Lucy said that she didn't know her name was Lucy Correa *Azevedo* until after her stepfather's death, when she inherited property and had to use her legal name. For the sake of clarity, however, I have used both surnames.

2 Lucy Correa Viera, personal interview, 4 Feb 1997.

3 Lucy Correa Viera, personal interview, 18 July 1995.

4 Nilda Rego, "Galvin Family Roots Run Deep on Mount Diablo," *The Valley Times* 3 May 1997: E5.

5 "Train Frightens Horses Driver Instantly Killed," *Contra Costa Gazette* 6 Mar 1909: 1.

6 "Undertaker Controversy," *Contra Costa Gazette* 13 Mar 1909: 8.

7 Contra Costa Superior Court Case #3197, filed 14 May 1909.

8 "Mrs. Azevedo Not Guilty of Bigamy," *Contra Costa Gazette* 27 Jan 1906: 1.

9 Viera, 4 Feb 1997.

10 Fred Bloching, personal interview, 21 Jan 1997.

11 Viera, 4 Feb 1997.

12 Viera, 4 Feb 1997.

13 Viera, 4 Feb 1997.

14 Viera, 4 Feb 1997.

15 Mary Viera Delamater, personal interview, 4 Feb 1997.

16 Maria E. Camposeco, "Clayton Woman Gets Delayed Diploma," *The Valley Times* 12 Feb 1996: 1.

17 Viera, 18 July 1995.

18 Camposeco 1.

19 Viera, 18 July 1995.

a "Undertaker Controversy."

b Viera, 4 Feb 1997.

The Morning Side of Mount Diablo

BORN IN 1819 in the Cherokee Nation, Alabama, near the Tennessee River, Jeremiah Morgan was on the move for much of the first 40 years of his life. His parents, Nathaniel and Mary Ellis Morgan, moved their family to Illinois when Jeremiah was nine. Two years later they relocated to a different Illinois county. After leaving home at age 17, Jeremiah Morgan lived consecutively in Wisconsin, Missouri (where he married Sarah Ellis), Texas, Missouri again, back to Wisconsin, and Iowa. In 1849 he left his wife and five young children in Jackson County, Iowa, and headed west to the California gold fields. He and six companions outfitted an ox-drawn wagon and joined a wagon train. Arriving at Bidwell's Bar on the Feather River six months and a day after setting out, they mined for gold, but Jeremiah earned far more money hunting wild game to feed fellow miners than he did hunting gold ore. Discouraged, he left on a steamer from San

Jeremiah Morgan, from a family tintype. Courtesy of Bill Morgan.

179

Francisco in September 1850 and journeyed through Panama on the way back to his family in Iowa.

He could not stop thinking about the wide-open spaces of California, however, and in April 1853 he packed up his family for another overland journey to California, again by wagon train. The present-day Morgan family still owns two shot and powder flasks made of copper that he brought with him. Settling first in Ygnacio Valley, Jeremiah recorded a claim on 15 October 1855 for 160 acres of what he contended was government land but was actually part of the *Rancho Arroyo de las Nueces y los Bolbones,* or *Rancho San Miguel* as it was sometimes called. He built a home and began farming. Tax records of 1860 showed that he still owned 92 acres in Ygnacio Valley.

During a hunting expedition in 1856, Jeremiah Morgan discovered a forested wilderness on the east flank of Mount Diablo that intrigued him. It was not only beautiful but ideal for stock raising—and it was not part of a contested Mexican land grant. By October 1857 he had erected a barn and a two-story house[1] on section 10 T1S/R1E and had brought his family to what is now named "Morgan Territory" in his honor. He liked to call the area the "morning side of Mount Diablo." He hauled redwood timbers for his buildings by ox-drawn wagon. Family lore suggests that the redwood came from the Santa Cruz mountains, but until 1860 redwood was available closer, in the Oakland hills. The original barn, much patched and mended, and a granary remain at the home site. Jeremiah's great-grandson Bill Morgan, who now owns that property, commented, "No two boards are the same width or thickness. All original nails are cut nails."[2] The roofs of the two outbuildings, now sheet metal, were shake shingles. The granary stored bulk grain after it had been threshed. When grain was needed later for feed, farm workers shoveled it out of the small square doors. Earl Thollander

featured the granary, with the old barn in the background, on the cover of his book *Barns of California*. Bill Morgan told this story about Thollander's drawing: "One of my daughters will never forgive him. My kids had 4-H lambs, and he had them hold them. This one daughter held her 4-H lamb, which is a pet, by the granary, and he sketched it out. Well, then when the picture came out in *Barns of California* . . . the lamb is there, but Sue isn't."[3]

Jeremiah also built a springhouse on a base of dressed stone. The spring that supplied water was "up the canyon a ways and it was a gravity water system. . . ."[4] Later, a well was dug nearby. The springhouse was a storage area for potatoes and apples as well as a place "to cool milk, to skim the cream . . . and also to make butter."[5] In the county tax records of 1877 and 1880, the Morgans listed 1,640 and 2,472 pounds of butter respectively, produced at their ranch. The Morgan home and the wooden frame top of the springhouse burned to the ground in 1932.

Jeremiah Morgan first estimated his "territory" as 10,000 acres, but in 1857 Alonzo Plumley acquired possessory title to half of Jeremiah's original tract.[6] Later, after the official first survey by the U.S. government in 1862, Jeremiah's land claims were reduced to 2,000 acres—equivalent to about three and one-half sections. In July 1901 he claimed section 10, section 16, and the SW¼ of section 3 (all in T1S/R1E).

Jeremiah had at least six siblings, and at least two brothers came west with him. An older brother, Jesse, a skilled carpenter, probably built the barn that still stands on the east side of Morgan Territory Road not far from Marsh Creek Road. The 1880 census listed Jesse Morgan with the Riley family. Jesse filed a pre-emption claim on 156 acres of section 4 T1S/R1E, citing settlement in December 1873.[7] He died in Morgan Territory on 26 October 1891. Another older brother, Josiah, lived in Morgan Territory with his wife, Johanna, and six children. The 1870 census listed him there as a tanner, but a poem written by one of his descendants suggested that he spent much of his time looking for gold. By 1880 a divorced Johanna was living in Clayton; four of the children were still at home.

Albert C. Morgan, a grandson of Josiah "Joe" Morgan, sent a poem in 1946 to his Clayton relatives about Morgan Territory and the three brothers who had immigrated west:

And They Called It Morganland

T'was in the time of long ago
Into this valley came Jerry, Jessie and Joe,
Joe was a miner in search of gold
He said in these hills there is wealth untold
I'll search these hills and with pan and pick
I'll sift the sand of Old Marsh Creek
That perchance I'll find in some hidden bend
The storied rainbows end.
So he went at his task with the highest hopes
He blasted the rocks of Diablo's slopes
He tunneled the hills, he dug in the ground
But the end of the rainbow he never found
So he wandered to another land
To dig for gold in its shining sand.

Jessie, a carpenter like our Savior of old
He built the house for the young and the old
And though he gathered not wealth or fame
Every one blessed him who spoke his name.
So he toiled on in life's endless mill
Till he was laid to rest on Laurel Hill.
Jerry, the farmer, said in his quiet way
Into this valley I've come to stay.
I'll clear this land with ox and plow
And on these hills I'll raise the horse and cow.
He worked at his farm in sun and rain
Till the valley was covered with growing grain
His crops he hauled to far off mills
And his cattle grazed on a hundred hills.
Many children came to bear his name
And he gathered a store of wealth and fame.
As time rolled on he was laid to rest
On the sloping side of Laurel Crest. . . .

Jeremiah had 16 children by his first wife, but only six were still living in 1882. When Sarah died in 1869, he married again, this time to Louisa Riggs. They had one son. Several of his children stayed in the local area, including Isaac, who had 14 children. All but one of Isaac's 14 survived to adulthood, and many present-day residents of Clayton, Byron, Brentwood, Marsh Creek, Livermore, and Morgan Territory are related to the Morgan family. In 1962 Isaac's son Denny Morgan estimated the family at 176 members; 110 of them attended that year's annual reunion on May 27 at Curry Creek Park.[8]

Swine were a major source of income for Jeremiah Morgan. According to tax records, he raised 37 pigs in 1854, 75 in 1855, 160 in 1864, 125 in 1876, 100 in 1877, and 75 in 1890, allowing the animals to run wild on open range and fatten up on the fall acorn crop. Then they were rounded up and driven like cattle to Oakland, where they were put on a barge bound for the slaughter yards in San Francisco. "It would take us a week to a week and a half," Isaac recalled for a newspaper interview in 1945, "to drive the pigs, 150 head or more at a time, down to Oakland by way of Lafayette and Orinda."[9] In later years the closer destination for the drive was Danville, where the pigs could be loaded on a train. Today's feral pigs in Mount Diablo State Park are probably descendants of escapees from 19th century ranches. Landowners on the west side of Morgan Territory Road can testify to their occasional destructive nocturnal visits to hillsides and gardens.

Jeremiah Morgan also raised horses, black Angus cattle, and sheep. He registered his brand JM with the county on 16 August 1858. By 1872 he was paying taxes on 40 horses, 25 stock cattle, 1,800 sheep, and 1,400 lambs. In Concord he also raised carp, which he sold at his Concord butcher shop along with his own beef. Great-grandson Bill Morgan described those days before refrigeration: "Everybody had butcher shops.

'Man against might'

"The villain in Jeremiah's idyl was an unexpected monster made of iron. The railroads were thrusting westward and by a congressional act, the U.S. government granted the railroad companies every other section of land along their tracks. To independent, individualistic Jeremiah Morgan, this was intolerable. He decided to fight! It was a case of man against might. After long litigation and expenditure, Morgan lost his case and most of his land." [a]

They would butcher beef, and they had to distribute it so they had wagons. They'd have people with wagons who would go around in like Clayton, Martinez, Concord, and sell you [beef], all fresh, and you'd eat it that day. Well, he [Jeremiah] had his fish pond and so along with the meat, he'd have fish."[10]

An excellent marksman, Jeremiah hunted deer, grizzly bear, and elk to support his growing family. The price of bear meat in the 1850s was one dollar per pound.[11] East Bay historian Nilda Rego wrote, "In the late 1850s Jeremiah Morgan . . . could almost support his family by hunting bear and selling the meat."[12] Slocum's county history reported that Morgan killed 46 bears in one year alone.[13] In October 1869 the *Contra Costa Gazette* mentioned that Jeremiah Morgan "brought to town . . . the huge paws of two large grizzly bears killed by him last week in the Livermore mountains."[14] By 1874 grizzly bears had disappeared from the Black Hills and Morgan Territory, but Morgan descendants continued Jeremiah's hunting tradition.[15] On Labor Day weekend in 1906, 10 Morgan family members, including Jeremiah's son Isaac, camped out in the family orchard while on a Mount Diablo hunting trip.

In 1860 and 1880 Jeremiah raised 100 bushels of Indian corn and 100 bushels of barley. He sold 2,500 pounds of grapes from his one-acre vineyard in 1880. He also sold 75 cords of wood and 800 dozen eggs. For the 1880 agricultural census, he claimed 2,000 improved and 1,500 unimproved acres. In both years he grew wheat and hay.[16]

As noted, Jeremiah Morgan's property claims were cut after the U.S. survey of 1862. But the greater threat to his real estate was the desire of the federal government to subsidize railroad building. In Morgan Territory and its surrounding countryside, most of the odd-numbered sections along the railroad routes had been deeded to Charles McLaughlin in 1870 as part of the 111,527.27-acre compensation he received from the federal government for constructing the Western Pacific Railroad.[17] Even though Morgan had much earlier claims, McLaughlin was awarded the land. By the time of his death in Clayton on 27 January 1906, Jeremiah Morgan had lost or sold all of his property.

Denny Morgan said of his grandfather Jeremiah, "He was of a gentle nature, one who did not want his horses whipped. My older sisters and brothers remember him as having them around him in front of the fireplace on a bearskin rug, telling them stories."[18] He was 5 feet 10, according to the voting register. Early Contra Costa County history books say that Jeremiah Morgan was illiterate; his signature does not appear on any deeds or tax records. In a court interview in 1898, Jeremiah was questioned about this:

> Q: Do you read or write?
> A: I cannot, not a word, I don't know a letter.
>
> Q: You don't write your name?
> A: No sir, never in my life.[19]

His illiteracy may be the reason for his nurturing of the Morgan Territory schoolhouse so his

Jeremiah Morgan's original barn, in 1996. Photo by Anne Homan.

children would have an education. Teachers often boarded at the Morgan home. Jeremiah never held any official government positions; nevertheless, he had a great deal of influence in his community, and newcomers frequently came to him for advice. He generously acted as witness for a number of neighbors to pre-emption and homestead proofs, which necessitated trips to the San Francisco General Land Office. The portrait of Jeremiah Morgan in Slocum's 1882 county history, taken from a tintype still owned by the family, shows a handsome, open face with wrinkles around his eyes testifying to a life spent outdoors.

Isaac Morgan, Jeremiah's youngest child by his first wife, continued his father's stock-raising traditions on land he acquired along Morgan Territory Road. Born in 1862, Isaac attended Morgan Territory School with his brothers and

sisters. Denny Morgan wrote in a memoir about his father, "When eight years old he rode the range with his saddle horse, and a few years later he became a plowboy, doing all types of work on the ranch with the hand of a veteran."[20] One of Isaac's schoolmates, Jane Howard, became his wife in 1884. The only time he spent away from California was a trip to Arizona when his brothers Bill and Ben were copper mining there. However, "along in the early Spring I got a letter from my girl so I turned around and came back. . . ."[21]

Shorter than his father, standing about five foot seven, Isaac Morgan had brown hair and blue eyes. After his marriage, he served as a school trustee for the Morgan Territory School District for more than 52 years. His obituary noted: "A public spirited citizen, he was recognized as one of the stable and substantial residents of the

'Marsh Creek Chowder Club and Marching Society'

Willard Morgan's son Bill once thought that all the community get-togethers with county officials were a waste of time. "But, what I finally realized later on, when I was going to college and whatnot, what they would do, when local issues occurred, rather than a letter-writing program, they always had this big barbecue. They would invite the supervisors, and sometimes they'd even get three out of the five. The county supervisors would come. Then was the chance and it was all a one-to-one verbal thing, put a jug of wine down in between them. And I remember the old guys, my dad and some of them, they really would go at it with these fellas, you know. We have a problem, we don't agree, how do we [solve it]? And apparently it was a political thing for the community. . . . They settled the issues right there.

"And my dad used to say, and I didn't understand it for a long time, if you start writing letters back and forth, the next thing you do, both sides hire a lawyer and you're in court trying to resolve it. But this way they could resolve the problem." [b]

county. He served on numerous grand and trial juries, but never ran for public office, although he was often asked to do so."[22] After learning he had a terminal illness he entered a Berkeley hospital for treatment, but five days later he demanded to return to Morgan Territory. Besides his wife and 12 surviving children, at his death on 20 February 1946 Isaac Morgan left 40 grandchildren and 12 great-grandchildren.

Isaac's son Willard grew up in Morgan Territory and also attended the local school. He worked on the family ranch, helping his father and brothers raise mostly sheep and cattle. In a

break with family tradition, Willard married not an Episcopalian but the daughter of Catholic immigrants from the Azores, Anne Correa Azevedo, sister of Lucy Viera. Willard and Anne had to cope with some prejudice on the part of both families and eventually moved away to Antioch for several years. Their son, Bill, remarked, "When I grew up, I didn't know . . . the difference between the Portuguese and the Anglos, you know. Never knew it. But apparently, a generation before my time there was real awareness of this. . . . They [his parents] were somewhat outcasts."[23] The Morgan family had lost Jeremiah's original home site on section 10 along Morgan Territory Road because his second wife could not pay off some bank loans. The parents of Anne Correa Azevedo Morgan bought the property at a bank sale, but the land returned to the Morgans when Anne inherited it after her mother's death in 1936. The Correa Azevedos had built a new house on the site of the one that burned, and Willard moved his family to that house from Antioch in 1934. They survived the Depression years by ranching and with supplemental income from Willard's working on county road gangs. Because Isaac had neglected to re-register the JM brand, he had had to choose a new one, a broken eight, which Willard continued to use. Bill Morgan recalled the land-poor status of his family, similar to that of other Morgan Territory Road residents: "Nobody had a great deal of cash money. When I was a kid here, my folks had land but never any money, you know, and I don't think that's understood at all now, how you're living really with no money. Just raise what you can."[24] Besides bringing up their son, Bill, Anne and Willard Morgan generously took two nieces into their family.

Like his father and grandfather, Willard Morgan was a force in the community, but not through elected positions. Son Bill—also christened Willard—described the quiet but intense politicking that went on behind the scenes at the barbecues held by the local Marsh Creek Fire Patrol and Improvement Association, nicknamed the Marsh Creek Chowder Club and Marching Society. "In the summer months we'd meet every month and have a little barbecue. And then in the fall we'd have a big . . . 'Family Barbecue.' Sold tickets, we'd raise enough money at that one party and usually [hold it] here at Curry Creek Park."[25]

Born in Antioch in 1930, Bill Morgan came to Morgan Territory with his parents in 1934. He attended Morgan Territory School with many of his cousins. His aunt Marie Morgan was his teacher for all grades through the eighth. Having graduated from UC Berkeley at age 19, she came to teach at Morgan Territory. "We don't know how it happened: she ended up marrying my uncle," Bill said with a laugh.[26] Marie taught at the one-room school for 15 years, from 1929 to 1945. According to Jack Gleese, in the early years she drove a 1929 Ford Club Coupe with a rumble seat. Her yearly salary in 1929 was $1,250.

Bill Morgan recalled clearly one of his teacher's lessons. "I remember one of the girls came screaming out of there [a separate room that contained the school library] and the teacher went in—there was a big rattlesnake laying on the books. And Marie, she was interested in and taught us at a real young age, natural history. And I remember her coming out with a rattlesnake. . . . I don't know how old it was, but she had a glove on. But she had it behind the head and she's holding it and she's showing it. All the parts of a rattlesnake and why we should not kill them.

"Because at that time, the kind of community standard, when you saw a rattlesnake he was a threat so you killed him! Got a hoe. But she didn't believe in that."[27]

Bill played the usual tricks on the teacher, including turning the clock ahead two hours so that the teacher let school out early one day,

'The coyotes harvested the sheep'

"When I grew up here we always had a band of sheep until, really, I shouldn't be nasty, but the do-gooders came in, and they stopped the Fish and Wildlife from trapping the coyotes. And the coyotes harvested the sheep, but that's after we were married; Naomi remembers guarding the sheep all night. Put them in the corral, and they'd [the coyotes] still come in, right in the corral. And it was illegal to shoot a coyote." [c]

After a pack of wild dogs killed 48 sheep in one night in their corral, Bill and Naomi Morgan decided to quit raising sheep. They have noticed that wild animals have also been affected; the quail and deer populations have decreased significantly, probably because of the increasing numbers of coyotes.

"They stopped trap-controlling the predators. They wiped out some of the farming operations as we said with the sheep. But the deer! There are very few deer now; there used to be a lot of deer around here when I was a kid. . . . And it goes back to this cycle thing; the biologists talk about 'the cycle.' . . . These coyotes, the population's increasing and increasing now, and they have less and less to eat. So as they do, they're wiping out everything else, the birds, the quail, hardly any quail you know now compared to what there used to be. And at some point . . . there will be just a jillion coyotes here, and then they'll get rabies or something in them. And it will wipe them all out. And then it [the cycle] will start again." [d]

probably to her relief as well as the delight of her mischievous student.

Motorcycle and sports car enthusiasts sometimes scheduled rallies along Morgan Territory Road, and the residents disliked the resulting traffic and noise. If Bill knew ahead of time that a motorcycle club was coming, he did his best to discourage future outings. "I would let the cattle out of the corrals and feed them in the middle of the road. When the motorcycles came by, they not only got muddy, but also a good undercoating of cow manure."[28]

After his grandparents moved into a new house they had built next to Morgan Territory Road, Bill enjoyed stopping there on his way home from school to eat a piece of his grandmother Jane Morgan's famous elderberry pie. Bill's teacher outside of school was his father, from whom he learned the arts of stock raising and dry farming. After attending Morgan Territory School with its average of 10 students for eight years, Bill adjusted to a student body of 1,000 at Mount Diablo High School. After high school, he earned a civil engineering degree and worked for the state department of agriculture while continuing to help his father with the ranch.

Bill met his future wife, Naomi Emmerman, at a party in Berkeley. In an earlier incident, Naomi and some friends from the university had chosen Morgan Territory Road for a picnic. In one version of the story, the villain was Bill, but he insists it was another "redneck" rancher: "She and a couple of her girlfriends were picnicking out here somewhere and it actually wasn't me, it was one of the neighbors came by and ran 'em out. . . . So she unjustly accused me [at the party] of this, and when I met her she was a little upset with these landowners and farmers in the area who run everybody out indiscriminately."[29]

The physicist from New York City and the California rancher fell in love and became the fourth generation of Morgans to raise their family in Morgan Territory. Some adjustments were necessary, of course, just as in any marriage. When Naomi suggested that they might have a vegetable garden, she "envisioned a little vegetable garden for the family. And Bill went out with a little tractor right through the little gate here.

And he put in a 'little garden for the family,' and I spent the whole summer bringing food down to senior citizens. I didn't know where to dispose of it—they locked the doors along the road when they saw me coming down! They didn't want any more!" Their daughter Cheryl laughingly added, "We raised 4-H steers on eating zucchini." Bill downplayed the problem: "Just a minor culture clash."[30] When he was growing up in the Depression years, the vegetables from the family garden were essential and were not only eaten fresh but canned and preserved for the rest of that year's food supply.

Naomi also had to adjust to Morgan Territory's one-lane road. She commuted round-trip over the road to her Lawrence Livermore Laboratory job until her retirement. One day on the Levy grade, she hit a chicken in front of George Cardoza's house. She brought the dead chicken up to the Cardozas' door, and they thought it a big joke that "the lady that bombs through here" had brought the evening's dinner. With the lingering cadences of her Queens, New York, accent, Naomi insisted, "I never did understand why they thought that was so funny. You know, I killed a chicken. Picked it up and brought it to them. Told them I'd pay for it. And they just thought that was hysterical."[31] She admitted to missing city life occasionally. Bill enjoys teasing her about her first visit back to New York after moving to Morgan Territory. "She kept talking about how great the weather was in New York— so she finally made the trip back. After her visit she came home shaking her head, saying, 'It's amazing how the weather has deteriorated in New York since I left there!'"[32]

The Morgans designed their home together, Naomi recounted, with Bill "taking care of the technical details and me looking out for the housekeeping angles. We planned it on the concept of a large circle with square kitchen and adjoining pantry in the center. Breakfast-family room, living room, and dining room revolve

No prettier places

Standing near the steps of Morgan Territory School about a year before his death, Isaac Morgan mused, "I've been around here a great many years, and maybe there are prettier places, but I don't think I am ever going to see them. Maybe there aren't any, after all." [e]

around them."[33] A large natural stone fireplace links the interior to the outdoors. Their site is on a hilltop with a breathtaking vista, but the house is invisible from the road. Bill also built a new red barn across the road from the old home site, and he invented another brand for his own cattle, a W over an M. He still runs some cattle and raises walnuts. Around 1965, he and his father stopped running sheep because of predators such as coyotes and stray dogs, which run in packs.

Bill and Naomi Morgan and their two daughters, Cheryl and Suzanne, have concerns about the changing community along Morgan Territory Road. "The thing that's changing it is the public acquisition of all the land here. And my concern is that . . . all the park agencies have plans for acquisition; they want to acquire more. . . . And, you know, a lot of people support this. 'Oh, we'd like to see the wild area.' But as far as the community, I think we're in real trouble because we have very few voters now, 200-some homes . . . [including] Marsh Creek. And we're just being voted into oblivion. And at some point, it's all going to be public land. . . ."[34]

In 1988 Bill and Naomi sold most of section 15 T1S/R1E to Save Mount Diablo, which transferred the 631 acres to Mount Diablo State Park. This sale made the first connection between the state park and Morgan Territory Preserve.

Another change, Bill noted, is that very few children of his parents' generation have made his choice—to continue working the land. The De-

pression years were hard for everyone. Perhaps young people blamed farm life and opted for other careers. World War II probably hastened the process by forcing young people into arenas far from home—the military, the factory, the business world. All of the local one-room schools are closed. The two that were actually on Morgan Territory Road are gone—no longer available for community get-togethers. The old chowder group with its hospitable diplomacy began to fade away as most old-timers sold their properties.

"Not a one of them has . . . [remained on the land]; sometime in the '20s or '30s they sold the last of the land out . . .," Bill said. "These people were old. . . . And they'd try and come back, like the Joseph family, have their annual picnic. I'd take my dad over there because he wasn't driving then. And he'd meet all these people and none of them had been here for 30 years, you know, and they remembered it, but their kids sure don't. I don't know them, they don't know me.[35]

1 Karana Hattersley-Drayton, "Morgan Territory: Interview with Bill Morgan and Family," for the East Bay Regional Park District, 2960 Peralta Oaks Ct., Oakland, CA 94605, 7 Nov 1996: 32.

2 Willard "Bill" Morgan, personal interview, 19 May 1997.

3 Morgan, May interview.

4 Hattersley-Drayton 36.

5 Howard N. "Denny" Morgan and Grace L. Morgan, "Morgan Territory," mimeograph, 1962, 1.

6 *History of Contra Costa County, California* (San Francisco: W.A. Slocum, 1882) 467.

7 San Francisco General Land Office, Cash Entry 4915, National Archives, DC.

8 Denny and Grace Morgan 5.

9 Jim Ritch, "Morgans, Pioneer Territory Pair, to Mark Anniversaries," *Oakland Tribune* 22 Feb 1945, 17.

10 Hattersley-Drayton 39.

11 Nilda Rego, "Morgan Settled 10,000 Acres on the Morning Side of Diablo," *The Valley Times* 9 Apr 1989: 5A.

12 Nilda Rego, "Hunting Changes from a Way of Life to a Hobby," *The Valley Times* Fashion/Lifestyle Section 16 Feb 1992: 6.

13 Slocum 468.

14 "A Hunter's Trophies," *Contra Costa Gazette* 2 Oct 1869: 3.

15 Rego, "Hunting Changes."

16 1860 and 1880 US Agricultural Census, Contra Costa County.

17 Mary Praetzellis, Suzanne B. Stewart and Grace H. Ziesing, *The Los Vaqueros Watershed: A Working History* (Rohnert Park, CA: Sonoma State Univ Academic Foundation, 1997) 34.

18 Denny and Grace Morgan 2.

19 Superior Court Contra Costa County Case 2836, 16 Nov 1898, Max Blum vs Jeremiah Morgan, box CC112 Clayton, at Contra Costa County Historical Society.

20 "I. Morgan Dead at 84," *Contra Costa Gazette* 21 Feb 1946, 8.

21 Ritch 17.

22 "I. Morgan Dead."

23 Hattersley-Drayton 9.

24 Hattersley-Drayton 49-50.

25 Hattersley-Drayton 11.

26 Hattersley-Drayton 6-7.

27 Hattersley-Drayton 6.

28 Morgan, May interview.

29 Morgan, May interview.

30 Hattersley-Drayton 50.

31 Hattersley-Drayton 53.

32 Sara Maloney, "The Morgan Family's Home," *The Tri-Valley Herald, Brightside* 8 July 1979: 5.

33 Maloney, "Morgan Family's Home."

34 Hattersley-Drayton 47.

35 Hattersley-Drayton 48.

a Sara Maloney, "A History of Morgan Territory Road," *The Tri-Valley Herald, Brightside* 8 July 1979, 2.

b Hattersley-Drayton 11-12.

c Hattersley-Drayton 24.

d Hattersley-Drayton 54.

e "Death Takes Patriarch of Morgan Territory," *Oakland Tribune* 21 Feb 1946: 5.

Ranching with "Pard"

BETWEEN 1850 AND 1867 Sarah Cottrell Howard had eight children, five of whom died before the age of five. One of the three who lived to adulthood suffered an accident as a toddler that left him unable to speak.[1] For the remainder of his long life, most of it spent on Morgan Territory Road, William Henry Howard had the mind of a child.[2]

According to family tradition, Sarah Cottrell had been an upstairs maid in the home of the wealthy Howard family in England.[3] But when she and Robert Rymer Howard were married in Derbyshire, England, at Bakewell Church on 21 October 1849, the marriage record showed "mechanic" as the occupation of both Robert and his father, also Robert Howard.[4] The baptismal records of their children at Manchester Cathedral list Robert as a spindle maker, further eroding the traditional tale of great wealth.[5] Perhaps he was studying to be a mechanic and meanwhile earning wages in a local industry. The Howards had two sons before William's arrival on 31 August 1854; one died just before Christmas 1853, one just after. Following the birth of a daughter, Elizabeth Caroline, in June 1856, the couple had two more sons who died as infants, one at the age of four months and the other at one month. A second daughter, Jane Ellen, was born near the end of October 1863. When Jane was six weeks old, the family left England for New York City, where they stayed for about four years. Their last child, another daughter, was born and died there in 1867.[6]

The New York City Directories listed Robert Howard, seaman 1866–67 and engineer 1867–68. He served on steamers carrying passengers and freight from New York City to Panama and back.[7] About 1868 the family moved to the Isthmus of Panama. Robert Howard stayed on

their steamer as its engineer, sailed around Cape Horn, and arrived at the west coast of Panama some time later. Family lore suggests mother and children disembarked and traveled across the isthmus by horseback. More likely, however, with a five-year-old, they rode the Panama Railroad, which had been completed in 1855 and which ran from Colón on the Gulf of Mexico to its western terminus at Panama City. New York City financiers had built the railroad to facilitate the journey for travelers eager to reach California, and from 1855 to 1869, 600,000 people traveled the railroad.[8] The 48-mile train trip lasted four hours and cost each passenger $25 in gold, the only payment accepted by the ticket agents.[9] Whether from horseback or from a train window, young Jane remembered seeing large snakes hanging from trees in the jungle.

On the west coast of Panama, the Howards lived for four years with friends in a large hilltop house overlooking the Pacific Ocean.[10] Robert Howard found work as an engineer on coastal steamers that made round-trip runs between Panama and Central American ports for the Pacific Mail and Steamship Company. Typical cargo consisted of mail, half a dozen passengers, coffee, animal hides, balsam, cochineal, indigo, and lumber.[11]

In 1872 the family said farewell to their Panamanian friends and steamed up the coast to San Francisco. Charles Ensor, an Irishman who was also a ship's engineer, married the Howards' older daughter, Elizabeth, on 4 October 1873 at the Church of the Advent in San Francisco. San Francisco Directories listed Robert Howard in the city from 1874 until 1877. The 1875–76 directory showed him as the first-assistant engineer on the Pacific Mail SS *Winchester*. The Pacific Mail and Steamship Company had maintained its northern California headquarters and repair facilities in Benicia from 1850 until 1869, when they were moved to San Francisco.[12] According to the published recollections of an early resident, a number of employees of the company came across the Carquinez Strait to hunt, to chase and capture wild horses, and to claim land in Contra Costa County.[13] The Howards and Charles Ensor likely heard of property available in Morgan Territory from fellow employees. In April 1874 Charles Ensor bought the NE¼ of section 4 T1S/R1E on Morgan Territory Road.

While the extended family's house was being built, the Ensors and Howards stayed at the Clayton Hotel.[14] Other hotel residents may have had an exciting time: Jane brought with her an unusual pet, a monkey from Panama. The animal lived to a great age and later enjoyed pestering dogs at the Howards' ranch. One piece of precious furniture shipped around Cape Horn for the family was a rosewood piano. Made in Boston by T.W. Vose and Company, the instrument has two keys fewer than a regulation keyboard. Robert Howard, who was said to possess a beautiful voice, had sung in the Manchester Cathedral choir in England; quite likely he or others in that 19th-century family also played the piano. The Bloching family later bought the piano, and recently their descendants donated it to the Clayton Museum, where it has pride of place in the parlor.

Robert Howard purchased the SW¼ of section 8 T1S/R1E from Francis D. McGuire in 1879. Howard and Ensor applied for a brand, a combination of H and E, in February of the same year. Robert Howard's seagoing career had meant long absences from his family. Fellow seaman William H. Taylor, who also settled in Contra Costa County, testified to the land office about the constant travels of his friend: "I knew him [Robert Howard] first in N. Y. City. . . . He was a steamship engineer and followed the sea constantly up to 1880. He was at sea 9/10 of the time."[15] Howard apparently intended to settle down permanently on land, where he could be close to his family.

The Howard family's move to Morgan Territory also lessened pressure on their childlike son, William, who was now 20 years old and increasingly the butt of unkindness in crowded San Francisco. Like a child, although he did not understand all the implications of the teasing, he knew enough to feel hurt. In rural Contra Costa County neighbors seemed more tolerant. William's nickname in Morgan Territory was "Pard." Many afternoons he waited patiently at his ranch gate near the road to visit with schoolchildren as they walked home in the afternoon. He was helpful around the ranch, performing chores such as chopping wood for the stove. Several people who remembered him mentioned that he usually wore rubber boots, which he invariably had put on the wrong feet. And with the easy friendliness of a carefree child, he giggled often.

The 1880 census taker found the Howard family at their new ranch on June 22. In that year the record showed that they paid taxes on the NW¼ and SW¼ of section 8. They also paid taxes on a sewing machine, three vehicles, nine horses, three colts, three cows, 23 stock cattle, 20 hogs, poultry, and a crop of barley. The Ensors' tax record that year for the NE¼ of section 4 reveals similar numbers of cattle, horses, hogs, and poultry in addition to 40 acres of wheat and 10 acres of barley.

Two years later the *Contra Costa Gazette* reported that Robert Howard had been "hauling manure from his barnyard with a pair of young and but partially broken horses, when they took fright and ran. Turning in at a gateway near the house, the wagon collided with one of the posts and Mr. Howard was thrown from his seat to the ground, where the heavy wagon passed over him with crushing effect."[16] Along with other severe injuries, he had several skull fractures. He died at

On their 62nd wedding anniversary, Isaac and Jane Howard Morgan posed in front of the valley oak where they were married. Photo courtesy of the Morgan family.

age 55 on 8 March 1882. Ranching was and is a dangerous business.[17]

Soon after her husband's death, Sarah Howard requested that the court make Jeremiah Morgan guardian of her "imbecile" son.[18] Through his mother and his guardian, William Howard applied for a homestead grant on the NW¼ of section 8 T1S/R1E, which was approved in October 1883. However, because of a debt of $385 to storekeeper Charles Rhine of Clayton, the court forced the Howard family to sell William's 160-acre homestead on section 8 to the highest cash bidder in 1884. Their friend William H. Taylor bought the property for $1,000.[19]

By 1890 Sarah Howard owned the NE¼ of section 4—property that had belonged to the Ensors. In September 1884 Charles Ensor had signed a deed in Ireland selling Sarah half share of the property for two shillings because of his "natural love and affection" for her. In another deed dated a year later, he gave her the other half

as well. The Ensor family had traveled to Ireland by 1882 and decided to remain there, living at the Ardress country estate near Armagh, Northern Ireland, property of the Ensor family since the 1770s. Their oldest son, Charles Howard Ensor, inherited the late 18th-century house and sold it to the National Trust in 1963. The elder Charles Ensor died at age 44, but his wife, Elizabeth Howard Ensor, stayed at Ardress to raise their 14 children, who eventually scattered across the globe to Canada, South Africa, Scotland, and the United States.

Sarah Howard's daughter Jane "Jennie" Howard attended Morgan Territory School and met the young Morgans there, including her future husband, Isaac. Eager to obtain his marriage license, Isaac attempted to cross an overflowing Pacheco Creek in Martinez on his horse and had to be rescued by a passerby.[20] On 20 March 1884, two years after the death of her father, Jane Howard and Isaac Morgan were married under

At the annual Morgan family reunion, about 1983: (l. to r.) Denny Morgan, Pat Morgan, Ada Morgan Hansen, Edith Morgan Frank, Willard Morgan. Photo courtesy of the Morgan family.

the spreading valley oak near her family home. A reporter for the *Contra Costa Gazette* interviewed her in 1948: "A photograph of Isaac shows him wearing a wedding suit of dark cloth, a figured velvet waistcoat and standing open collar with a diamond horse show pin in his cravat. Describing her gray silk wedding dress, made with widely sweeping skirt and 'polonaise,' Mrs. Morgan explained, 'That was a long basque, with lots of buttons down the front. I well remember because I had to make all those button holes.'"[21]

After the wedding Jane and Isaac Morgan supported Jane's mother and brother and lived on section 8 in the Howard home back on Curry Creek Road. Life was primitive there, with no running water, but grandson Bill Morgan remembered that "a lot of living and eating" took place on their large screened-in porch.[22] Sarah Howard helped with all the chores of ranch life, including watching over her grandchildren, and

William helped with heavy ranch work. In 1910 Sarah either had a blood clot or suffered an injury that led to gangrene in her leg. A doctor had amputated one of her toes in April, but the infection spread. She died in late June.[23] William continued to live with his sister and brother-in-law until his death in 1940. Isaac and Jane sold the old Howard place in 1937 and built a home on section 4 next to Morgan Territory Road. The Rubino family now owns this site, and the Morgan home is gone. Bill Morgan recalled that the enormous valley oak still on the property once had many deer and elk antlers nailed in its bark from hunting expeditions. He believes that antlers from the last tule elk killed on Sherman Island were in the collection.

Jane Morgan and her sister Elizabeth both had 14 children. "I made all the children's clothing and baked 23 loaves of bread at a time in an outdoor oven," Jane recalled in the *Contra Costa*

Jane's sidesaddle

In 1948, octogenarian Jane Howard Morgan, mother of 14, recalled her girlhood love of horseback riding: "I loved to ride and never thought a thing of jumping fences on the sidesaddle." And what became of the sidesaddle? Jane smiled. "I sold it and bought a baby carriage!" [a]

Gazette article. "When there was sickness, we helped one another. As there were no hospitals and few doctors, midwives took care of the babies."[24] All of Jane's eight sons and six daughters were delivered safely and remained reasonably healthy until 17 October 1918, when Albert died of influenza at Fort Lewis, Washington, where he had been stationed in the army. Looking back on her experiences, Jane observed, "I think girls and boys were better off in the old times. . . . They have more opportunities now but they do not take advantage of them. We had no autos, movies nor high schools."[25]

Jane Morgan's favorite holiday was Christmas. "For years we had a Christmas dinner in this room, which was built so we could all get together. As the family grew, 84 of us sat down to Christmas dinner. It was wonderful! But . . . the family is so large now that we have an annual picnic."[26] Outliving her husband by three years and her brother by nine, Jane died peacefully of natural causes at age 84, surrounded by family, on the 65th anniversary of her marriage—20 March 1949. The Morgan family picnic is still held each year on the first Saturday in June.

1 Contra Costa County Superior Court Case #328, 24 Mar 1882, at Contra Costa County Historical Society.

2 Willard J. "Bill" Morgan, personal interview, 19 May 1997.

3 Also spelled variously Cothrell and Cotterill. On her marriage record, however, she signed her name "Cottrell."

4 Marriage #461, page 231.

5 Manchester Cathedral, Manchester, Lancashire, England, Baptismal Record #7, page 420, 17 Sep 1854; #3, page 440, 19 Oct 1856.

6 Sadie Adams, phone conversation, June 1997.

7 Notes written by Lili Morgan, 4 Sep 1970. Photocopy at Clayton Museum, Clayton, CA.

8 Walter LaFeber, *The Panama Canal* (NY: Oxford U P, 1978) 12.

9 Lucius Beebe and Charles Clegg, *The American West* (NY: E.P. Dutton, 1935) 72.

10 Bill Morgan interview.

11 In the San Francisco city directories for 1875 and 1876, Howard was listed as serving on the S.S. *Winchester.* Cargo information from various issues of the *Panama Daily Star and Herald,* including 11 Mar and 10 Apr 1875: 2. *History of Contra Costa County, California* (Los Angeles: Historic Record Co, 1926) tells of Howard serving on steamers that ran between Panama and San Francisco.

12 Robert Bruegmann, *Benicia: Portrait of an Early California Town* (San Francisco: 101 Productions, 1980) 8.

13 G.B. Drummond, ed. *Recollections: Early Life in the San Ramon Valley As Related by Prof. James Dale Smith, Headmaster, Livermore College* (Oakland, CA: GRT Book Printing, 1995) 4-6, 32-35, 100-101.

14 Lili Morgan notes.

15 San Francisco General Land Office, Homestead Entry 2290.

16 "Fatal Accident," *Contra Costa Gazette* 11 Mar 1882: 3.

17 In 1996 agriculture was the second most dangerous occupation in the U.S. after construction. *Statistical Abstracts of the U.S. for 1996* (DC: Bureau of the Census).

18 Superior Court Contra Costa County Case 328, 24 Mar 1882, box CC112 Clayton, at Contra Costa County Historical Society.

19 Superior Court Case, 10 Oct 1884.

20 Howard "Denny" Morgan and Grace L. Morgan, "Morgan Territory," mimeograph, 1962, 1.

21 Agnes N. Groom, "Life is Mellow for Beloved Pioneer of County; 'Progress Parade' Has Been Rich," *Contra Costa Gazette* 1 Mar 1948: 2.

22 Bill Morgan interview.

23 "Hospital Notes," *Contra Costa Gazette* 23 Apr 1910: 4. Contra Costa County Death Record, Family History Library microfilm #1294350.

24 Groom 2.

25 Groom 2.

a Groom 2.

The Olofson family, 3 November 1901: parents Sylvester and Louise, with children (l. to r.) Edith, Adella, and Oliver. From the Wright family collection.

Curry Creek Park

MOTTLED SYCAMORE TREES cast shade over the rectangular swimming pool, which is being filled with dirt.[1] The large leaves are quiet in the windless heat of summer. Small stone fireplaces and an old baseball field are visible. South of the pool, live oaks and more sycamores rise from the banks of Curry Creek, a little stream that by late August usually has dried up before its junction with Marsh Creek. The steep flank of Mount Diablo's North Peak climbs away to the northwest. The creek is named for James Curry, who "engaged in stock business" here between 1858 and 1860.[2]

From about 1925 until 1938, Sylvester Olofson opened up this portion of his property along Curry Creek to families and organizations on summer weekends. People came from all over the East Bay, traveling out Clayton Road to Marsh Creek Road and up Morgan Territory Road to Curry Creek Park to picnic, swim, hike, and camp. On Saturdays Sylvester came down on horseback from the ranch house two miles upstream to collect 25 cents a car from each group. At first water fun was limited to the creek itself. The cement pool was added in 1933, along with public dressing rooms and lavatories. Sylvester Olofson's grandson re-opened the picnic grounds from 1946 through 1979.

J. Peter Olofson, Sylvester's father, had run away at age 14 from his native Stockholm, Sweden, and found work aboard ship as a deck hand. About three years later, in 1848, he arrived in San Francisco and began working at the docks as a stevedore loading and unloading ships. Probably he did a little dabbling in the gold mines. By 1857 he had met and married Clarissa Marsh, who had recently immigrated with her family to Oakland from Liverpool, England. Clarissa's granddaughter recalled that even late in life Clarissa added an "h" at the beginning of cer-

tain words, for example "happle" for "apple." When Peter became a naturalized citizen in 1864, he was still a San Francisco resident.

Ten years later, although Peter was still working on the San Francisco docks, he and Clarissa moved their family to East Oakland, settling eventually on 21st Avenue. In March 1886 Peter applied for a 138-acre homestead in the Mitchell Canyon area southwest of Clayton, and his older son, Alfred, applied for a homestead on neighboring property, the NE¼ of section 34 T1N/R1W. Alfred's proof described his land as rough and mountainous, fit only for grazing.

Alfred stayed in Oakland at the family residence and continued to work as a printer, but Peter retired from his work at the docks. By September 1886 he and Clarissa had moved to the ranch land on a high ridge overlooking Walnut Creek. In his 1891 proof for the San Francisco General Land Office, Peter itemized a house, barn, corral, and outbuildings as well as 30 acres under cultivation. He received the patent for the property on 21 June 1892.[3] The voting register for that year recorded Peter Olofson at age 61 with gray eyes and gray hair. He stood about five feet nine inches tall. Also that year the Oakland city directory listed him as a farmer rather than a stevedore. Olofson Ridge is still a landmark on the western boundary of Mitchell Canyon.

Peter became blind in his old age, and a few years before his death the family convinced him to move with Clarissa down from the isolated hills to a Clayton cottage. His obituary notice in 1903 praised Peter's character: "He was noted for his industry, frugality and integrity and possessed to a high degree the three attributes that are indispensable in the make-up of a good citizen—a good neighbor, a loving husband and an affectionate father."[4] Clarissa's obituary in 1913 named five daughters and two sons, including two sets of twins who survived her. The couple are buried side by side at Live Oak Cemetery in Clayton.

In 1904, divorce and spousal abuse were rarely public items, but in March of that year Clarissa Olofson testified in her daughter Laura's divorce case in Contra Costa County Superior Court that Laura's husband drank excessively and was abusive to her. The court documents read: "On a certain day in July, 1899, the defendant struck this plaintiff with his fist, bruising her face and blackening her eye; that on or about Dec 23d 1899 the defendant kicked this plaintiff violently on her hip rendering same sore and lame thereby; that the defendant has on numerous occasions threatened this plaintiff with great injury and violence and thus keeping the plaintiff in constant fear. . . ."⁵

Laura added that she was afraid to live with her husband and that he was not supporting her. He reportedly earned a decent wage as a blacksmith but used the money to buy liquor. The court granted Laura her divorce in 1905, and four years later she married rancher Joe Stockfleth, a steady and respected member of the Clayton community. This happy relationship endured.

Peter and Clarissa's son Sylvester was born in San Francisco in 1867 and moved with the family to Oakland. By 1886 he had become a printer for the *Oakland Tribune*; two years later he was commuting to San Francisco as a printer for the *Daily Report*. Sylvester married Louise Fake of Oakland in 1892. His father-in-law gave them some property, and Sylvester built a two-story home on 21st Street in Oakland not far from the residence of his father. A doctor recommended that because of health problems Sylvester should get away from the dust and chemicals in the printing environment. At a tax sale in December 1895, Sylvester and his brother, Alfred, bought from the bank the east half of section 8 T1S/R1E along Curry Creek. Sylvester gave up printing

and moved to Morgan Territory with his family. Edith Olofson Wright believed that her father traded the Oakland house for his share of the land cost. In 1906 Sylvester and Alfred bought the NW¼ of section 4 T1S/R1E, which had previously been the property of the Norman family and included the land pre-empted by Jesse Morgan in 1873. The Wright family still calls this part of section 4 the "Jesse quarter." The census taker in 1900 found Sylvester and Louise Olofson in the Morgan Territory Precinct with daughters Edith and Adella and son Oliver.

The family's first home on the ranch was a rundown one-bedroom cabin. For $50 Sylvester bought the old Nortonville schoolhouse, which had been abandoned since most of the coal mining families moved away.⁶ He hauled the schoolhouse to the ranch and hired his brother-in-law to build a new house, using the schoolhouse lumber. Edith remembered her new home well: "[The schoolhouse] was torn down and rebuilt and we had a nice home with running water in a sink and drain boards and pantry—three bedrooms—a living room—a big kitchen and a porch all across the front with a cellar under the kitchen and living room."⁷ Son Oliver was born in the new house in 1898 and Albert in 1904.

Plants were suspended from roof rafters along the porch. A stand outside held a basin of water and towels for the males to wash up; Louise and the girls washed inside at the sink. The outside washstand also was the storage place for shoe polish, to spruce up everyone's shoes before a trip into town. "Town," Edith explained, meant either Clayton, which "had a post office, a store and five saloons," or Concord.⁸ The bathtub had cold running water; hot water for the weekly bath on Saturday was heated on the stove. The cool cellar held canned fruits, vegetables, and meat as well as salted salmon. The family also stored fresh milk there and skimmed the cream off in the mornings. Louise Olofson washed clothes outdoors in large tubs on the porch. She had to boil

Edith (l.), Oliver, and Adella Olofson, c. 1898. From the Wright family collection.

"everything that needed whiteness—sheets, bath towels, petticoats, dish towels, bureau scarfs. She scrubbed on a scrub board. . . ."[9] Edith described her own wardrobe as a girl: "We bought shoes with strings or buttons that came up past our ankles—stockings that covered our legs and petticoats that flounced our dresses and I had a crocheted petticoat—we all wore hats—even to school."[10]

Many of their clothes were hand-me-downs as the family struggled to make a go of the ranch. A previous tenant had left old beer bottles on the property. The Olofsons cut the tops off to make the bottles suitable as jelly containers. In rainy weather, when Sylvester could not work outside, he put new soles on their shoes or mended harness. He and Louise would not buy anything on credit. Summing up the lifetime philosophy of

Cousins (l. to r.) Oliver and Ray Olofson, and Nettie Fake and Adella Olofson, c. 1910. From the Wright family collection.

her parents, Edith noted, "Pa never wanted anything he couldn't pay [for] and Ma didn't want anything either."[11] They planted an orchard and several fig trees. A typical breakfast consisted of cooked apples and hot mush, served with bread and coffee. Often supper was mush again, this time with milk or syrup. Noon was the larger meal, with vegetables and meat or fish. The children attended Morgan Territory School, walking about a four-mile round trip each day.

As Sylvester worked outdoors on the ranch, his health slowly improved. Martin Wright, older son of Edith Olofson Wright, remembered his grandfather and grandmother very well, because every year his parents sent him out from Oakland to the Curry Creek ranch for the summer. "My grandfather Sylvester, he came out of the printing office, and he was not too healthy.

He came up there on the ranch, and he worked out in the open and plowed the fields and raised the grain and rounded up all the cattle. . . . He sold cattle, and he was working alone, and he just thrived on it. He got his health back. It was just amazing."[12] Martin's grandmother Louise had become deaf at an early age and was dependent on the large unwieldy hearing aids of those days. After finishing her housework, she loved to read magazines with romantic stories. Their daughter Edith said of them: Pa was "a very gentle man. He never hit us, except once he hit Ollie at the table for doing something he shouldn't. . . . Ma was always serious. Pa would laugh at us and laugh when people came to visit."[13] Neighbor Jack Gleese remembered Louise as quiet and shy. He characterized Sylvester Olofson as neat and nice, not a boastful person. Jack's father worried that a fire might start at the picnic grounds, but Sylvester always made sure that the campers used the stone fireplaces and extinguished their fires properly.[14]

Sylvester and Alfred Olofson invested in land and cattle together, but it was Sylvester who did all the work on the Curry Creek ranch. Alfred and his family rarely even visited from Oakland. Alfred still worked as a printer, for the *San Francisco Post,* and he later became a linotype operator. Nevertheless, when they sold cattle, the two brothers shared the profits equally. At roundup time neighbors would all pitch in; Sylvester especially depended on the help of the Morgan boys. Louise Olofson's brothers and sisters frequently visited with their families, bringing gifts of food from the city and enjoying the ranch property where they could relax and pick wildflowers, mushrooms, or berries. Edith reminisced about hunting with her Uncle Walt Fake for squirrels, deer, quail, and doves.

Every Sunday, whether company was expected or not, Sylvester had an unvarying routine, according to his grandson Martin. "My grandfather wasn't really religious, but every Saturday night he had a bath in the pantry. They didn't have hot water. Grandma would boil up four or five pots of hot water and dump them in the tub, and he'd take a bath every Saturday night. And Sunday morning he'd shave and dress up. He wouldn't work. He wouldn't work on Sunday.

"There was no company, nobody's around, and I was a little kid there, of course, so we'd take the cat and the dog and the pig went with us and the lamb. There was three or four animals always. And we'd walk down the road . . . shoes shined and all this. Never see a soul, except me. . . . He was a different guy on Sundays."[15]

Martin slept with his grandfather in a big double bed on the porch. Sylvester slept there, winter and summer, his whole life on the ranch. When Martin visited, he was given a nightshirt and hat, a sort of bonnet with strings to tie under

Martin Wright enjoyed helping his grandfather Sylvester on the Olofsons' ranch:

"When I was a little boy and just started to school, I'd come here in the summertime and help my grandfather with fencing and many other farm problems. . . . I was pretty small, so he'd harness up the team, and hook 'em up to the sled, and I would play with the dog. And then I would get on the sled, and he'd drive the team and we'd go way up the hill, and then he would dig the post holes. He had the posts, and he had the wire. He'd dig the post holes, and I'd stop playing with the dog. He loosened up the dirt with the crowbar, then I would get on my hands and knees and take the dirt out. . . . We had to dig these holes about two feet deep, and so that was my big job, taking that dirt out. And then when we put the post in, I pushed the dirt back, and then he would tamp it down with a big crowbar." [a]

As Sylvester aged, however, their roles reversed. "Then, years went by, my grandfather got old, and I was in my prime. And so, I would go up there in the summertime, and we would do the same thing, except that I would harness the horses and hook 'em up to the sled and load all the posts and the wire. And he would sit and play with the dog. Then he would ride on the sled. I'd drive the team up to where we were working, and I'd take the crowbar and dig the holes, and he'd go down on his hands and knees and take the dirt out. . . ." [b]

his chin, to sleep in, just like his grandfather's. On Sunday mornings while they still lay in bed, his grandfather sang old songs to him. At night before they turned in, they walked down to the creek edge, and Sylvester talked aloud to the stars, saying goodnight to deceased relatives, es-

199

pecially remembering his daughter Adella.[16]

Sylvester and Louise's other daughter, Edith, had married George Ross Wright of Oakland on 29 June 1917 during his World War I service. In 1918 while Edith was living in Texas with her husband, the younger daughter, Adella, died of the flu in Oakland, where she had been working to help in the war effort. Edith and George had some difficulties and separated for several years. With her two small sons she came back to live with her parents at the Curry Creek ranch and taught at Morgan Territory School in 1921 and 1922. She had attended normal school after high school years in Oakland and Fremont, acquired the credentials for teaching, and taught for four years at a one-room school before her marriage. Edith's published memories of the country school and teaching there are positive, but her son Martin remembered otherwise. "When my brother got ready to go to school, she didn't want him to go to school here at Morgan Territory schoolhouse," Martin recalled. "They [the pupils] were too rough, too rowdy, had too many bad habits. So she decided, by golly, I'll try that [marriage] again to get the kids away from having to go to school at this little country schoolhouse where they only have two or three books and a lotta bad words."[17]

Edith did remark in her memoirs that "I learned all my swear words from the Morgans." She and Martin and his brother moved back to Oakland to live with her husband, but Martin came to stay at Curry Creek every summer. Two daughters were born in Oakland soon after the move.

One summer day when Martin was about 11 or 12, he and his grandfather came upon a huge rattlesnake—probably three to four inches in diameter—underneath a dead tree. Sylvester climbed the tree with a forked post and caught the snake behind the head. He attempted to kill it by pressing on the post, but he could not get enough leverage. He called Martin over, "Motty,

you gotta come up here, climb up here and hold this snake down so I can get something and kill it." So Marty climbed the tree and held the post on the neck of the snake. "I didn't have a lot of weight, and it was like riding a bucking horse as I'm trying to hold that snake." Finally, his grandfather came back with an ax and dispatched the reptile, which had 14 rattles. "It just seemed to me that I was holding that snake for an hour—it was probably more like five or 10 minutes, but I had nightmares for a dozen nights after that."[18]

Sylvester had a stroke in 1938 and no longer allowed outsiders to use his property for picnics. In 1941 he suffered a heart attack while repairing a pump and fell face down into the creek, where he died. After his death Louise Olofson had a house built closer to Morgan Territory Road on section 4. Remembering long-ago shopping expeditions, Martin's wife, Dorothy, laughed and noted wryly that she was probably double-parked and definitely pregnant as she waited in her car for Louise to emerge from one of the two Concord grocery stores. An extremely thrifty shopper, Louise would sometimes want to be ferried back and forth four times between the two stores before she settled on the better price. She outlived her husband by 12 years.

After Sylvester Olofson's death, his heirs and his deceased brother's family squabbled over the property for five years. When Martin Wright returned home from his World War II service as a naval officer aboard a minesweeper in the South Pacific, a sign advertising the Curry Creek property for sale had been displayed on the fence along Morgan Territory Road for over a year. Martin and Dorothy decided to buy it, but that was not an easy task. Dorothy recalled, "We borrowed money from every relative who smiled at us, and got a bank loan, too, though that was really hard to arrange."[19] Martin added, "I had to go to—I forget what it was—123 banks trying to get a loan to buy the park; well, maybe it was

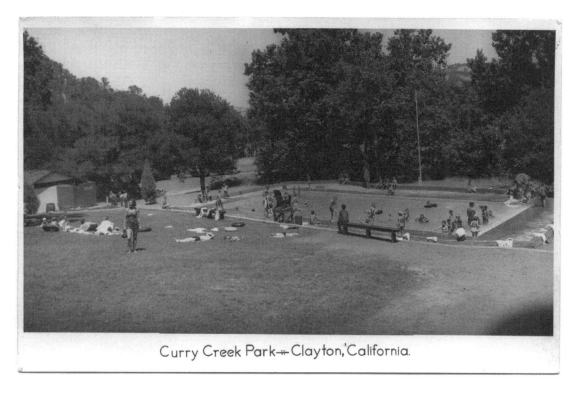

Curry Creek Park -+- Clayton, California.

Among Dorothy Wright's responsibilities at Curry Creek Park was serving as lifeguard (standing, left, c. 1956). From the Wright family collection.

23. At any rate, we had a heck of a time."[20] Finally successful in negotiating the loan, the Wrights moved to the property in 1946.

Dorothy went from a wartime job as head of the Women's Personnel Department for Point Richmond's Standard Oil Refinery to cooking on a wood stove and keeping house in a one-room cabin with only one layer of wood planks for walls. Their plans to improve the cabin got a jump-start when Dorothy almost immediately became pregnant. With five children arriving in short order, the last two a set of twins, the family usually remained two rooms behind in their construction efforts. At first the only available bathroom was in the swimming pool dressing area. By degrees, however, they enlarged the cabin and added amenities. They reopened Curry Creek Park to the public, still charging only a nominal fee. Near their cabin, not far from the pool, they built a snack bar. Martin had a full-time job until 1961, so much of the day-to-day operation of the park fell on Dorothy's shoulders. The children helped as they grew older, especially in summers when organizations as well as individual families came for picnics, barbecues, and swimming, seeking relief from the hot weather. The Wrights also hired local teenagers. Martin was responsible for all building, development, and maintenance on the ranch, but often on weekends, three great-uncles from the Fake family came out from Oakland to help. One was a master plumber, another a finish carpenter, and

On a Thanksgiving hike, 1957: sister-in-law Eunice Wright (l.) with Dorothy and Martin Wright, and a group of Wright siblings and cousins. From the Wright family collection.

the third a master cabinetmaker. Martin stressed that without their help, the venture would not have been a success. Another money-saver was the venison from Martin's hunting.

Although Curry Creek is a dormant stream in late summer, it shows another side to its personality in the spring. Draining the entire northeast side of Diablo's North Peak, it often floods in heavy rains, notably in 1955, 1958, and again in 1962. The creek bed is deep near the Wrights' home, but in those three years the creek overflowed its banks and a little water crept into the house. Once the rain starts, the creek rises abruptly. Dorothy described the sudden deluge: "It is very exciting. It sounds like an avalanche, with the big timbers [carried in the flow] coming down."[21] Usually a four-by-four at the bot-

tom of the door was enough to keep most of the water out of the house.

But one flood season was more than merely exciting. The brimful creek was rushing by and Dorothy was working in the house when she heard panicked screams from her two older daughters, five-year-old Claudia and four-year-old Diana. The two, along with their 18-month-old sister, Cindy, had been playing in front of the snack bar near the creek. Dorothy raced out, jumped into three-and-a-half feet of rushing, freezing water without pausing to think, and just managed to grab her sputtering youngest daughter, Cindy, who had fallen into the rain-swollen creek. Dorothy was six months pregnant with the twins, Tom and Judy, at the time.

The Wrights eventually retired; the last oper-

Just another springtime flood at the Wrights' place:

Dorothy Wright "recalled a time when their son Tom was stationed outside the back door [on a four-by-four intended to guard against water entering the house], and the force of the water was making the timber waver gently under his feet. His older sister, Diana, went out to replace him, and when Dorothy looked out a while later after dark, Diana was standing with the water swirling around her ankles, wearing an old sombrero, reading a book [by flashlight—by this time the storm had caused their electricity to go out]. 'What are you doing?' called Dorothy. 'Studying my Spanish,' Diana called back. 'Heck, there isn't anything else to do out here.'" c

ating season for Curry Creek Park was 1979. Between 1980 and 1982, Dorothy and Martin subdivided their property, selling 25 acres with the trailer park, five acres with the original house and pool, and five acres that included the old ball field and picnic area. One of the new owners has finished filling the swimming pool with dirt, and signs on Marsh Creek and Morgan Territory roads now advertise a private Curry Creek Trailer Park, open to members only.

Martin died suddenly on 14 September 1999. A few months later Dorothy contacted Save Mount Diablo. "I want the public to be able to ride and walk up to the mountain," she said, "and my property will allow it."

Save Mount Diablo announced in March 2001 that it had signed an option agreement with Dorothy to acquire the remaining 76 acres of the Wrights' land for $640,000. If the funds are raised in time and the sale goes through, "a life estate agreement will allow Dorothy to live out her life on the property [and] the Wright and Olofson families will be given continual access to 'the Gathering Place,' a family monument high up between Wright and Curry canyons." [22]

1 Dorothy and Martin Wright supplied much of the information in this chapter in an interview on 5 Mar 1997 and in subsequent conversations.

2 *History of Contra Costa County, California* (San Francisco: W.H. Slocum, 1882) 546. Possibly Edward Curry also had settled in the area for a while.

3 San Francisco General Land Office, Homestead Entries 4341 and 4332, National Archives, DC.

4 "Death of Peter Olofson," *Contra Costa Gazette* 28 Nov 1903: 2.

5 Condie vs. Condie, Contra Costa County Superior Court Case #3597, 1904-5, at Contra Costa County Historical Society, Box CC18, Clayton.

6 In another note, Edith Olofson Wright claims the schoolhouse was from Somersville, but the Somersville schoolhouse was still in use in 1903. Edith says that her brother Oliver was born in the new house. Oliver was born in 1898, so her notation of Nortonville must have been correct.

7 Edith Olofson Wright's memories are from several handwritten sheets preserved by her family. On one of them she states that she is writing them at age 87; that would have been about 1980.

8 Edith Wright's notes.

9 Edith Wright's notes.

10 Edith Wright's notes.

11 Edith Wright's notes.

12 Martin Wright, personal interview, 5 Mar 1997.

13 Edith Wright's notes.

14 Jack Gleese, personal interview, 26 Nov 1996.

15 Martin Wright interview.

16 Martin Wright, conversation, 2 Feb 1998.

17 Martin Wright interview.

18 Martin Wright interview.

19 Meg Burges, "The Wrights of Curry Creek," *Contra Costa Times* 27 Apr 1966, 24.

20 Martin Wright interview.

21 Burges 24.

22 "Wright Canyon & Curry Creek / Talking to the Stars, Saying Goodnight to Loved Ones ...," *Diablo Watch* Spring 2001: 1, 6.

a Martin Wright, conversation, 19 May 1997.

b Martin Wright conversation 1997.

c Burges 24.

Chet and Gertrude Anderson, c. 1941. Courtesy of Bob and Irene Justice.

Caretakers of the Past

WARMTH FROM the brightly polished antique wood stove fills the kitchen, and the aromatic pulse of perking coffee signals the hospitality of the owners. Tiny-paned windows, framed in wood, overlook the back yard and the nearly dry bed of Marsh Creek in October. Above windows near the ceiling of the service porch, old-fashioned photographs of people long dead line the walls. Each room of the house reveals a love of old things—pieces of cut glass, lace doilies, a wooden wall telephone, a lamplighter hanging from the huge native stone fireplace, snowy white linen on the dining table, old sheet music open on the piano. This house is a museum, lovingly cared for by its owners, Irene and Bob Justice. The Justices are caretakers of the inheritance willed to them in 1993 by Conrad Chester "Chet" Anderson and his wife, Gertrude: the 1941 house, its contents, and a five-acre lot. In another sense the responsibility of the Justices transcends the material. Irene realizes this when she says, "Our only legacy is that someone remembers us."[1]

Chet and Gertrude Anderson both lived well into their 90s. In 1986, when Chet was 89, he stayed in a nursing home for nine months because poor circulation had culminated in large leg ulcers. He was miserable—he hated being away from his home on Morgan Territory Road. Bill Morgan, a good friend, worried about Chet's condition. Bill had met Irene Justice while she was caring for his uncle as a private-duty, home-care nursing aide. Bill took Irene to visit with Chet, and Irene promised "Mr. Anderson," as she always called him, that if he would go home, she could cure his ulcers. "So I brought him home," Irene said. "Within six months we had his legs completely healed. Of course, [the ulcers] just kept happening, but I kept on top of it, and it never got to the point where he had to be hospitalized again."[2]

Irene's husband, Bob Justice, was working as a ranger for the California State Park System. For nine years he had been stationed at Stinson Beach, for 11 years at Brannon Island. For the last 10 years of his career, he worked at Mount Diablo State Park. At the time of Chet Anderson's need for home nursing care, the Justices were living in Mitchell Canyon south of Clayton. Irene spent an eight-hour working day at the Andersons' and returned each night to her own home, but she was always on call.

Chet Anderson was a big, hearty man who had worked for Western Pacific as a civil engineer. After his retirement in 1941, he worked for Shell Oil, a night job at a pumping plant near the Marsh Creek Detention Facility off Marsh Creek Road. The pumping plant closed down, so Chet applied to the Contra Costa County Sheriff's Department and started another job as the guard in charge of the night shift at the Marsh Creek facility. He never carried a weapon, not even a nightstick. His size alone made him an intimidating person. But whereas some guards by their nature seemed to antagonize the prisoners, Chet was known as a caring person. Other guards might spend their time writing up reports while the prisoners were locked down. When Chet was in charge, however, the inmates considered him a friend.[3]

Chet Anderson had heard of Morgan Territory from his friend Sylvester Olofson. He first came out from Oakland to visit the area in 1918 and promptly fell in love with it. Chet and Gertrude Grace Frey were married on 7 July 1925. On 20 September 1938 they paid Mary Correa Azevedo Cardoza $12,000 for 435 acres on Morgan Territory Road, part of section 33 T1N/R1E. After tearing down the existing old ranch buildings, they built a barn and then a garage into which they moved in 1938 while their house was being

The Andersons' hayfield, c. 1941. Courtesy of Bob and Irene Justice.

built. Final construction costs for the house in 1941 were $6,500. The Andersons raised horses, sheep, cattle, and pigs and grew hay to feed the animals. Their hayfield was a level plot just north of their house site. George Frank remembered haying there after he got out of the army in the late '40s.

"Up there on the flat, Chet had a big ranch. We used to come there, and we'd bale hay for him," George Frank said. "Bob Morgan [Isaac Morgan's son], he would come and had this team with a stationary baler, y'know. Then Bob would take, and he would buck the hay into the press. . . . And then Chet would come out in the afternoon, and we'd eat.

"Oh, we'd get up in the morning and eat about 3:30, 4 in the morning, and then we'd go out to work. We'd start as soon as we could see to poke the wires, we'd go to work. We'd bring a lunch, a breakfast-like lunch; we'd have that about 8:30. At lunchtime my mother would bring a hot lunch out for all the guys, for the whole crew. And it'd be a pot of beans or stew, or something like that. And she'd also bring a 3:30 or 4 o'clock lunch out. Y'know, Chet Anderson, he'd go up to Curry Creek Park and buy some beer and bring it down to go with our lunch. He was real nice. . . ."[4]

The Andersons planted new grapevines, cared for the ones already growing on their property, and sold the grapes to the De Martini Winery in Clayton. Mary Cardoza, who sold the land to the Andersons, had inherited it from her father, Antone Correa Azevedo. Mary married and divorced John Maio, then Tony Baeta, and then married Frank Cardoza.[5] Jack Gleese remembered that the Baeta family had many fruit trees on the property—cherry, apple, pear, apricot, peach, and plum—as well as different types of grapes. "They were old vines, and they were huge. The trunks on those vines must have been eight or 10 inches in diameter."[6] Part of the vineyard was planted in wine grapes, part in table grapes. Bill Morgan recalled tokay and muscat as well as the Spanish mission grape.[7] Several mission grape vineyards on Morgan Territory survived even as late as 1950. They had escaped the grape mite that destroyed early vineyards in the Clayton area.[8] Tony Baeta allowed neighbor children to help themselves to the grapes as long as they did not throw them around and waste them, Jack Gleese said.[9]

If the grapevines were as old as both Bill and Jack believed, then of course the Baettas had not planted them. The property had first been purchased in 1871 by John H. Weber,[10] an immigrant from Denmark, with agricultural college scrip. Possibly he planted the vines that Bill and Jack remembered. In his 1867 pre-emption claim Weber noted that he had planted an orchard and vineyard on his ranch.[11] By the 1880 agricultural census he had a two-acre vineyard producing 5,000 pounds of grapes and 200 gallons of wine yearly.

A small grove of walnut trees planted by the Andersons is producing large, flavorful nuts even now, in 1999. Several other still-productive walnut groves stand at the northern end of Morgan Territory Road. Henry Frank planted walnut trees in the '30s that are still growing near Leon Drive along Morgan Territory Road.[12] Bill Morgan remembered that many other groves existed in the 1930s and 1940s.[13] In the '50s Bill Morgan dug out old mission variety grapevines in order to plant his walnut orchard.

In their early years on Morgan Territory Road, Chet and Gertrude Anderson enjoyed dressing up for evening jaunts into San Francisco or Oakland with two couples from the Olofson family. They liked to stay down at Carmel, and on one vacation traveled to Vancouver by train. On another train trip in 1939 they stopped at the Pontiac factory in Michigan and bought a car which they drove home. Early photographs show their delight in the outdoor life available in Morgan Territory. But Gertrude gradually developed the symptoms of agoraphobia, probably after her father's death in October 1941.

Remedies today can usually treat this fear of crowds successfully, but in those days people, even Gertrude herself, did not understand her affliction. "Well, people would drive in to see Chet, you know, and she'd be in the yard and when she'd see the car coming, she'd run in the house and shut the door," said Bob Justice. "The 'Mystery Woman' was what people called her—she was very, very reclusive."[14] During the last 25 years of her life, she rarely left the one room in the house that she called her own. Most agoraphobics are women, and before the advent of modern drugs and therapy, many, like Gertrude Anderson, turned to alcohol to relieve their panic. Their families were obviously affected as well. Chet ran all the household errands, did all their shopping. Their social life became nonexistent.

Chet enjoyed many hours of sharing his family history and his collection of old photographs with Irene Justice when she was his home care nurse. As children in 1845, his Irish grandmother, Mary McGill, and her brother and sister had been put on a boat bound for America to escape the effects of the Irish potato famine.[15] Irene commented, "That must have been difficult—put your children on a ship and say goodbye to them."[16] The Quakers were active during the famine in giving humanitarian aid to the Irish, and when Mary arrived in this country, she boarded and worked as a servant in a Quaker home. To the end of her life, she always used the pronouns of an earlier time, such as "thee" and "thine." In New York about 1863,[17] she married Irishman Thomas Anderson, who had immigrated in 1860.[18] Thomas and Mary came cross-country to Oakland and eventually moved to the Piedmont area near the intersection of Redwood Road and Anderson Avenue, where they bought over 700 acres of land. They had five sons who first helped them run a wood and coal business, and later the Anderson Brothers' Dairy. Their third son, also named Thomas, was Chet's father. He married Laura Gottwals, who was of German descent, and they had two sons, Chet and Walter. Walter died at age 41 of peritonitis just as Chet and Gertrude were settling in on Morgan Territory Road.

Mary Anderson had outlived her husband by 26 years when she died in 1939. At her death at approximately age 94, she left an estate worth over $96,000. Anderson family rumor had her still playing the stock market on the day she died.

Bit by bit through the years, Chet sold all his property in Morgan Territory except for the five-acre house lot. He first sold land on the west side of the road in 1964 and sold the last acreage in 1988. New owners subdivided these properties. After Chet retired from his job at the Marsh Creek Detention Facility, he often frequented the Clayton Club saloon. Longtime neighbor Dorothy Wright told the following story: "As usual, Chet was sitting at the bar nursing a beer. A stranger came in, pulled out a gun, and threatened the patrons and the bartender. 'This is a hold-up. Everybody put your wallets on the table and don't cause any trouble. This is a hold-up. Now I'm really serious about this,' the man said, or words to that effect.

"And Chet, who was about five sheets to the wind, looked over at him, and he says, 'You son of a bitch,' and he picks up his mug of beer and threw it at him. The robber's gun went off acci-

'I'm going to burn the house down . . .'

Gertrude Anderson's nephew and heir did not have the love of the 1941 house and its contents that Chet Anderson had. Irene Justice told of his visit to Chet one day: "'Well, when I inherit this piece of property,' he says, 'I'm going to burn the house down and everything that's in it.' And Mr. Anderson, after the nephew left, he says to me, 'Well, I worked three jobs just to build and pay for this property.' He says, 'I can't stand the thought of it being burned down and all the contents in it being burned down, so honey, you're going to inherit it.' I says, 'Please, don't do that! I don't want it. I don't want to get in the middle of a family argument. I just want to take care of it.' He insisted, 'You love this old place and all the things in it.'"[a]

dentally, but no one was hit. And everybody's hollering, and the bartender's trying to come around the end, and Chet's still gonna take this guy 'cause he's not gonna rob *his* bar.

"The robber turns and races out of the bar. One of the other customers runs out after him just as the Clayton police come around the corner. They see the second guy running, and they think he's the one trying to flee the Clayton Club, so they tackle him and bring him down. By the time it's all over, the real robber got away, of course. Chet became a real western town hero. He saved the Clayton Club and all the patrons."[19]

Irene Justice took care of Chet Anderson for four years, until his death at age 93 in 1990. His care grew more difficult when—six feet tall and weighing 230 pounds—he became wheelchair-bound. Two of his few comforts were having several drinks of Wild Turkey and visiting with Bill Morgan. But Chet chafed more and more about his isolation and immobility. One night Bill was shocked to hear Gertrude's voice over the telephone. By now she was most often withdrawn. Chet had gone out in the afternoon, she said, and had not returned. Bill came over to find that Chet had fallen out of his wheelchair into the creek. He had taken a portable phone with him, but the phone had fallen out of reach when the wheelchair went over. "He was just plain mad at me and the world," Bill said, in describing the situation.[20] Beside his own problems, Chet worried increasingly about what would happen to his wife after his death. With her agoraphobia, a nursing home would be a frightening place. Irene promised him that she would continue to take care of Gertrude, which she did until Gertrude died in 1993, three years after Chet's death. Chet Anderson's amended will specified that after Gertrude's death, Irene and Bob Justice would have the house and the remaining five acres.

Since his retirement from Mount Diablo State Park in 1991, Bob has not been bored or searching for activities—taking care of the Anderson property is a full-time job. In 1993 when the Justices moved in, the property was falling apart. The elderly Andersons had not been able to take proper care of it for many years. Dry rot in the roof meant that Bob had to replace the rafters. Huge fallen tree limbs lay on top of the roof. Not one of the drains was working properly. The basement was full of trash. Directly in front of the house is a huge valley oak tree, seven feet in diameter; it is estimated to be between 350 and 400 years old. Irene affectionately calls the old tree "Mother." Just keeping Mother trimmed and in good health so that she does not fall on the house costs a small fortune. The Justices are not wealthy, and they worry that someday they will not be able to afford the upkeep of the property and the rising taxes. In that case they will have to move, but they are torn about what to do with their museum. Who would be the caretakers of this legacy? Even if they could somehow fit all the contents of the house into a new place, they

Bob and Irene Justice under the huge old valley oak tree they affectionately refer to as "Mother." 2001 photo by Don Homan.

feel that would not be right. The collection belongs here on this site.

Irene showed me an engraving above a china cabinet of two frolicking white kittens. Mr. Anderson knew, she said, that this was her favorite picture in the house. Every morning when she comes in to make breakfast, that picture always hangs a little askew, as if in greeting.

1 Irene Justice, personal interview, 13 Oct 1997.

2 Irene Justice interview.

3 Bill Morgan, personal interview, 31 Oct 1997.

4 George Frank, interview at Old Timers' Luncheon, Clayton Museum, 1 Dec 1997, sponsored by the Clayton Historical Society.

5 Mary received her divorce from John Maio on 12 June 1900 on the grounds of mental and physical cruelty (*Contra Costa County Deeds* 86:66).

6 Jack Gleese, personal interview, 26 Nov 1996.

7 Bill Morgan, phone conversation, 18 Dec 1997.

8 George A. Pettit, *Clayton: Not Quite Shangri-La* (Martinez, CA: Contra Costa County Historical Society, 1996) 65.

9 Jack Gleese interview.

10 Sometimes the Weber family spelled their name "Weaver," a direct translation into English.

11 San Francisco General Land Office, Agricultural College Scrip 143, TX, National Archives, DC.

12 Phyllis Frank, Clayton Old Timers' Luncheon, 7 Oct 1996.

13 Bill Morgan, phone conversation, 18 Dec 1997.

14 Robert Justice interview.

15 Chet Anderson told Irene Justice that his grandmother came to the United States in 1845 at age 6, but the 1900 and 1910 US census records for Oakland, ED 325, sheet 17, line 57 and ED 26, sheet 18A, respectively, have her immigration date as 1852, which would make her about 13. In order for her to have retained the Quaker language, the earlier year was probably correct. On her son Franklin's death record, her surname was spelled Magill (CA #11671).

16 Robert Justice interview.

17 The 1900 US census for Oakland lists 34 years of marriage; the 1910 lists 47 years.

18 According to the 1900 US census for Oakland, he immigrated in 1860. The 1910 census lists the year as 1851. The 1880 census, unlike the others, lists his birthplace as England (ED 7, sheet 22, line 21).

19 Dorothy Wright, personal interview, 1 Dec 1997.

20 Morgan, interview 31 Oct 1997.

a Irene Justice interview.

Quicksilver and Its Aftermath

DULL AND REDDISH brown, the pond to the west of Morgan Territory Road, not far from its intersection with Marsh Creek Road, reflects the steep east side of Mount Diablo's North Peak. Intermittent piles of brick-red slag, left from over a century of mining for quicksilver—today we call it mercury—interrupt the greenery of the steep slope. The silence and heat are oppressive. Water is at a premium on Morgan Territory during the month of August, but no birds, fish, or amphibians disturb the unblinking surface of the pond. Acid leaching from the old mine tailings of crushed cinnabar has killed most of the aquatic insect life. The area that holds the pond was bulldozed expressly to catch seepage from the mountainside and protect the watershed from contamination. During heavy winter rains, how-

No Fishing

The poison of mercury and acid spreads at least 10 miles downstream to Marsh Creek Reservoir, which officials closed to fishing in 1980 when testing revealed significant amounts of mercury in bass, sunfish, and catfish.[a]

ever, the overflowing pond sends tainted water into a Marsh Creek tributary. Environmental news reporter James Bruggers wrote in 1994 that investigators had found almost 20 years earlier that Dunn Creek, flowing into Marsh Creek just below the mine, was "highly turbid and ex-

Mercury mine tailings in Morgan Territory, 1998. Photo by Anne Homan.

tremely lethal to aquatic life." Dunn Creek's thick brown water was described then as having the color and consistency of butterscotch pudding.[1]

To clean up the mine and surrounding area with sediment capping would cost approximately $10 million. Current owners Jack and Carolyn Wessman, who naively bought the property for a country retirement home in 1974, described their experience as "the American dream gone wrong."[2] In 1990 the Central Valley Regional Water Quality Control Board granted the Wessmans an exemption from the Toxic Pits Cleanup Act.[3] The Water Board had faced a fiscal dilemma, according to James Bruggers: "If it enforced the cleanup act, the Wessmans would have gone bankrupt and the mine would have gone to the state, with taxpayers taking over responsibility."[4] Various quicksilver mining companies that had leased the area either have long since gone out of business or have no assets left to seize. Meanwhile, the Wessmans continue to cooperate with authorities, gradually capping the tailings with soil and plants so that rainwater will leach more slowly through the ground before reaching open streams. But the couple acknowledged their frustration. "There have been lots of [government] studies done," Carolyn Wessman noted, "and nothing's left over for remediation."[5] Her husband remarked to the most recent task force investigating the problem, "You people dwell on studies and all, but I want to fix it."[6]

Long before anyone claimed ownership of the property, Native Americans collected the cinnabar ore to extract vermillion, which they used for red body paint and which was probably a major item for the local Volvon tribe to trade with their neighbors.[7] The area in Morgan Territory that contains the ore extends over parts of sections 28, 29 and 33 T1N/R1E. John H. Welch was the first settler to locate a cinnabar claim here, in 1863 during the copper mining rush. He claimed to have explored and prospected the land

in 1862.[8] The Welch Quicksilver, Silver, and Copper Mining Company was incorporated 17 July 1863 and issued 4,800 shares of stock.[9] In a court case filed on 18 July 1868, claims by the Mount Diablo Quicksilver Mining Company prevailed over Welch's company, run by trustee Samuel Phillips. A number of local claimants testified against Welch Quicksilver, Silver, and Copper Mining Company, including L.A. Hastings and Charles Rhine. At the time about 25 men had been working at the Welch mine, and various machinery such as a boiler, a steam engine, retorts, and a crusher are mentioned.[10] When Welch's company lost its case, Samuel Phillips won a judgment against Welch for Phillips's $10,000 investment, and the county sheriff closed the mine. After ownership of the mine had changed hands at least three times, Welch bought it back again in November 1874 with a new corporation, the Welch Consolidated Quicksilver Mining Company.[11]

On 20 July 1874, E.J. Ryan recorded a claim that he called the California Quicksilver Mine.[12] After selling all his mining interests to Welch in January 1875,[13] Ryan became superintendent of Welch's new Consolidated Quicksilver Mining Company, which now started to work on the old Welch claim.[14] The *Contra Costa Gazette* reported in January 1875 that the company had "expended about $10,000 up to the present time, and expect to have their furnaces completed and ready for smelting by the latter part of February. They are running two tunnels for the cinnabar deposit. . . . Mr. Ryan seems a very candid man of good judgment, and he appears very well satisfied that the company have a good prospect."[15] By July 1875 the *Gazette* reported that the mine had made several quicksilver shipments, the last one amounting to 16 flasks.[16] A flask is a metal cylinder approximately 15 inches long, holding 75 pounds of the liquid metal.

In November 1875 William Rider Powell claimed he owned the mine property. He had ap-

After residue from the Mount Diablo Quicksilver Mine furnace killed all the trees in a half-mile radius, this taller furnace stack was erected higher on the mountain, c. 1935. From the Ray Blomberg collection.

plied for a patent for the NE¼ of section 29 T1N/R1E in December 1874, and he asserted that he had filed a placer mining claim on the same property in October 1866.[17] In this court case, the Welch Consolidated Quicksilver Mining Company claimed that E.J. Ryan, its mine superintendent, had lived and worked at the mine "with a force of men" since March 1875. The case was settled out of court, but threats of litigation continued.[18] From 1875 through 1877, Ryan ran the mine with good success. At some point during this three-year period, it produced 85 flasks of mercury per month. In 1888 the mine was still the subject of litigation, and Ryan had left.[19] Eventually, the mine was closed. When Victor Blomberg and two partners leased land for their Mount Diablo Quicksilver Mine in 1929, the remains of the Welch/Ryan mine furnace and condensing chamber were still standing.

Knut Victor Blomberg had come to this country from Sweden in the early 1900s. He was one of the younger sons in a farming family with 14 children; only the eldest son would inherit land, so Victor decided to emigrate. His own younger son, Raymond, told how his father met his future Swedish bride during their sea voyage on the liner RMS *Baltic* to New York: "He found out my mother's brother had a bottle of brandy in his trunk. So, he got to know him."[20] Anna Maria Bergman and her brother were natives of Gøteberg, a large seaport, where their father worked in an iron foundry. "My mother was the oldest of 10," Raymond noted, "and they [older daughters] were stuck with the family then. They had to stay there and take care of the little kids, you know. So she got out."[21]

After arriving in San Francisco, the couple worked for two or three years before marrying. Anna cooked for a wealthy family in the city; Victor crewed on local sailing scows delivering hay around the bay. Later, he and a cousin worked at various construction jobs. In 1915 the Rhodes-

Just what is cinnabar?

Mine operators Jack Mony and John Johnson knew little about mercury ores or mining, Ray Blomberg said. "They put a big piece of rock in Mr. Johnson's dump truck, a little white dump truck, and hauled it to Sacramento and got it assayed. . . .They saw sparkling in the rock. They thought that was the cinnabar."[b] The assayer set them straight—this was excellent ore, but the red-colored rock itself, not the sparkling material, was cinnabar.

Jamieson firm hired Victor to work with dredges and marine equipment, and the Blombergs moved to Napa, where their two sons, Harold and Raymond, were born. By 1929 when he left Rhodes-Jamieson, Victor was the dredger foreman at their sand and gravel company at Eliot, and the family had moved to Sacramento. Victor's farewell recommendation letter from Rhodes-Jamieson read in part, "Mr. Blomberg has proven to be a very capable man in this line, and we recommend him highly—he has had years of experience, is efficient and trustworthy."[22]

Two men named Jack Mony and John Johnson had heard of a sand mine for sale near Byron in Contra Costa County. They talked Victor into becoming a possible partner in the mine, but it sold before they made a bid. In the process, they learned of the old Welch/Ryan mercury mine for sale, and the partners leased 40 acres on Mount Diablo from Joseph Tonge in 1929.

Unlike other metals, mercury remains a liquid at room temperature. The name quicksilver derives from its beautiful silver color and the fact that the heavy liquid moves—thus seeming quick, that is, alive, rather than inert or dead. The usual price of mercury per flask in 1929 was about $100. In the period 1930-1931 Blom-

Knut Victor Blomberg with rows of mercury flasks; each flask held 75 pounds of mercury. From the Ray Blomberg collection.

berg and his partners produced 58 flasks of quicksilver from cinnabar ore taken from old tunnels of the Ryan mine.[23] More rich bearing ore was eventually discovered about half a mile northeast, downhill from the Ryan mine. In 1932 Edward A. Howard granted Blomberg and his partners a five-year lease with an option to buy this second site. The partnership named the new site the Mount Diablo Quicksilver Mine. After incorporating their company in Nevada on 4 August 1931, they sold stock to raise cash for new construction.[24]

By 1935 the price of a flask of mercury had dropped to $30. The deepening financial depression forced the three to lease their mine to C.W. Erickson. When a mine is leased, the new firm takes over the operation but the original company receives a royalty based on sales. Under Erickson's management, a "glory hole" at the Mount Diablo site produced 730 flasks of quicksilver.[25] *Special Report 80* of the California Division of Mines and Geology noted, "The ore in this shoot was quite rich in metacinnabar as well as cinnabar, and is said to have once yielded 48 flasks of quicksilver in 48 hours."[26] Residue from the furnace chimney killed all the trees for half a mile around, and mine neighbors were upset. As a result of their complaints, the company built a much taller stack higher on the mountain in about 1935. Meanwhile, they leased an additional 60 acres from Howard and began putting up a larger capacity 40-ton Gould-type furnace. However, by the time the furnace was finished all concerned had run out of money. In 1936 Erickson in turn sold his lease to the Bradley Mining Company.

Victor Blomberg remained at the mine, working as foreman for Bradley. Philip W. Cox was the general superintendent. Under Bradley ownership, according to *Special Report 80*, "Ore taken from these workings yielded 10,455 flasks of quicksilver between 1937 and 1948, making the Mount Diablo quicksilver district rank ninth in U.S. production for the period 1940–1952. . . ."[27] The value of all mercury mined in this area through the years is placed at $1,564,069.[28] During World War II, the price of a flask almost doubled, to a high of $192 in 1943. The *Oakland Tribune* touted the wartime uses of the metal as an anti-fouling paint to keep marine organisms from growing on ship hulls and as an essential ingredient in the manufacture of medical equipment and of detonators for torpedoes and aerial bombs.[29] A newspaper article published on 8 May 1941 praised the 30 men who had been working in three shifts at the Mount Diablo mine without a break since Christmas Day to supply mercury for Great Britain's war effort.[30]

The men mined ore in an open surface pit, with about seven benches, as well as underground, with four levels connected to a shaft with a 45-degree slope. An engine pumped water constantly to keep the shaft from flooding, and in the beginning the pumped water was simply allowed to drain straight into Dunn Creek. After a suit brought by neighbors, authorities insisted that mine owners run pipes from the workings up to a ridgetop where the water sprayed out over the landscape. Because the water was extremely corrosive, pipes had to be concrete-lined stainless steel. At present, water in the abandoned mine has inundated its shaft and all tunnels.

The process of extracting mercury from cinnabar (mercury sulfide) began with filling the firebrick-lined, 35-foot oil furnace with crushed ore.[31] While the six-foot diameter furnace rotated, its temperature was increased until the ore became white hot. The sulfur oxidized to sulfur dioxide, allowing the mercury to sublimate. Resulting mercury vapor flowed into condensers that cooled it down until the pure metal reverted to its normal liquid state. Vats under the condenser collected the heavy liquid. Victor Blomberg always bottled all the mercury himself. Although only five foot eight, he was exceedingly strong and easily carried two vats at a time, each filled with 150 pounds of mercury. Carefully, always being aware of the poisonous nature of the metal, he poured the liquid mercury from a vat into two flasks. Asked if his father ever had any problems with mercury poisoning, Ray Blomberg laughed. Victor lived to the age of 92 and was driving until age 87.

The furnace crew worked in three eight-hour shifts, morning, afternoon, and night. Underground mining was in two shifts, morning and afternoon only. Work continued seven days a week, no holidays, no overtime. Furnace shift records entered in an old school copybook for 1941 show that the men worked straight through on Thanksgiving and Christmas Day. Clarence Webb, Pat Russell, E.W. Witt, and Hugo Bosco competed against each other as they manned the hot furnace, noting carefully the number of slag cars removed. On one page Witt complained, "Hugo you can't make a square joint in the track round by putting grease on it. Please fix the track so we can use it." Retaliating on another page, someone added "B.S." and "Big Stuff" in front of Witt's name. When Witt noted a record 31 ore cars on his shift, another worker put three large question marks by the figure. Witt replied, "Don't forget punk I was using the small car, thanks to pretty boy 'Hugo the sheik.'"[32] Some 45 people worked at the mine in its heyday during World War II. The single men had a cookhouse for meals, and the Bradley Company built 12 cabins to house workers. Victor Blomberg rented out the cabins, made repairs, and performed various caretaker duties.

Many local young men joined the work crew. After he graduated from high school in 1938,

The 6-foot diameter furnace at the Mount Diablo Quicksilver Mine. Courtesy of Contra Costa County Historical Society.

Martin Wright worked underground at the mine for about six months. At the end of the afternoon shift at four o'clock, the miners would set off an explosion and leave for the day. Martin's lonely task from six in the evening until two in the morning was to muck out the resulting loose rock. The job meant almost constant shoveling at the 300-foot level. He had to fill an ore car, then push it out through the tunnel to the shaft where he dumped the ore into a funnel called a "pocket" that had a closure at the narrow end. Although the air was cool underground, by the time Martin was ready for his lunch break he was sweating profusely. When he emerged from the mine in winter weather to eat topside, he was soaking wet and soon freezing.

On the day shift, tram cars were lowered down the sloping shaft with a cable hoist and filled with the ore from the pocket, then pulled back up to the surface. Early one evening, someone from the afternoon crew was still pulling up the last tram car even though Martin was already at work. Martin had just finished emptying ore into the pocket and luckily had moved back somewhat into the tunnel when the cable hoist broke and a fully loaded tram car roared down the shaft, destroying everything in its path.[33]

Victor and Anna Blomberg had moved their family from Sacramento to Morgan Territory in 1929. Victor built a house with two bedrooms, a kitchen, and a living room with a native stone fireplace, on acreage leased from the Howards. The family had a huge barbecue pit where Ray remembered Victor as a master at outdoor cooking. "He was a great guy," Ray said of his father. "He was very fair, very fair. When we grew up, he

'That's why I never smoked'

Ray Blomberg did not recall hearing of any serious accidents at the mine. Inspectors sent by the Bureau of Mines were strict about enforcing regulations. Special Report 80 *noted in 1963: "The gases methane, hydrogen sulfide, and sulfur dioxide are common underground in the Mount Diablo mine. They present no hazard, however, where modern ventilating techniques and electric lamps [powered by a battery backpack] are used."[1] "Of course," Ray said, "you couldn't smoke underground. I think that's why I never smoked. As a kid, I'd see these miners sneaking a smoke—[that could] blow the whole place up."[c]*

was the boss, but he was very fair."[34] Irmgard Cox, wife of mine superintendent Philip Cox, described Victor as a "jolly old Swede" and Anna as a "marvelous cook." Anna fixed Swedish dishes— potato salad, pickled herring, meatballs. Traveling salesmen knew they could find a delicious meal with the Blombergs, although some of them did not know what they were eating. After polishing off a meal of sliced tripe, one salesman told Anna, "This is the best creamed chicken I have ever eaten."[35]

Swedish friends would often come over, and Victor loved to converse in his native language. Ray laughed and said, "All the Swedes would get together, you know, and talk about the old country, how good it was. That would make my mother madder'n the devil. She'd say, 'There's a boat leavin' every day.'"[36] As Ray and Harold grew up, their mother insisted on English being spoken in the home. Ray's wife, Fran, recalled, "If you wanted to converse, you did it in English. . . . Consequently, her accent was very light, about like Ingrid Bergman."[37] Victor's accent remained strong throughout his life.

The two boys attended Morgan Territory School, and Ray, like many other former students, praised the teaching abilities of Marie Rosenblatt Morgan. "That school was just wonderful!"[38] He liked the intimacy of such a small student body and the fact that with multiple grades in the same room, the younger students learned informally from the older ones because they heard all the oral lessons. Ray was the only graduate in 1935. He noted that life in Morgan Territory was "pretty darn lonesome sometimes," so the boys cherished any visitor.[39] Finding their jersey milk cow every afternoon was one of Ray's chores. "I'd come home from school. Howard's beef cattle were on the place.[40] Our cow would run with the herd. The beef cattle were spooky. I'd actually have to crawl up the little creek or something to get close to her. Put a chain on her and take her home. . . . She could have roamed miles, you know, up the mountain, but she never went up the hill, thank goodness."[41]

They cut wood for the kitchen stove and to sell. In summer they moved the wood stove outside onto a patio area. Rattlesnakes were plentiful, and one day Anna saw a huge one on her patio barbecue table. "She was mad—that snake wasn't going to get away with that!" Ray said. "She got a big ax and chopped [the snake] in two. She saved it as long as she could to show people. She was so proud of that."[42] At first they had an outhouse, but then Victor made a "shower house" that contained a toilet and shower and facilities for indoor laundry. Anna did a great deal of canning and loved to redecorate the interior of the little house. Smiling, Ray said that the walls probably had 14 different coats of paint. Ray and his brother both worked at the mine. Ray started at 16. "My dad was the boss. I did most everything, everything no one else wanted to do. Made $3.50 a day."[43]

The price of a flask of mercury plummeted again after World War II, and the Bradleys sold gravel made from a conglomerate called graywacke taken from a site near the old Ryan mine. Bradley Mining Company sold its lease to Ronnie B. Smith in 1951. In the early 1950s, two suits were brought against the operators of the mine. Owners of Marsh Creek Springs, a recreational area downstream, complained of careless deposit of the tailings. "Marsh Creek is now badly discolored and filled with excessive mineral substances," causing damage to their swimming pool and drinking water, the suit said.[44] The other suit, brought by the administrators of the estate of Edward A. Howard, alleged illegal dumping of mine tailings in section 28 and construction of a dam that created sediment run-off onto Howard's property.[45] Several other investors leased the mine after Smith. In 1955 Blomberg and his partners sold the mine and property to the Cordera Mining Company for $140,000.

Victor Blomberg kept three and a half acres for himself, moving to a site down the mountain nearer Morgan Territory Road. By this time Anna was in a rest home in Concord. In 1972 Victor moved into a one-bedroom house in the backyard of his son Ray's Concord home, which made it easier for him to visit Anna. Although Victor had the privacy of his own home, Ray and his wife, Fran, were close by if needed. Every morning at eight o'clock Victor fed Anna her breakfast at the nursing home. Afterward he would visit with the Cox family on his way home. "He had a little red truck, I remember," recalled Irmgard Cox. "When I'd see it turn the corner, I'd say, 'Here comes Vic!' He always loved to visit over coffee laced with bourbon."[46] His daughter-in-law Fran noted, "He was a great person to have around, not demanding. I still had to cook a few Swedish things on Sundays, but I had had a good teacher [Anna]."[47] Anna Blomberg died in 1974, Victor 10 years later.

According to Ray, his older brother, Harold, was the smart one in the family, going on to study at Heald Business College, and then be-

coming a CPA. Harold suffered from severe diabetes and died at age 50 in 1969. Ray became a heavy equipment operator and later in his career a salesman of heavy equipment. He enjoyed traveling and the challenge of selling. Ray and Fran have two daughters and a son. After retiring and moving from Concord to the Gold Country town of Sonora, Ray said, he realized that he no longer had the urge to travel. A passerby can recognize their home by the ore cart in front.

Contra Costa County perseveres in its efforts to alleviate problems at the mercury mine site. From 1995 to 1997, Darell Slotton of the University of California at Davis used the latest measuring technology to conduct intensive studies of the reservoir, creeks, and wildlife affected by mercury contamination. He concluded, "The mine area itself was the clear source region for the mercury, with an estimated 88 percent of the total input of mercury to the upper watershed traceable specifically to the current exposed tailings piles."[48] Based on the recommendations of Slotton, the Contra Costa County Department of Public Works is seeking a state grant for an ecosystem restoration. Cost of the proposed project is $1,406,000, considerably less than previously proposed options. The project would include diverting several creeks, grading the site so that it is less steep, adding several feet of soil cover, and planting grass and native species of other vegetation. This Morgan Territory location is by no means the only mercury contamination site in the Bay Area or the state, and the county hopes that successfully cleaning it up would benefit more than the Marsh Creek watershed. The 1997 Contra Costa County report noted, "If a relatively low cost approach is significantly effective, that will be very useful information for the wider goal of statewide mercury remediation."[49]

1 James Bruggers, "No Cleanup in Store for Mercury Mine," *The Valley Times* 3 July 1994: 1A.

2 Bruggers, "No Cleanup," 4A.

3 Bruggers, "No Cleanup," 1A.

4 Bruggers, "No Cleanup," 4A.

5 James Bruggers, "Plants Might Cut Mine Pollution," *The Valley Times* 11 Feb 1995: 8A.

6 Bruggers, "Plants," 8A.

7 Robert F. Heizer and Adam E. Treganza, "Mines and Quarries of the Indians of California," *California Journal of Mines and Geology*, 40 (July 1944): 312.

8 San Francisco General Land Office, Mining Entry 51, National Archives, DC. Welch's affidavit swearing to the exploration was dated 27 Mar 1875.

9 The Contra Costa County Historical Society has a certificate from the company worth four shares, which were issued to Robert Lewis Jr. on 9 Dec 1865. According to the certificate, the organization was started in 1863.

10 Welch Quicksilver, Silver and Copper Mining Company vs. The Mount Diablo Quicksilver Mining Company, filed 18 July 1868 in Contra Costa County District Court, 15th Judicial District. Materials available at Contra Costa County Historical Society, file box CC6.

11 Mining Entry 51.

12 *Contra Costa County Land Claims*, Vol. 5, page 633. In local accounts the name of the mine is usually spelled Ryne, Rine or Rhyne. Perhaps confusion arose because of the well-known Rhine family of Clayton who did own some nearby property. Also, in 1865 and probably for longer, Charles Rhine was secretary of the Welch Quicksilver, Silver and Copper Mining Co.

13 Mining Entry 51.

14 "Mt. Diablo Quicksilver," *Contra Costa Gazette* 26 Dec 1874:3.

15 "The Quicksilver Mine," *Contra Costa Gazette* 2 Jan 1875: 3.

16 "The Quicksilver Workings," *Contra Costa Gazette* 3 July 1875: 3.

17 Announcement of patent registration, *Contra Costa Gazette* 12 Dec 1874: 4.

18 The Welch Consolidated Quicksilver Mining Company vs. William Rider Powell, filed 18 Nov 1875 in Contra Costa County District Court, 15th Judicial District. Materials available at Contra Costa County Historical Society, file box CC6.

19 William Irelan Jr., State Mineralogist, "Contra Costa County," *Annual Report of the State Mineralogist*, no. 8 (ends 1 Oct 1888), State Mining Bureau: 162.

20 Ray Blomberg, personal interview, 30 June 1997.

21 Blomberg interview.

22 From letter owned by Ray Blomberg.

23 "Geology and Mineral Deposits—Mt. Diablo," *California Division of Mines and Geology, Special Report 80* (1963) 20, 23.

24 Nilda Rego, "Mount Diablo Miners Try Luck With Mercury," *The Valley Times* 13 Sep 1997: D5. Articles of Incorporation, filed in Carson City, NV on 4 August 1931, given to the Contra Costa County Historical Society by Ray Blomberg in November 1998.

25 "Geology and Mineral Deposits—Mt. Diablo," 23.

26 "Geology and Mineral Deposits—Mt. Diablo," 23.

27 "Geology and Mineral Deposits—Mt. Diablo," 23.

28 "Geology and Mineral Deposits—Mt. Diablo," 23.

29 "Mount Diablo Quicksilver to Aid Defense," *Oakland Tribune* n.d.

30 "Mount Diablo Quick-silver Mine Working Day and Night As a 'Defense Industry'" 8 May 1941. Newspaper (not named) article saved in scrapbook owned by Ray Blomberg.

31 This furnace was first used in early 1938. Clyde P. Ross, *Quicksilver Deposits of the Mount Diablo District, Contra Costa County, CA*, State Department of the Interior, Bulletin 922- B: 33.

32 The copybook is owned by Ray Blomberg.

33 Martin Wright, personal interview, 5 March 1997.

34 Blomberg interview.

35 Irmgard Witt Cox, personal interview, 5 Sep 1997.

36 Blomberg interview.

37 Frances Blomberg, personal interview, 30 June 1997.

38 Ray Blomberg interview.

39 Ray Blomberg interview.

40 These cattle belonged to Edward A. Howard, no relation to ship's engineer Robert Howard.

41 Ray Blomberg interview.

42 Cox interview.

43 Nilda Rego, "Depression Has Effect on Mount Diablo Mercury Mines," *The Valley Times* 20 Sep 1997: D5.

44 Contra Costa County Civil Case 58077, 8 June 1953.

45 Contra Costa County Civil Case 57662, 13 Apr 1953.

46 Cox interview.

47 Frances Blomberg interview.

48 Darell G. Slotton, Shaun M. Ayers and John E. Reuter, *Marsh Creek Watershed 1995 Mercury Assessment Project Final Report*, Contra Costa County, CA, March 1996: 60.

49 "Mt. Diablo Mercury Mine Site Remediation and Mercury Export Reduction Project," Attachment E, *Marsh Creek Watershed Mercury Assessment Project, Second Year (1996) Baseline Data Report*, Contra Costa County Department of Public Works, July 1997: 7.

a Bruggers, "No Cleanup," 1A.

b Blomberg interview.

c "Geology and Mineral Deposits—Mt. Diablo," 24.

d Blomberg interview.

Summer Cabins

FEW CURRENT RESIDENTS of Morgan Territory Road wrest their living from the land. Most do not have enough acreage, and even those who do—longtime ranching families like the Morgans, Cardozas, and Morrises—supplement their agricultural efforts with other careers. In the first half of the 1900s, some East Bay families who bought property in Morgan Territory did not plan to raise beef cattle or grow walnuts for a living. In pleasant weather only, they commuted from busy metropolitan lives to second homes in the restful hills. The Howard, Hink, and Stadelhofer families are among these summering owners.

HOWARD FAMILY

Barely noticeable under a rich supply of weeds, a stone barbecue fireplace is crumbling behind what is probably Jesse Morgan's old barn. This fireplace remains the only clue to the outdoor social life of the Howard family who once lived here. Edward A. Howard began acquiring property along the road in 1905 when he bought the William Ryder Powell estate, the NW¼ of section 29 T1N/R1E.[1] In 1932 Howard leased part of the land to Victor Blomberg for mercury mining. Step by step, Howard also bought pieces of sections 28, 32, 33, and 36.[2] He built a summer home for his family east of the road near the stone fireplace.

Edward Howard was born in San Francisco but lived most of his life in Oakland. His father, John R. Howard, a physician, moved the family to Oakland in 1876 when Edward, his younger son, was 12. Edward graduated from the University of California at Berkeley in 1886,[3] just after the death of his father.[4] Soon he became a partner in an Oakland lumber business, which sometime after 1898 moved to San Francisco. By 1908 he was president of E.A. Howard and Company, dealing in hardwood, lumber, cabinet woods, and flooring.[5]

After hiring Manuel Mendoza as year-round caretaker, Edward Howard did run beef cattle on his country property with the help and advice of Sylvester Olofson. When Edward and Daisy Howard and their four children spent time on the Morgan Territory property, horseback riding was a favorite activity. Mendoza would catch and saddle the Tennessee walkers for the family. Neighbor Dorothy Wright's memory of E.A. Howard was clear: "I saw him on horseback once, and he was very impressive. He wore a hat—not a cowboy hat, but a fedora style. He looked very distinguished, with a neatly trimmed mustache and goatee."[6] Accustomed to the rough-and-tumble school of ranch riding as a boy, Martin Wright described Howard's riding clothes as "outfits I never saw before in my life."[7]

The Howards and the Sylvester Olofson family were neighbors who helped one another in their isolated community. The Olofsons' daughter Edith Wright wrote a note to Daisy Howard in 1953. The Wright family saved Edith's rough draft:

"When going thru some of mother's papers after she passed away last May I came upon a letter from Mr. Howard to 'Pa' telling him there was no charge for the diving board sent for the swimming pool, because of little favors including 'farm advice' from him. The keeping of that friendly note is typical of the esteem in which the Olofson family held you and your family. We were so proud to claim you as acquaintances and especially proud of Mr. Howard's trust and respect for Pa. . . . I still have the haviland china tea set you sent Mom and the inlaid wooden boxes you gave Dell and me. . . . I remember riding 'Bessie.'

"But this note is just to tell you that we

deeply appreciated your kindness and even without that letter to remind us, we think of you and Mr. H. as very wonderful people—and we wish you a most happy Xmas."

Edward Howard was an active horseman even past the age of 80. He was a founder and director of the Oakland National Horse Show and an active member of the Oakland Trails Club, and held trotting races on a track at his Morgan Territory property.[8] He died on 26 June 1947 at his Oakland home on Fairmount Avenue. Besides his country property in Morgan Territory, he owned the lumber company, timberland in Lake County, shares in Union Oil and Western Pacific, and various city lots in Oakland. Also listed in his will was his 1937 Buick Special Sport Coupe.[9] The Howards' house in Morgan Territory burned to the ground in the 1960s; of the old buildings only Jesse Morgan's white barn and the weed-covered barbecue survive. Their property was sold and subdivided into ranchettes for horse owners.

HINK FAMILY

John Frederick Hink came to the United States in 1869 as a draft evader from militaristic Prussia. His native state of Holstein had been annexed from Denmark three years before. By 1872 he had opened his first dry goods store in San Francisco, with four employees. Ready-made clothes did not exist, but the store sold items for women that included whalebone corsets and high-button shoes. He opened a Berkeley store in 1904 with his son, Lester "L.W." Hink, then 19 years old, as manager. Father and son had very different ideas on how to do that job. One day L.W. took his father aside and firmly told him, "Either you run the store or I run the store."[10] His father gave L.W. the keys and never interfered again. Ten years after the original Berkeley opening, Hink's was in the larger space it would occupy for the next 63 years, a Berkeley landmark at the corner of Shattuck and Kittredge. By 1949

Hink's had 542 employees. L.W. Hink remained in charge from the opening of the Berkeley store until his retirement in 1975 at age 90.[11] L.W. Hink, his employees insisted, should be given credit for the success of the store. His "generosity of spirit, genius for business, involvement in community service" added up to a warm, charismatic CEO.[12] By the time his son Robert took over after L.W.'s death, however, the store was having economic difficulties, and Robert was unable to stop the trend. The Hink family sold the department store in 1977. On 1 Oct 1985 the new owners closed the doors of the beautifully crafted 1914 building with its marble and maple floors, intricate plaster cast ceilings, and solid brass doors.[13] Now it houses a 10-screen movie complex, somewhat the worse for wear.

Personnel hired by the Hinks tended to stay a long time, and often their children were hired as well. An employee who had been with the store for 34 years suggested that "Hink's was not a store; it was a family."[14] One of the nephews of J.F. Hink, John Jacob Hink, came to Berkeley from Schleswig-Holstein in 1911. He soon became merchandising manager for the store, retiring from that position in 1960.

In 1925 John Jacob "J.J." Hink bought 40 acres in section 29 T1N/R1E just south of the mercury mines in Morgan Territory.[15] George Pettit, who wrote about the Clayton area, noted, "His family had picnicked in the area a number of times, and when he found that an elderly Spanish-American lady, Macaria Arroya, was willing to sell 40 acres for $650 he couldn't resist the opportunity."[16] He built two homes on the property, one for his family and one for his father-in-law, John H. Gabriel. As with the Howards, J.J. Hink's wife, Leola, and their four children would stay throughout the summer in Morgan Territory, with J.J. visiting on weekends. Ray Blomberg remembered that the Gabriels lived there practically year-round. One day, after a blast at the mercury mine, John Gabriel came over to complain to the Blombergs. According to Ray's version of the event, Gabriel had been "lying there in his chaise lounge . . . outside. We set a blast off. There was a stump involved. Those pieces would fly forever. He was lying there and a piece of wood . . . landed right along side of him. He came [over to the mine] carrying the wood back."[17] John Jacob "J.J." Hink died at age 75 on 21 January 1971 at his Berkeley home. The 40 acres was acquired by Mt. Diablo State Park in September 1982.

STADELHOFER FAMILY

Many hot sulphur springs once existed on the slopes of Mount Diablo and its associated foothills. Possibly these springs represented the dying stages of activity that produced the quicksilver deposits.[18] In 1875 Bareges Sulphur Springs, on what is now Heather Farm Park in Walnut Creek, had bathhouses open to the public on weekends. Pine Canyon Sulphur Spring was located four miles north of Danville at the western base of Mount Diablo. There is a sulphur spring on the east slope of North Peak. Ferndale Springs, six miles southwest of Martinez, included a hotel and cottages in the late 1800s and offered mineral baths of soda, sulphur, and magnesia water. The most famous in the East Bay is Byron Hot Springs, where natural salt springs, as hot as 140 degrees, were visited by the California Indians long before a fancy hotel was built nearby.[19]

Another sulphur spring, more secluded and now less celebrated, is on the NW¼ of section 12 T1S/R1E, about 2.5 miles south of Marsh Creek Road. Owned for the past half-century by the Stadelhofer family, it has an early history as a resort.

Louis and Minnie Seemann of Oakland bought this quarter—known as Sycamore Springs—from its previous owner, J.W. Jarvis, in 1886.[20] Born in Germany in 1851, Louis Seemann had immigrated to the United States in

1870. He was five feet six, with hazel eyes and dark hair. Minnie was born in New York of German parentage. When Minnie Seemann applied for a homestead for Sycamore Springs' 160 acres in November 1905, she estimated the value of the property at $4,000.[21] The dirt access road that follows Sycamore Creek into the hills was dubbed Fern Canyon Road by the Seemanns but now goes by the less euphonious name of Hog Canyon Road.

At the site of Sycamore Springs, about 1,000 feet in elevation, three canyons come together in a small flat area. The *Richmond Record* included the resort on this site in its listing in 1906 of interesting local spots: "Among the many places for one to pass the summer days for recreation and enjoyment of country life is the well-known resort of Sycamore Springs. . . . It is the mecca for the lovers of camp life. . . . The sulphur spring water has been tested and proven to possess medicinal properties of high curative quality."[22] A patron could choose hot or cold sulphur springs or pure spring water. The Seemanns advertised hunting in season, mountain climbing, and "every outdoor occupation imaginable within call."[23]

Besides outdoor campers, the Seemanns could accommodate 25 boarders in their two-story home. Minnie Seemann was praised for setting a "splendid table." Many fruit tree varieties had been planted on their property, and the house was "shaded by the favorite European trees—lindens and walnuts. Here is the haunt of Mrs. Seemann's pigeons, which flock about her on call and feed from her hands. A dish of delicious squabs is frequently served to the household."[24] One large linden and many walnut trees still shade the area. Pigeon potpie and squab were prized dishes in those days. Today's homeowner more often seeks methods to frighten annoying pigeons away from the roof. In earlier times, however, pigeons were encouraged to roost on farms and ranches. Jesse Morgan's barn, built around 1885, contains pi-

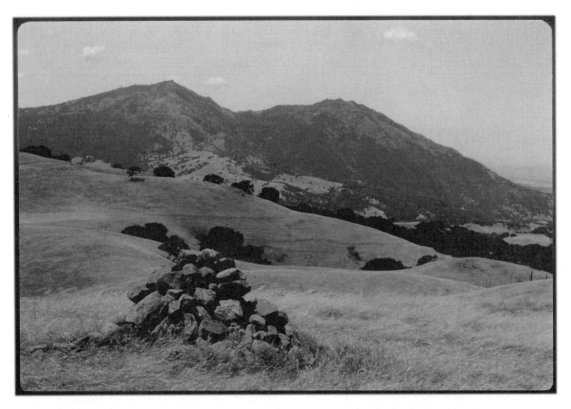

The Stadelhofer family cairn, at the highest point on their Sycamore Springs property. 1999 photo by Anne Homan.

geon doors and, inside under the roof, nesting boxes. Phillippa Clyma baked pigeon potpie for visitors. Catherine Clyma's friend Kate Doyle wrote in 1905 of her savory memories: "Cassie, I so often think of [your mother] and her potpie."[25] A year earlier, Kate had written of her disappointment in her own culinary arts: "I tried to make a pigeon potpie like your mama's for dinner last evening. It was nice, but didn't quite suit me as well as hers did."[26]

Stage drivers met the train at Brentwood twice a week during the season to bring visitors 12 miles to Sycamore Springs. On 24 June 1909 Sycamore Springs sponsored a grand ball; "a large attendance was expected from Clayton, Byron, Brentwood, Marsh Creek and Antioch."[27] The

Seemanns hosted another dance at their "mountain resort" on 24 July 1909.[28]

The Seemann family left Sycamore Springs about 1911. In December 1910, they sold their property and paid off two mortgages amounting to $2,350.[29] Minnie died at age 55 in 1915. Louis died in Antioch in 1919; he had been the caretaker at Riverview High School. The property was sold to a number of different owners; at various times someone built an outdoor dance floor and a poorly designed swimming pool that collapsed. In the late 1920s and the 1930s, local young people attended Farm Bureau picnics and dances at the springs.[30]

When Fidelis Frederick "Fred" Stadelhofer and his wife, Stella, bought the Sycamore Springs property in the 1940s, the only remnants of previous owners were a small outbuilding, the dance floor, the walls of the old pool, exotic trees, and a rock fireplace that had been the centerpiece of the Seemanns' home.[31] The spring on the property was still gushing at five to six gallons a minute.[32] On 1 May 1945 the Stadelhofers bought the remaining three-fourths of section 12 from Daniel Conner.[33] It had been in the Foskett family for 18 years, from 1922 until 1940, and had earlier been the ranch of Joseph Bent Nunez and his family, who had left to run dairy farms in the Central Valley. Traces of the Nunezes' old cabin still exist, and access to the property is possible on old dirt roads from Morgan Territory Road.

Fred's father, Frederick Carl Stadelhofer, son of a master glazier, was born in Konstanz, Germany, in 1869 and settled in the area of St. Louis, Missouri, after his 1886 immigration to the United States. The younger Fred married Stella Newton on 17 August 1922, and they moved from Webster Groves, a suburb of St. Louis, to Seattle, and then to Berkeley, where work was available after a disastrous $9 million fire on 17 September 1923 that destroyed more than 1,000 buildings and left 6,000 people homeless.[34] Their daughter, Virginia, was born in Webster Groves, but their two sons, John and yet another Frederick ("Fritz"), were born in Berkeley. Stella's parents soon followed Fred and Stella to Berkeley from St. Louis.

Fred worked for a while for the Byron-Jackson Pump Company as a machinist, then decided to open his own contract machine shop. He had an old Chevrolet engine up in the rafters to supply power for his machinery. When son Fritz was 10, his responsibilities were to sweep the floors, run the drill presses, and climb up in the rafters to oil the machinery. Fritz described his father as "very friendly, a philanthropist, a fine old earthy person. He left a trail of good feeling wherever he went."[35]

One day while doing pump work in the shop

for a customer, Fred thought of making jet pumps for home water systems. Berkeley Pump Company was incorporated in March 1937. By 1978 Berkeley Pump's buildings had spread over 12.5 acres in the industrial heart of Berkeley near Sixth and Bancroft. The firm manufactured a variety of pumps, mostly for agricultural irrigation. Ralph Rhoda, who joined the company in 1939, designed a pump that made jet boats possible. When Fritz returned from a stint in the Air Force during World War II, he started his official 50-year career working with his father at Berkeley Pump, and Fritz's son, Eugene, worked as a mechanic and foreman in the Berkeley shop for 18 years. When Transamerica bought out the company in 1978, Berkeley Pump had manufacturing and sales branches all over the United States from Atlanta to Portland, as well as international branches.

Fred Stadelhofer had envisioned "a country place" for his children, "a play place, somewhere with recreation not too far from Berkeley."[36] After he bought the Sycamore Springs quarter, Fred's younger son, Johnny, and Fred's father-in-law built a cabin, incorporating the original rock fireplace of the old Seemann home into the new structure. Later, Fritz helped add on a bathroom and another bedroom. The family also worked together on building a smaller swimming pool, using two of the original walls. Eugene, born in 1948, was practically raised at the ranch, which was "heaven for a kid."[37] He had horses to ride, the pool to swim in. His grandfather bought some used Oakland playground equipment and brought up two big slides and a merry-go-round. In addition, they had a trampoline. Eugene learned to drive on dirt roads in a 1942 war-surplus Jeep. His father had stood in line for three days in Benicia to buy it.

About 1970 Fred and Fritz managed to put their section of land under the protection of the Williamson Act, passed with the intention of preserving open space. In order to qualify, the landowner must have at least 100 acres. The family pays taxes based only on the agricultural value of their property. Section 12 is too covered with trees and chaparral to be of much agricultural use except for running a few cattle, so their taxes are low. Eventually, the family founded the Sycamore Springs Corporation, which now owns the property.

Eugene Stadelhofer and his family still enjoy going to the springs to relax. He has maintained many dirt roads that carve through section 12. As his jeep, a Suzuki now, crests a steep hillside meadow not yet contaminated by the star thistle that is invading some areas, Mount Diablo rises abruptly in front of him, so close he almost seems to be driving straight into its chaparral. From this highest point on the property, about 2,200 feet, he can see the Clymas' almond orchard, the mothball fleet in Carquinez Strait, and—on especially clear days—the Sierra. On his jeep trips, Gene notes game trails for future bow-and-arrow deer seasons and mends the vandalism of wild pigs at the springs. The old resurrected swimming pool continues to beckon in the heat of California summers. Modern amenities such as telephones and PG&E electricity do not exist here. Lost mountain bikers frequently knock at the Stadelelhofers' cabin door. And at least figuratively, representatives of the East Bay Regional Park District and Save Mount Diablo, interested in acquiring more parkland, are knocking, too.

1 George A. Pettitt, *Clayton: Not Quite Shangri-La* (Martinez, CA: Contra Costa County Historical Society, 1996) 79

2 *Contra Costa County Official Records* 1291: 508-515; 2088: 55.

3 "Edward Howard, Noted Horseman, Lumberman, Dies," *Oakland Tribune* 26 June 1947: 2.

4 Oakland Death Certificate 6572, from listing at the Oakland Public Library.

5 *San Francisco City Directory* 1908.

6 Dorothy Wright, personal interview, 4 Jan 1999.

7 Martin Wright, personal interview, 4 Jan 1999.

8 Martin Wright, personal interview, 5 Mar 1997.

9 *Official Records* 1291: 508-515.

10 Martin Halstuk, "It Began with Whalebone Corsets. . . .," *Oakland Tribune* 29 Jan 1978: n.p.

11 Nancy Nordahl, "Although the Store Has Closed, Former Employees of Hink's Still Get Together," *The* [Berkeley] *Voice* 20 Nov 1985: 4.

12 "Although the Store Has Closed."

13 Nancy Nordall, "The History of Hink's," *The* [Berkeley] *Voice* 20 Nov 1985: 4.

14 "Although the Store Has Closed."

15 *Contra Costa County Official Records* 13: 180.

16 Pettitt 79. Another spelling of the surname was Arraya.

17 Ray Blomberg, personal interview, 30 June 1997.

18 Clyde P. Ross, *Quicksilver Deposits of the Mount Diablo District, Contra Costa County, CA*, State Dept of the Interior, Bulletin 922-B.

19 Mae Fisher Purcell, *History of Contra Costa County* (Berkeley, CA: Gillick, 1940) 390.

20 *Contra Costa County Deed Book* 49: 283.

21 *Contra Costa County Homestead Book* 4: 359.

22 William L. Metcalfe, compiler, *Contra Costa County Under the Vitascope* (Richmond, CA: *Richmond Record*, 1 Jan 1902) n.p.

23 "Sycamore Springs A Place of Recreation," a one-page photocopy of a newspaper article, circa 1906, n.p.

24 "Sycamore Springs."

25 Kate A. Doyle, letter to Catherine Clyma, 9 Sep 1904.

26 Kate A. Doyle, letter to Catherine Clyma, 7 July 1905.

27 "Clayton Notes," *Contra Costa Gazette* 24 July 1909: 3.

28 "Marsh Creek News," *Byron Times* 6 Aug 1909: 1.

29 *Contra Costa County Satisfaction of Mortgages* 10: 476-77. *Contra Costa County Deed Book* 160: 154.

30 Willmetta Frank Mann, Old Timers' Luncheon, Clayton Museum, 3 Nov 1998, sponsored by the Clayton Historical Society.

31 Eugene and Victoria Stadelhofer, personal interview, 12 Dec 1998.

32 Frederick "Fritz" C. Stadelhofer, videotaped interview, 7 Sep 1990.

33 *Contra Costa County Deed Book* 816: 421.

34 "Nearly 100 Blocks Are Devastated; Still Fear Several Lives Are Lost," *Berkeley Daily Gazette* 18 Sep 1923: 1.

35 Fritz Stadelhofer interview.

36 Fritz Stadelhofer interview.

37 Eugene Stadelhofer interview.

Know Your Place

TALL WINDOWS spread bright sunlight through the schoolroom. To one side an old stove takes away the spring chill. Chalk squeaks on individual slate boards as students finish their arithmetic assignments. Eagerly, hands shoot up when the teacher asks a question. Mistress Kurtz calls on a girl in a blue bonnet who stands and curtseys before giving her correct answer.

The hickory stick is not needed for discipline this day in May 1999. Joan and Don Kurtz have captured the full interest of their students. During April and May each year, volunteers re-enacting a 19th-century school day teach weekday classes at the restored Tassajara School on Finley Road, a one-room school built in 1888. Joan Kurtz started the program in 1995; by 1999, about 20 volunteer teachers and 14 San Ramon Valley elementary schools took part. Students attending are third-graders who are studying a required California history unit. To prepare for their 1888 school day, they will have found a costume, made a lunch pail, memorized an older version of the Pledge of Allegiance, and learned the classroom rules and punishments. Participating in such activities as writing with pen and ink, reading from *McGuffey's Third Reader,* and rolling a hoop at recess, the youngsters learn history firsthand.

The Tassajara One-Room School Program is sponsored by the Museum of the San Ramon Valley and supported by the San Ramon Historical Society, the San Ramon Valley Fire Protection District, and the San Ramon Valley Firefighters Association. These organizations and volunteer teachers are demonstrating to young people that history exists not only between the covers of a book or on the walls of a museum, but in our communities. That little white building with a bell tower under the walnut trees has a meaning.

Neighbor to neighbor

"When a guy down the road had a bad tractor accident," Bill Morgan recalled, *"word spread up and down the road he needed help. So a bunch of us neighbors went up to the house to put in a water system he couldn't finish because of the accident. . . . It's pretty much been that way up here over the years."* [a]

Knowledge of local history, including natural history, enriches our lives, and Morgan Territory Regional Preserve, a link in a much larger area of open space, is a wonderful natural resource. As a new century commences, we have another invaluable resource. In 1900 only 44,762 Americans were 90 or older; today, 1.4 million people in this country are 90 to 99, and an additional 64,000 are at least 100.[1] Ninety-seven-year-old Mary Bettencourt Lumpkin, a 1916 graduate of Tassajara School, returned one year to share her memories with the third-graders. Many other senior citizens, including Thornton K. Taylor, Antoinette Morris, and Lucy Viera, who were in their 90s, have contributed greatly to my knowledge of Morgan Territory and its residents. Their stories are irreplaceable, not only for the sake of tracing family genealogy but for learning the flavor of a time.

Although most U.S. citizens live in urban areas, the romantic American dream of a little place in the country still persists. My husband half-seriously has suggested that future Morgan Territory Road residents be required to take an aptitude test that would reveal impossibly rose-colored views of country living. This is a beautiful place, close to nature, but it is also the place

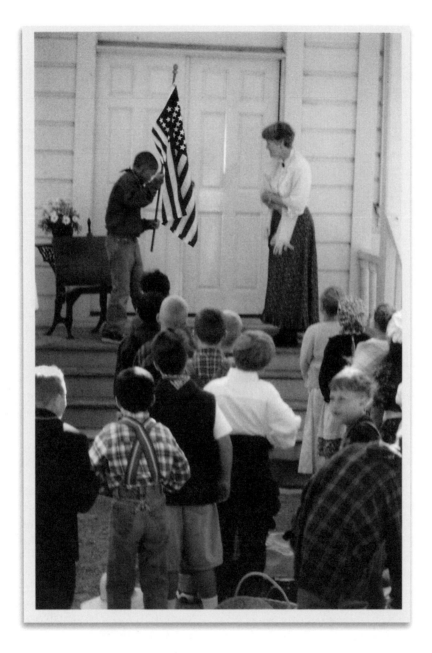

Teacher Joan Kurtz, in period costume, looks on as a visiting third-grader positions the flag, May 1999. Photo by Don Homan.

"Oh, say, can you see?" Sunbonneted pupils pay close attention to the flag ceremony at the restored Tassajara School, May 1999. Photo by Don Homan.

where household cats keep disappearing, where the wind can send the roof sailing, where the well gives up in the dry season and mud slides slither over the road in the wet season, where gophers eat all the seedlings, where people go bankrupt trying to make a living raising Arabian horses, where Mary's soccer practice is in town a harrowing 20-minute drive away, where old Morgan Territory mercury mines are sending poison into a Brentwood reservoir. Most residents along Morgan Territory Road now live on small properties carved out from the quarter sections, but to buy even a small property and move here without understanding reality is indeed foolish.

Gradually, people learn their lessons about this place. Some families leave, but those who stay meet the practical challenges and develop a special camaraderie. Fourth of July and Halloween celebrations at the firehouse. Training to fight fires and administer medical aid—and yes, actually fighting fires. "Town hall" meetings with the Contra Costa Water District. These and other cooperative occasions help create a community feeling.

Old-timers and newcomers continue to find harmony, despite varied cultures and backgrounds, in this somewhat primitive, at times harsh, but always beautiful rural setting.

1 Susan Levine, "Centenarians Recall Years of Rapid Changes," *The Valley Times* 19 Jan 1999: A12.

a Linda Davis, "Time Doesn't Spare Morgan Territory," *The Valley Times* 3 Dec 1989: C1.

Acknowledgements

Special thanks to my husband, Don Homan, for all his help, including the use of his photographs; and to my brother, James Marshall, my friends Walt and Robin Morgan, Seth Adams of Save Mount Diablo, and my editor, Jackie Pels of Hardscratch Press, as well as designer David Johnson. ❧ Thanks also to the Black Diamond Mines staff, the Contra Costa County Historical Society, the Livermore Heritage Guild, the Livermore-Amador Genealogical Society, the Institute for Historical Study, the Clayton Museum, Dr. Adrian Praetzellis, Karana Hattersley-Drayton, Dr. Randall Milliken, Ron Crane, and Dr. Philip Manwell, who so kindly supported my project. ❧ Thanks to countless helpful librarians and archivists. ❧ Perhaps the biggest thanks of all should go to family, friends, colleagues, and neighbors who listened patiently to my enthusiasm and encouraged me to continue.

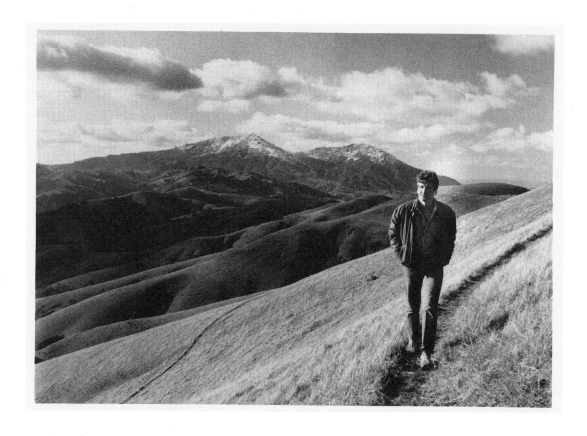

The late Bob Walker at work, with a view of Riggs Canyon and Mount Diablo (self portrait © IDG Films/Oakland Museum).

ANNE MARSHALL HOMAN, shown interviewing Antoinette Gattorna Morris in 1997 for the chapter titled "'Guv'nor' Al Morris and His Little Genovese," has lived in Livermore for 30 years, the last 20 on Morgan Territory Road. After earning her teaching credential and an M.A. in English literature at Holy Names College in 1973, she taught a variety of English classes at Livermore High School. In 1996 she retired and began work on *The Morning Side of Mount Diablo*, her first book. She belongs to a number of local historical societies as well as the Institute for Historical Study, a community of independent and academically affiliated scholars. Her articles about San Francisco Bay Area history have appeared in several magazines, and some of her haiku have been published in the poetry journal *Frogpond*. She is currently at work on her second book, an alphabetical history of the city of Livermore.

BOB WALKER, whose photographs appear on the front cover and on pages 3, 10, 20-21, and 232, came to the San Francisco Bay Area in the early 1980s after graduating from Oberlin College. Through his persuasive photography and boundless enthusiasm, he became influential in the preservation of local parklands. His usual technique was to use very slow film and shoot in late afternoon light. He served as president of the San Francisco Bay Area chapter of the Sierra Club for two years and on the board of Save Mount Diablo. He was director or committee member of many local environmental groups. His photographs have been published in newspapers and magazines and exhibited in many venues. From 3 March to 24 June 2001, a major show was held at the Oakland Museum of California, where his photographs are preserved in the archives. He died in 1992, at age 40, but the influence of his work continues.

Bibliography

ORAL HISTORY

Adams, Sadie. Telephone conversation. June 1997.

Basso, Ernest and Dorothy. Personal interview. 19 Feb 1996.

Bloching, Fred. Personal interview. 21 Jan 1997.

Blomberg, Raymond and Frances. Personal interview. 30 June 1997. Correspondence. 1997-1999.

Buffo, Cal and Beverley. Personal interview. 23 Nov 1998.

Butterfield, Mary. Personal interview. 20 May 1996. Telephone conversations. 1995-6.

Clary, John. Assistant Fire Chief, East Diablo Fire District. Telephone interview. 7 Oct 1997.

Cox, Irmgard Witt. Personal interview. 5 Sep 1997.

Delamater, Mary Viera. Personal interview. 4 Feb 1997.

Dempsey, Norma Bloching. Personal interview, telephone conversations and correspondence. 1995-1999.

Dias, Will and Marge. Personal interviews. 21 Sep 1995; 12 Nov 1996.

Frank, George. Old Timers' luncheon. 7 Oct, 1 Dec 1996 at Clayton Museum, sponsored by the Clayton Historical Society.

Frank, Phyllis. Old Timers' luncheon. 7 Oct 1996 at Clayton Museum, sponsored by the Clayton Historical Society.

Ghera, Jean. Personal interview and telephone conversations. Oct 1996.

Gim, Brigette and Harry. Personal interviews and phone conversations. 1995-6.

Giovanni, Dorenda Bloching. Personal interview. 21 Jan 1997.

Green, Olive. Personal interview. 23 May 1996.

Gleese, Jack and Rose. Personal interviews, phone conversations and letters. 1995-9.

Grisel, August. Telephone interview. 9 July 1996.

Hargraves, Juanita Robles. Personal interview and telephone conversations. 1995-6.

Hardiman, Carol. Personal interviews. 1995-6.

Hattersley-Drayton, Karana. "Interview with Jack Gleese," Sonoma State U Anthropological Studies Center, for the Contra Costa Water District. 9 Sep 1995.

—. "Interview with Juanita Robles Hargraves," Sonoma State U Anthropological Studies Center, for the Contra Costa Water District. 9 Nov 1995.

—. "Morgan Territory: Interview with Bill Morgan and Family," for the East Bay Regional Park District, 2960 Peralta Oaks Ct., Oakland, CA 94605. 7 Nov 1996.

—. "Morgan Territory: Interview with Ida (Cardoza) Taylor," for the East Bay Regional Park District, 2960 Peralta Oaks Ct., Oakland, CA 94605. 12 July 1996.

—. Report on Oral History Completed Under the Historic Treatment Plan for Construction of the Los Vaqueros Dam and Reservoir and Related Requirements, Los Vaqueros Project. Rohnert Park, CA: Sonoma State U Academic Foundation, 1996.

Homan, Donald. Personal interview. 6 Oct 1997.

Hubbell, Claire Miller. Personal interview. 20 Oct 1998.

Joyce, Sandy. Personal interview. 19 Jan 1998.

Justice, Robert and Irene. Personal interview. 13 Oct 1997.

Koopman, Melinda Robles. Telephone interview. 1 Sep 1995.

Krebs, Joe. "News at 6." NBC. WRC, Washington, DC. c27 Feb 1996.

Lake, Roger and Suzanne. Personal interviews. 20 Mar, 5 Oct 1997.

Lamee, Dorothy Reinstein. Personal interview. 29 Aug 1996. Telephone interview. May 1996.

Lawrence, Richard. Telephone interviews. 25 July, 23 Aug 1996. Personal interview. 23 Feb 1999.

Lindner, Manfred. Personal interview. 8 Jan 1999.

Mallory, Denny and June. Personal interview. 4 May 1997.

Mann, Willmetta Frank. Old Timers' luncheon, 3 Nov 1998, Clayton Museum, sponsored by the Clayton Historical Society.

Morgan, Willard "Bill" G. Personal interviews. 19 May, 4 July, 31 Oct 1997. Telephone conversations.

Morris, Antoinette Gattorna. Personal interviews. 11 Feb 1995, 9 Sep 1996, 31 Jan 1997, 31 May 2000. Conversations 1995-1999.

Murray, Carole Cardoza. Personal interviews and phone conversations. 1995-1996.

Murray, Michael. Personal interview. 17 Sep 1996.

Pederson, Minnie. Telephone interview. 4 Sep 1995.

Rasmussen, Gordon. Personal interview. 9 Sep 1997.

Reinstein, Vera Jensen. Personal interview. 9 Sep 1997.

Robles, Bernard. Personal interview. 2 Dec 1998.

Robles, M. Ronald. Personal interview and telephone conversations. 1995-6.

Schneider, Beatrice and Tim. Telephone conversation. 21 Apr 1996. Personal interview. 15 June 1996.

Schneider, John T. Telephone interview 24 Sep 1995.

Scurran, Erin. Telephone interview. 14 Oct 1997.

Shepherd, Les and Mary. Personal interview. 9 July 1995.

Silva, John R. Personal interview. 13 Oct 1995.

Smith, Omery. Telephone interview. 1 May 1996, 18 Sep 1996. Correspondence. 1996-1999.

Stadelhofer, Eugene and Victoria. Personal interview. 12 Dec 1998.

Steiner, Beth. Telephone interview. 7 Oct 1997.

Tawney, Hazel Franco. Personal interviews. 28 Oct 1997 and 23 June 1998. Correspondence 1997-1999.

Viera, Lucy Correa Azevedo. Personal interviews. 18 July 1995; 4 Feb 1997.

Waters, John. Personal interview and mine tour. 26 Feb 1997.

Wright, Dorothy. Personal interview. 1 Dec 1997.

Wright, Martin. Personal interview. 19 Mar 1997.

Wright, Martin and Dorothy. Personal interview. 5 Mar 1997; 4 Jan 1999.

PERIODICALS AND VARIOUS PAPERS

"Andrew F. Burke Is Dead at 79." *San Francisco Chronicle* 20 Mar 1964: 26.

Bank of Martinez sales document, 14 Dec 1895, Xerox copy.

Beaudin, Tom. "A Practical Approach to Fighting Tassajara Fires." *The Valley Pioneer* 10 May 1978: 21.

Bohme, Frederick G. "The Portuguese in California." *California Historical Society Quarterly* 35 (1956): 233-252.

Boudreau, John. "Call It Beast Bay: Ancient Animals Found Hospitable Home Here." *The Valley Times* 4 June 1995: 4A.

Bruggers, James. "Hidden Indian Culture Dug Up at Los Vaqueros." *The Valley Times* 25 July 1995: 5A.

—. "Maintaining the Mountain." *The Valley Times* 1 Dec 1996: 4A.

—. "No Cleanup in Store for Mercury Mine." *The Valley Times* 3 July 1994: 1A.

—. "Of Ghosts and Grizzlies." *The Valley Times* 12 May 1993: 4A.

—. "Plants Might Cut Mine Pollution." *The Valley Times* 11 Feb 1995: 8A.

Burges, Meg. "The Wrights of Curry Creek." *Contra Costa Times* 27 Apr 1966: 24.

Camposeco, Maria E. "Clayton Woman Gets Delayed Diploma." *The Valley Times* 12 Feb 1996: 1.

Cardoza, Joseph Souza and Lucy Bent Nunez. Wedding Certificate. 16 Dec 1895. (In possession of Ida Cardoza Taylor).

Christy, Iola J. "Clayton Stories." *Clayton Chronicles* Jan 1998: 5.

Contra Costa Gazette. Incomplete run at the Contra Costa County Library in Pleasant Hill. 1860-1900, 1905-1923, 1926-1963.

Davis, Linda. "Time Doesn't Spare Morgan Territory." *The Valley Times* 3 Dec 1989: 1, 2C.

Debley, Tom. "Group Aims to Block Diablo Development." *Concord Transcript* 28 Jan 1972: n.p.

Denison, James. "From the Arena to the Hall of Fame." *The Sunday* [Monterey] *Peninsula Herald Weekend Magazine* 25 Apr 1982: 3-6.

Drummond, Gary. "Laddsville." *The Livermore Roots Tracer.* Livermore: Livermore Area Genealogical Society, Oct 1997: 686.

"Edward Howard, Noted Horseman, Lumberman, Dies." *Oakland Tribune* 26 June 1947: 2.

"Estate of Manuel Garcia." *Byron Times* 8 July 1910.

Foote, Timothy. "1846: The Way We Were—and the Way We Went." *Smithsonian* Apr 1996: 38-51.

"Geology and Mineral Deposits—Mt. Diablo." *California Division of Mines and Geology, Special Report 80* (1963): 20-26.

Groom, Agnes N. "Life is Mellow for Beloved Pioneer of County; 'Progress Parade' Has Been Rich." *Contra Costa Gazette* 1 Mar 1948: 2.

Hagemann, Herbert L. Jr. "Abstract Of Title—Rancho el Valle de San José," reprint from *Pacific Historian* May/August 1965. Amador-Livermore Valley Historical Society, n.d.

Hallissy, Erin. "Firefighters Slowing Diablo Blaze." *The Valley Times* 16 July 1981: 1A.

—. "Fire Stopped After Burning 2,400 Acres." *The Valley Times* 17 July 1981: 1.

Halstuk, Martin. "It Began with Whalebone Corsets... ." *Oakland Tribune* 29 Jan 1978: n.p.

Harvey, Dennis. "8200 Highland Road, Livermore Country Living on 3 Acres." San Ramon, CA: Prudential California Realty, March 1997.

Hedgecock, Catherine. "Copter Rescues Hiker Injured in 200-Foot Fall." *The Valley Times* 16 Jan 1995: 3A.

Heizer, Robert F. and Adam E. Treganza. "Mines and Quarries of the Indians of California." *California Journal of Mines and Geology* 40 (July 1944): 312.

Hightower, M. M. "Former Champion Cowboy." *Hoofs and Horns* Nov 1953: 11.

Hill, Ward. "Historic Architecture Assessment, Guirado House." 9 Sep 1996.

"History of the Parish of St. Catherine of Siena, Martinez, CA." Mimeograph.

Irelan, William Jr. "Contra Costa County." Annual Report of the State Mineralogist 8 (ends 1 Oct 1888). CA State Mining Bureau: 162.

Lake, Roger. "Tassajara Good-by Dinner." 8 June 1990.

Leiser, Ken. "If They Don't, No One Will." *The Valley Times* 6 Nov 1986: 4B.

Levine, Susan. "Centenarians Recall Years of Rapid Changes." *The Valley Times* 19 Jan 1999: A12.

"Livermore," Crofutt's New Overland Tourist and Pacific Coast Guide 1880.

Livermore Echo. Incomplete run on microfilm. Livermore Public Library. 1887-1918.

Livermore Enterprise. Incomplete run on microfilm. Livermore Public Library. 1874-1876.

The Livermore Herald. Incomplete run on microfilm. Livermore Public Library. 1877-1904.

The Livermore Herald. Complete run on microfilm. Livermore Public Library. 1906 to date.

The Livermore Herald obituaries. 1900-1961. Livermore Heritage Guild, Carnegie Library, Livermore.

Livermore Rodeo Program. 1918-1993 Commemorative Issue.

Maloney, Sara. "A History of Morgan Territory Road." *Tri-Valley Herald*, Brightside 8 July 1979: 2, 4.

—. "The Morgan Family's Home." *Tri-Valley Herald*, Brightside 8 July 1979: 5.

Marinucci, Carla. "Tassajara Families Remain Calm While Firefighters Swelter." *The Valley Times* 6 July 1981: 3A.

Marks, Judie. "In a Nutshell, Acorns Are Manna for Many Creatures." *The Valley Times* 6 Nov 1996: 18A.

Marsh Creek Fire and Improvement Association Minutes and Memorabilia.

"Masks Donned to Ward Off Flu." *Tri-Valley News* 18 Jan 1976: 3.

Monitor 2 Jan 1875.

Morgan, Howard "Denny" and Grace Morgan. "Morgan Territory." Mimeograph copy 1962.

Morgan, Lili, notes, 4 Sep 1970. Photocopy at Clayton Museum, Clayton, CA.

"Morgan Territory to Be Park." *The Independent* 22 June 1975: 1.

"Motorcycle Proposal Outrages Ranchers," *The Independent* 30 Aug 1970.

"Mt. Diablo Geology and Mineral Deposits." *California Division of Mines and Geology. Special Report 80* (1963).

Mt. Diablo Quicksilver Mine, Articles of Incorporation. Nevada, 4 Aug 1931. Contra Costa County Historical Society, Martinez.

"Mount Diablo Quicksilver to Aid Defense." *Oakland Tribune* n.d.: n.p.

"Naturalizations," *Reese River Reveille* 20 Oct 1880.

"Nearly 100 Blocks Are Devastated; Still Fear Several Lives Are Lost." *Berkeley Daily Gazette* 18 Sep 1923: 1.

Nordahl, Nancy. "Although the Store Has Closed, Former Employees of Hink's Still Get Together." *The* [Berkeley] *Voice* 20 Nov 1985: 4.

—. "The History of Hink's," *The* [Berkeley] *Voice* 20 Nov 1985: 4.

Olofson, Peter and Clarissa Marsh. Wedding certificate. Stockton, 24 Sep 1857. Xerox copy.

Ortiz, Bev. "Mount Diablo As Myth and Reality." *American Indian Quarterly*. Fall, 1989: 457-470.

People, Bricks and Timber: The Story of St. Michael's Parish. Livermore, 1978.

Pollock, Sarah. "Bob Walker, the Evolution of an Artist." *Diablo*.

—. "Paradise Saved." *Diablo*. December 1992: 52-56.

Prorodeo Sports News. 20 Apr 1992: 19.

Rego, Nilda. "Depression Has Effect on Mount Diablo Mercury Mines." *The Valley Times* 20 Sep 1997: D5.

—. "Galvin Family Roots Run Deep on Mount Diablo." *The Valley Times* 3 May 1997: E5.

—. "Hunting Changes from a Way of Life to a Hobby." *The Valley Times* 16 Feb 1992: Fashion/Lifestyle 6.

—. "More Die in Flu Epidemic than in WW I." *The Sunday Times* 12 Sep 1999: C7.

—. "Morgan Settled 10,000 Acres on the Morning Side of Diablo." *The Valley Times* 9 Apr 1989: 5A.

—. "Mount Diablo Miners Try Luck with Mercury." *The Valley Times* 13 Sep 1997: D5.

Ritch, Jim. "Morgans, Pioneer Territory Pair, to Mark Anniversaries." *Oakland Tribune* 22 Feb 1945: 1.

Ross, Clyde P. *Quicksilver Deposits of the Mount Diablo District, Contra Costa County, CA*. State Department of the Interior, Bulletin 922-B.

Schneider, Johnie. "Ace Rodeo Rider Tells How He Tames Vicious Broncos." *Popular Science Monthly* Aug 1934: 24-26, 107.

Slotton, Darell G., Shaun M. Ayers and John E. Reuter. Marsh Creek Watershed 1995 Mercury Assessment Project Final Report. Contra Costa County, CA, Mar 1996.

—. "Mt. Diablo Mercury Mine Site Remediation and Mercury Export Reduction Project, Attachment E." Marsh Creek Watershed Mercury Assessment Project, Second year (1996) Baseline Data Report. Contra Costa Dept of Public Works, July 1997.

Sullivan, Raymond and John Waters. "History of Mount Diablo Coalfield." *California Geology* Mar 1980: 51-59.

"Surveyor Established Boundaries of Pleasanton Township." *The Livermore Herald-News*, Shopping Guide 18 June 1969: 8-9A, 13A.

"Sycamore Springs a Place of Recreation." Newspaper article, c1906.

"2 in Bank Accused of $8,000 Shortage." *San Francisco Examiner* 6 Oct 1916: 1.

Vallejo Documents. Bancroft Library, Berkeley, ms.C-B29.

The Valley Times. Complete run on microfilm at Livermore Public Library. 1980 to date.

Watson, Susan. "Bill Mott and Bob Walker Will Be Sorely Missed." *Diablo Watch*, Fall/Winter 1992: 4-5.

"Wright Canyon & Curry Creek: Talking to the Stars, Saying Goodnight to Loved Ones ..." *Diablo Watch*, Spring 2001: 1, 6-8.

Wright, Edith Olofson. Twenty pages of personal memoir. c1980.

THESES AND MANUSCRIPTS

Alexander, Wallis Bruce Jr. "The Historical Development of the Mt. Diablo Unified School District." MA thesis. Hayward State U, 1968.

Ballard, Margaret. "History of Coal Mining in the Mount Diablo Region, 1859-1885." MA thesis. U of CA Berkeley, 1931.

DeNier, Flora L. "Robert Livermore and the Development of the Livermore Valley to 1860." MA thesis. U of CA Berkeley, 1927.

Hattersley-Drayton, Karana. "Community, Conflict and Change: The Oral History of the Mount Diablo Coal Fields." MA thesis. U of CA Berkeley, 1996.

Stokle, John Gerald. "Mission San Jose and the Livermore Valley, 1798-1842," MA Thesis, U of CA, Berkeley, c1967-1968.

BOOKS

Almeida, Carlos. *Portuguese Immigrants*. San Leandro, CA: U.P.E.C., 1978.

Bancroft, Hubert H. *History of California*. Vol. 3. San Francisco: A. L. Bancroft, 1884-1886.

—. *History of California*. Vol 5. San Francisco: History Co, 1886.

—. *The Wild Tribes*. Vol. 1. NY: Appleton, 1875.

Bancroft Pioneer Register and Index. Baltimore: Regional Pub, 1964.

Bean, Walton and James J. Rawls. *California: An Interpretive History*. 4th ed. NY: McGraw-Hill, 1983.

Beebe, Lucius, and Charles Clegg. *The American West*. NY. E.P. Dutton, 1935.

Bennett, Virginia Smith. *Dublin Reflections*. Dublin, CA: Dublin Historical Preservation Assoc, 1991.

Bible belonging to Sarah Cottrell Howard.

Bidwell, John. *A Journey to California, 1841: The Journal Account in the Bidwell-Bartleson Party*. Ed. Doyce B. Nunis Jr., Santa Cruz, CA: Western Tanager P, 1991.

Bidwell, John. *Life in California Before the Gold Discovery*. Palo Alto, CA: Lewis Osborne, 1966.

Boessenecker, John. *Lawman*. Norman, OK: U of OK P, 1998.

Bronson, William. *The Earth Shook, the Sky Burned*. Garden City, NY: Doubleday, 1959.

Bruegmann, Robert. *Benicia: Portrait of an Early California Town*. San Francisco: 101 Productions, 1980.

Bryant, Edwin. *What I Saw in California*. 1848. Lincoln, NE: U of NE P, 1985.

Collier, George C. *A Narrative History of Contra Costa County*. El Cerrito, CA: Collier, 1983.

Drummond, G. B., ed. *Recollections: Early Life in the San Ramon Valley As Related by Prof. James Dale Smith, Headmaster, Livermore College*. Oakland, CA: GRT Book Printing, 1995.

Fredrickson, David A., Suzanne B. Stewart and Grace H. Ziesing, eds. *Native American History Studies for the Los Vaqueros Project: A Synthesis*. Rohnert Park, CA: Anthropological Studies Center, 1997.

Freedman, Bernard, compiler. *Death Notices of Contra Costa County, CA, 1860-1919*.

—, compiler. *Schools in Contra Costa County*. Vol. 1-4. Cuttings from the *Contra Costa Gazette*, 1996.

Ganz, Rudolf. *The Jews of California*. NY: Southern Jewish Historical Society, 1960.

Goodyear, W. A. *Coal Mines of the Western Coast of the United States*. San Francisco: A. L. Bancroft, 1877.

Hall, Frederic. *The History of San José and Surroundings*. San Francisco: A. L. Bancroft, 1871.

History of Alameda County, California. Oakland, CA: M. W. Wood, 1883.

History of Contra Costa County, California. Los Angeles: Historic Record Co, 1926.

History of Contra Costa County, California. San Francisco: W. H. Slocum, 1882.

History of San Luis Obispo County, California. Oakland: Thompson and West, 1883.

Jablonski, Edward. *America in the Air War*. Alexandria, VA: Time-Life, 1982.

Jelinek, Lawrence I. *Harvest Empire: A History of California Agriculture*. S.F. Boyd and Fraser, 1979.

Jones, Virgie V. *Historical Persons and Places . . . in San Ramon Valley*. Alamo, CA: Morris-Burt, 1977.

LaFeber, Walter. *The Panama Canal*. NY: Oxford U P, 1978.

Livermore Cemeteries. Livermore, CA: Livermore-Amador Genealogical Soc, 1988.

Margolin, Malcolm. *The East Bay Out*. Berkeley: Heyday Books, 1988.

—. *The Ohlone Way*. Berkeley: Heyday Books, 1978.

Maurer, Maurer. *Combat Squadrons of the Air Force, World War II*. DC: US Gov Printing Office, 1969.

Metcalfe, William L., compiler. *Contra Costa County Under the Vitascope*. Richmond, CA: *Richmond Record*, 1 Jan 1902.

Milliken, Randall. *A Time of Little Choice*. Menlo Park, CA: Ballena Press, 1995.

Mora, Jo. *Californios*. Garden City, NY: Doubleday, 1949.

Mosier, Dan. *Harrisville and the Livermore Coal Mines*. San Leandro, CA: Mines Road Books, c1978.

Mosier, Dan and Earle E. Williams. *History of Tesla*. Fremont: Mines Road Books, 1999.

Mutnick, Dorothy G. *Some Alta California Pioneers and Descendants*. Lafayette, CA: Past Time Pub, 1982.

Newton, Janet. *Las Positas*. Livermore, CA: Newton, 1969.

—. *The Livermore Valley 1878, 1889*. Livermore, CA: *The Livermore Herald*: 1988.

Northrup, Marie E. *Spanish-American Families of Early California*. Vol. 1. New Orleans: Polyanthos, 1976.

Oakland City Directories 1869-1943. Complete run. Oakland Public Library.

Oakley, Stuart. *A Short History of Sweden*. NY: Praeger, 1966.

Perkins, William. *Three Years in California*. Berkeley: U of CA P, 1964.

Pettitt, George A. *Clayton: Not Quite Shangri-La*. Martinez, CA: Contra Costa County Hist Soc, 1969.

Pitt, Leonard, ed. *California Controversies*. Arlington Heights, IL: Harlan Davidson, 1987.

—. *The Decline of the Californios*. Berkeley: U of CA P, 1966.

Praetzellis, Mary, Suzanne B. Stewart and Grace H. Ziesing. *The Los Vaqueros Watershed: A Working History*. Rohnert Park, CA: Sonoma State U Academic Foundation, 1997.

Purcell, Mae Fisher. *History of Contra Costa County*. Berkeley: Gillick, 1940.

Robinson, W. W. *Land in California*. Berkeley: U of CA P, 1948.

Rogers, Francis M. *Atlantic Islanders of the Azores and Madeiras*. North Quincy, MA: Christopher Pub House, 1979.

Salesbring, Albert and Jane. *Here Rolled the Covered Wagons*. NY: Bonanza, 1948.

San Francisco City Directories 1877-1925. San Francisco Public Library.

Santos, Robert L. *Azoreans to California*. Denair, CA: Alley-Cass, 1995.

Sawyer, Eugene T. *History of Santa Clara County, California, with Biographical Sketches*. L.A.: Historic Record Co, 1922.

Siig, Anna T. and G.B. Drummond, transcribers. *Recollections of a Pioneer Mother*. Livermore: Livermore Heritage Guild, 1995.

Stewart, George R. *The California Trail*. NY: MacGraw Hill, 1962.

Tutorow, Norman E. *Leland Stanford: Man of Many Careers*. Menlo Park, CA: Pacific Coast, 1971.

Vaz, August M. *The Portuguese in California*. Oakland, CA: I.D.E.S., 1965.

Waldman, Carl. *Encyclopedia of Native American Tribes*. NY: Facts on File, 1988.

White, Terence de Vere. *Ireland*. NY: Walker, 1968.

Williams, Jerry R. *And Yet They Come*. NY: Center for Migration Studies, 1982.

Woodham-Smith, Cecil. *The Great Hunger*. NY: Harper and Row, 1962.

RECORDS

Alameda and Contra Costa Counties Directory, 1871-2.

Alameda County Births, Deaths, Mortuary Records, Land Patents, Delayed Birth Index, Marriages. v.d. Microfilm series 1376376-1376381. Family History Library. Salt Lake City, UT.

Alameda County Marriages, 1853-1883. Recorder's Office. Oakland, CA.

Alameda County Land Records, deed books. v.d. Oakland, CA.

Alameda County Great Register, 1867-1882. Oakland Public Library. Oakland, CA.

Alameda County Record of Patents. Vol. B, 1876-1891.

Baptisms, 1864-1880. St. Leander's Catholic Church. San Leandro, CA.

Baptisms, 1850-1853. St. Mary's Catholic Church, Oakland. Contra Costa County History Society. Martinez, CA.

Baptisms and Marriages, 1776-1854. Mission Dolores, San Francisco, CA. Archdiocese of San Francisco, Chancery Archives, St. Patrick's Seminary. Menlo Park, CA.

Baptisms and Marriages, 1831-1877. Mission San José and Saint Joseph's Catholic Church, San Jose, CA. Archdiocese of San Francisco, Chancery Archives, St. Patrick's Seminary. Menlo Park, CA.

Baptisms and Marriages, 1777-1863. Mission Santa Clara and Catholic Church, Santa Clara, CA. U of Santa Clara Archives, Orradre Library. Santa Clara, CA.

Baptisms, Marriages and Deaths, 1853-1920. St. Catherine of Siena Catholic Church. Martinez, CA.

Baptisms, Marriages and Deaths, 1878-present. St. Michael's Catholic Church Records. Livermore, CA.

Burial Card Index, St. Michael's Catholic Church. Livermore, CA.

Cemetery Records of California, Vols. 1-4.

Contra Costa County Assessor's Map, Book 6: 28.

Contra Costa County Board of Supervisors' Minutes. Board of Supervisors' Clerk Office. Martinez, CA.

Contra Costa County Brands and Marks 1850-1917. Recorder's Office. Martinez, CA.

Contra Costa County Death Certificate #37; C. L. Abbot, Coroner.

Contra Costa County Death Records, 1873-1921. Microfilm series 1294350-1294351. Family History Library. Oakland, CA.

Contra Costa County Great Register, 1866, 1871, 1872, 1875, 1877, 1880, 1884, 1886, 1890, 1892, 1894, 1896, 1904, 1914, 1918. Microfilm at Family History Library. Oakland, CA.

Contra Costa County Justice Court, Sixth Township, #2061, 21 Dec 1899.

Contra Costa County Land Claims, Vol 5. Recorder's Office. Martinez, CA.

Contra Costa County Land Records, deed books. v.d. Recorder's Office. Martinez, CA.

Contra Costa County Land Records, mortgage books. v.d. Recorder's Office. Martinez, CA.

Contra Costa County Land Records, satisfied mortgages. v.d. Recorder's Office. Martinez, CA.

Contra Costa County Marriage Records, 1855-1941. Recorder's Office. Martinez, CA.

Contra Costa County Marriages, 1873-1887. Contra Costa County Historical Society. Martinez, CA.

Contra Costa County Miscellaneous Records. v.d. Recorder's Office. Martinez, CA.

Contra Costa County Naturalization Records. v.d. County Courthouse. Martinez, CA.

Contra Costa County Official Records. v.d. Recorder's Office. Martinez, CA.

Contra Costa County Old Road Records History Book, Vol. B. Dept. of Public Works. Martinez, CA.

Contra Costa County Patent Books. Vols 1-5. Recorder's Office, Martinez, CA.

Contra Costa County Poll Tax List. 1872-3. Contra Costa County Historical Society. Martinez, CA.

Contra Costa County Probate Records. Clerk's Office. Martinez, CA.

Contra Costa County Public School Catalogue, 1882, 1884, 1890. Contra Costa Library. Pleasant Hill, CA.

Contra Costa County Public School Catalogue, 1889. Clayton Museum. Clayton, CA.

Contra Costa County Road Books, Vols. 1-2, 4. Dept. of Public Works. Martinez, CA.

Contra Costa County School Board Ledger, 1876-1895.

Contra Costa County Tax Assessment Lists. Clayton 1854-1890. Contra Costa County Historical Society. Martinez, CA.

Contra Costa County Tax Assessment Lists. Danville, Tassajara and San Ramon District 2. 1850- 1903. Contra Costa County Historical Society. Martinez, CA.

Contra Costa County Tax Assessment Lists. Nortonville, Somersville and Morgan Territory. 1872-1908. Contra Costa County Historical Society. Martinez, CA.

England Census 1881 Reading, Berkshire County.

Index to Marriages (Men), 1851-1941, A to Mi. Contra Costa County Recorder. FHL film 1294354 item 6. Family History Library. Oakland, CA.

Livermore City Tax Assessment Lists, 1887-1905. Livermore Heritage Guild. Livermore, CA.

Oakland Deaths. Oakland Public Library.

Robert Graham Mortuary Records, 1880-1887. Livermore Heritage Guild. Livermore, CA.

San Francisco General Land Office files. National Archives, DC.

Stanislaus County Superior Court, Probate, filed 2 Dec 1915.

U.P.E.C. Membership Lists. Concord Council (#20). San Leandro, CA.

US Agricultural Census, 1860 and 1880. Contra Costa County, CA.

US Census 1840 Perry County, OH, population schedule.

US Census 1850 Jackson County, IA, population schedule.

US Census 1850 Washington County, IN, pop. schedule.

US Census 1860 Contra Costa County, CA, pop. schedule.

US Census 1860 Van Buren County, IA, pop. schedule.

US Census 1870 Alameda County, CA, pop. schedule.

US Census 1870 Contra Costa County, CA, pop. schedule.

US Census 1880 Alameda County, CA, pop. schedule.

US Census 1880 Contra Costa County, CA, pop. schedule.

US Census 1880 Lander County, NV, pop. schedule.

US Census 1880 San Francisco, CA, pop. schedule.

US Census 1880 Solano County, CA, pop. schedule.

US Census 1900 Alameda County, CA, pop. schedule.

US Census 1900 Contra Costa County, CA, pop. schedule.

US Census 1900 San Francisco, CA, pop. schedule.

US Census 1910 Alameda County, CA, pop. schedule.

US Census 1910 Contra Costa County, CA, pop. schedule.

US Census 1920 Alameda County, CA, pop. schedule.

US Census 1920 Contra Costa County, CA, pop. schedule.

US Census 1920 Stanislaus County, CA, pop. schedule.

TAPE

Portugal and the Azores. Video recording. Englewood, CO: Quantum Communications, 1991.

Stadelhofer, Frederick "Fritz." Interview. Video recording. 7 Sep 1990.

COURT CASES

Condie vs Condie. Contra Costa County Superior Court Case #3597, 1904-5. Contra Costa County Historical Society. Box CC18 Clayton. Martinez.

Contra Costa County Superior Court Case #328. Clayton 1882-1884. Contra Costa County Historical Society. Martinez.

Contra Costa County Superior Court Case #3197. Filed 14 May 1909. Contra Costa County Historical Society. Martinez.

The Welch Consolidated Quicksilver Mining Company vs William Rider Powell. Filed 18 Nov 1875 in Contra Costa County District Court, 15th Judicial District. Contra Costa County Historical Society, file box CC6. Martinez.

Welch Quicksilver, Silver and Copper Mining Company vs The Mt. Diablo Quicksilver Mining Company, filed 18 Jul 1868 in Contra Costa County District Court, 15th Judicial District. Contra Costa County Historical Society, file box CC6. Martinez.

General Index

hired hands and, 101. *See also* vaqueros

horses and, 31, 100, 175. *See also* vaqueros

horse training and, 59-60, 62, 90, 96, 101

houses

lack of amenities in, 45, 49, 124, 165, 201

style of, 82, 96, 161, 186-187, 196

missions and, 29-30

orchards, 42, 50, 140

by particular families. *See specific families in name index*

products of, 31, 32-33, 86, 97, 161

ranchos and, 31-33, 34, 35, 57, 62

sheep herding, **102**

shift from livestock raising to grain farming, 35

swine drives and, 181

tasks involved in, 32, 169, 174-175, 199

tenants and, 82, 110

typical crops, 35

typical livestock holdings, 35

weather and, 35

women and, 45, 73, 78, 153

Rancho Arroyo de las Nueces y los Bolbones, 25, 180

Rancho Cañada de los Vaqueros, 25, 32, 45, 47, 62, 105

Rancho El Niño, 79

Rancho el Valle de San José, 31

Rancho Las Positas, 32, 35, 165

Rancho Los Meganos, 32

rancho period

defined, 31

end of, 34-35

ranchos. *See also specific ranchos*

Native Americans and, 31, 32, 34

ranching and farming and, 31-33, 34, 35, 57, 62

rancho life, 31-32, 34-35, 36, 62, 64

rodeos and, 32

vaqueros and, 57

Rancho San Miguel. *See* Rancho Arroyo de las Nueces y los Bolbones

Rancho San Ramon, 31

religion

Catholic. *See* Catholicism

Native Americans and, 22, 29-30

Yaqui tribe and, 41, 44

Native American. *See* Native Americans, spiritual beliefs of

Rhodes-Jamieson firm, 214

reata, **170**

Riggs Canyon, 57

Robertson Park, 168

rodeos

abroad, 166

Livermore Rodeo, 78, 91, **164**, 165, 168

original, 32

riders, 153, 165, 166, 168, 169-170

Sacramento Rodeo, 170

Salinas Rodeo, 168

Romero Grant, 64

Roselawn Cemetery, 70, 146

Round Valley, 16

Rowell Ranch, 90

S

sailing and stevedoring. *See* work and labor, sailing and stevedoring

Saint Catherine of Siena, 47, 62, 151, 160

Saint Dominic's Priory, 47

Saint Joseph's Home, 90

Saint Mary's Catholic Church, 64

Saint Mary's College, 86

Saint Michael's Church and Cemetery

baptisms at, 62, 64, *163*

burials at, 45, 51, 54, 55, 59, 90, 123, *163*, 168

marriages at, 47, 54

mass at, 155, 166

schooling at, 74

Saint Stephen's Cemetery, 174

Salinas, Calif., 168

San Bruno National Cemetery, 92

San Francisco, Calif., 81, 86-87, 189-190, 196

San Francisco General Land Office, 36, 60, 86

San Francisco Normal School, 112

San Francisco Presidio, 62

San Joaquin River, 23, 25

San Joaquin Valley, 21

San Jose, Calif., 53, **54**, 62

San Jose juzgado, **52**

San Quentin Prison, 58

San Ramon Creek, 64

San Ramon Valley, 22, 34, 64

San Ramon Valley Fire Protection District, 130, 137, 138-139

San Ramon Valley School District, 139, 227

Save Mount Diablo, 126, 127, 187, 203

school districts. *See specific school districts*

schools. *See also specific schools*

Black Hills area and, 109-119

as community centers, 109, 118-119

corporal punishment and, 176

one-room schoolhouses. *See specific schools*

school elections, 54

teachers and. *See* teaching

scrip payment

agricultural college type, 36, 49, 54, 69, 86, 121, 207

defined, 36

military bounty land type, 36, 53, 55, 57, 63

settlers

American from outside California. *See* American migrants

Azorean immigrants as. *See* Azorean immigrants

French immigrants as, 49, 65

Genovese immigrants as, 73-74

Irish immigrants as. *See* Irish immigrants

Jewish immigrants as, 79-82

land claims and. *See* land claims; land grants

Mexican immigrants as. *See* Mexican immigrants

Mexican land grants and. *See* land grants

mortgages and. *See* mortgages and loss of land

Native Americans as. *See* Native Americans

Prussian immigrants as. *See* Prussian immigrants

rancheros and Californios as. *See* rancheros and Californios

Index of Names

The Morning Side of Mount Diablo

Project coordinator and editor: Jackie Pels
Book design and production: David R. Johnson

Indexes by Elizabeth C. Feil, ASI
Morgan Territory maps by David R. Johnson
Composition by Archetype Typography, Berkeley, California
Printed and bound at Thomson-Shore Inc., Dexter, Michigan
Alkaline-pH recycled paper (60-pound Glatfelter Opaque)

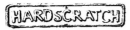

HARDSCRATCH PRESS

2358 Banbury Place
Walnut Creek, CA 94598-2347
phone/fax 925/935-3422

The front cover photograph of "the morning side of Mount Diablo" is by
the late Bob Walker, as are the title page cameo with Mount Diablo's two peaks,
the aerial panorama on pages 20-21, and the self-portrait on page 232.
Of the Morgan Territory views on page 10 (numbering clockwise
from upper right), photos 2, 5 and 6 are by Bob Walker.
All are © IDG Films/Oakland Museum of California.

The back cover vista of Morgan Territory Road as well as the
stormy-day rainbow on page 8 and the frontispiece panorama, pages 6-7,
are by Don Homan. The boy in the 1971 frontispiece photograph is
9-year-old Ted Homan. On page 10 (numbering clockwise from upper right),
photos 1 and 4—a view of the old Androws property (see "Seven Sisters")
and a sunrise over Los Vaqueros Reservoir—are by Don Homan;
photo 3, from the snow-covered deck of their Morgan
Territory home, is by Anne Marshall Homan.

Unless otherwise noted, the black-and-white snapshots and other
illustrations in the historical sections of the book, including the
back-cover portrait of Jeremiah Morgan from page 179, were generously
lent by the individuals and organizations named.

Printed in the United States of America

First printed June 2001

Hardscratch Press, Walnut Creek, California

Library of Congress Control Number 2001131402

ISBN: 0-9678989-2-7

9 8 7 6 5 4 3 2